THE
MARBLE ROOM

THE
MARBLE
ROOM

How I Lost God
and Found Myself
in Africa

BILL HATCHER

Lantern Books | New York | A Division of Booklight Inc.

2012
Lantern Books
128 Second Place
Brooklyn, NY 11231
www.lanternbooks.com

Copyright © 2012 Bill Hatcher

Library of Congress Cataloging-in-Publication Data

Hatcher, Bill.
The marble room : how I lost God and found
myself in Africa / Bill Hatcher.
    p. cm.
Includes bibliographical references (p.   ).
ISBN 978-1-59056-406-6 (pbk. : alk. paper) —
ISBN 978-1-59056-408-0 (ebook)
  1. Hatcher, Bill. 2. Christian biography—United States.
3. Spiritual biography—Africa, East. I. Title.
BR1725.H244A3 2012
204.092—dc23
[B]
                                    2012020219

Printed in the United States of America

Contents

contents continued

Author's Note

THIS IS A true story. It recounts the spiritual transformation I experienced while living in East Africa from 1994 to 1996. All places, events, dreams, and people described are real. However, as a courtesy to my ex-wife, I use a pseudonym when referencing her in the text. I also use a pseudonym when referencing my second housemate to avoid confusing him with another person of the same name. All other proper names used in the story are real.

In the interest of readability, loose translations of Swahili to English are favored where they occur in the story. For literal translations, see "A Glossary of Swahili Words and Phrases" at the end of the book. Phonetic pronunciations of Swahili words and proper nouns used in the story can also be found in the glossary.

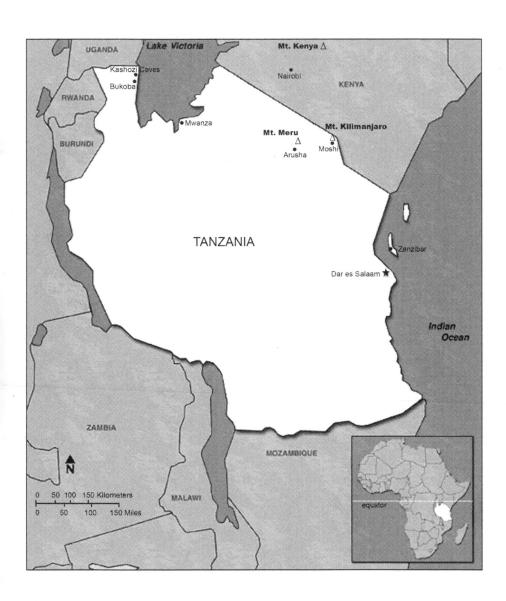

UGANDA   Lake Victoria   Mt. Kenya △

Kashozi Caves   Nairobi
Bukoba   KENYA
RWANDA

BURUNDI   • Mwanza   Mt. Meru   Mt. Kilimanjaro
                              △   △
                              Arusha   Moshi

              TANZANIA   Zanzibar

                              Dar es Salaam ★

                                          Indian
                                          Ocean

ZAMBIA

N
                              MOZAMBIQUE

0   50 100 150 Kilometers
                              MALAWI   equator
0   50   100   150 Miles

BOOK ONE
Death

CHAPTER 1

Fissures of Men

THERE WAS NO turning back. I had crossed a threshold, and what once gleamed like polished marble was now cold and dark and riven with flaws.

My breaths were short and shallow. I tried to swallow, but my throat seized shut in the thin, crystalline air. Blood surged through my temples and thumped against my knitted cap and helmet. Brad was somewhere ahead of me, maybe fifty feet, but the sun had been down for hours and I'd lost track of him. I was alone. Darkness closed in.

We had been climbing Mount Kenya for seven days, and had reached the summit twelve hours earlier. Descending from 17,000 feet, we had rappelled onto a narrow ledge that sloped off to the Lewis Glacier a half mile below. I was unroped and had no headlamp or flashlight. The moon was full, but the higher pinnacles and gendarmes surrounding me draped long shadows across the rock wall and ledge and stole all sense of depth. I was blind.

Temperatures were below freezing, but my face prickled with sweat. I panted. I stepped into the black. I reached for the invisible rock wall to my left and was reassured when I found it, but leaning sideways stole traction from under my feet. I took a timid step, and then another, but my next step turned on an unseen stone that shot into the void. I screamed and wheeled around. My feet pitched into the air.

Then my mind stopped. The sky filled with stars, glittering unconcerned, and an intense stillness surrounded me. Time stretched endlessly away. I floated in space, unattached, and I felt calm and peaceful. My breath misted my eyes and moistened the inside of my nostrils. The smell reminded me of my last supper: cold peanut butter.

"William!" Brad shouted.

Gravity returned. I crashed onto my backpack, face up, and my feet dangled off the ledge. I clawed for anything I could get ahold of. My pack was my only point of contact and it began grinding over the sloping surface. In a second or two, it would be too late.

It was January 1996, and I was approaching the end of life as I knew it. Without being conscious of it, I had tempted fate in ways that exploded my understanding of God, truth, and reality.

But would it be worth the price, even if I did survive?

A year and a half earlier, I had boarded a plane for East Africa. Until then I was little more than a racist, camo-ball-cap wearin', born-again Christian. I received the Holy Spirit as a child at the Pentecostal revivals in my small, southern Illinois town and raved at Christian rock concerts as a teen. At the age of twenty-four, I married the sweet, evangelical Baptist girl I had met at a local mall. In less than four years, I was divorced, childless, and bound for Tanzania as a Peace Corps volunteer. This profound shift was due to a series of fissures—tiny cracks that had spread in the bedrock of faith that was the basis of my entire worldview.

Growing up in the Bible Belt, I regarded Christian fundamentalism not only as true but as exclusively true and peerless. My God was the only god. He was good, all-powerful, all-knowing, and apparently a white American male. My beliefs were solidified at an Assemblies of God church, where my mother taught Sunday school and my father helped take offerings. As a boy of eight or nine, my life was bounded by dogmas that were beautiful, prejudiced, and absolute.

Every Sunday morning before church, I fed the livestock, took my turn in the shower, and poured myself a bowl of Golden Grahams. After breakfast, I clipped on a tie and scrunched down in the beanbag chair to watch either *The Hour of Power* with Rev. Robert Schuller or *CBS News Sunday Morning* with Charles Kuralt. Before long, my mom, dad, little sister, and I piled into our '72 Dodge Charger (with a 400-cubic-inch, V-8 engine, reminiscent of the General Lee from *The Dukes of Hazzard*), and drove down country roads hemmed about with fields of green sweet corn.

My dad sometimes smoked a pipe on the drive to church. He preferred Half and Half Pipe Tobacco—half burley, half bright—packed in a tin. Since the windows stayed up to protect my mom's teased-out, pageboy hairdo, swirls of smoke filled the car, which smelled like a mixture of chocolate, coffee, and my dad's English Leather aftershave. I liked the smells, even though the smoke made my eyes water. But my dad would just crinkle his eyes, reach for the AM radio, and find a down-home country-music ballad to entertain us on the half-hour drive.

We went to church every Sunday, and when a baptism, faith healing, or visiting gospel quartet was scheduled to perform, we fellowshipped at Wednesday evening revivals, too. We almost never missed church, despite the fact that gas prices had shot up from thirty cents a gallon in 1973 to sixty cents a year and a half later.

Our family was members of a white, working-class, conservative congregation. In every service, we prayed and sang and raised our hands to receive the Holy Spirit and glorify his holy name. It never occurred to me to ask why there weren't any black folks in our church, when over a quarter of the people in town—and over half of those in the greater St. Louis metro area—were African American.

Nevertheless, it eventually came up. One Sunday afternoon on the drive home from church, and after we had eaten lunch at York Steak House, my dad set the record straight. "Listen here," he said, shifting the toothpick between his teeth. "The Bible says that Noah's son, Ham, went down to Africa after the flood. And since they was all monkeys down there then, he married one of 'em and had kids. Now, that's how them niggers came to be, and that's why we don't mix with 'em. Period."

I was no expert on biology, but I had seen enough episodes of *Mutual of Omaha's Wild Kingdom* to learn that different species could not interbreed. Plus, the miniseries *Roots* and an episode of *The Brady Bunch* made it clear that black people were just as human as white people. After mulling it over, I decided to take my father's interpretation of the Bible with a grain of salt and lump it together with his many other discourses on wops, dagos, spics, wetbacks, and japs.

Incredibly, my dad's teachings yielded unforeseen benefits. Instead of strengthening my childhood worldview, they weakened it. Tiny nicks in my carefully sculpted outlook on life eventually made it vulnerable to total failure and collapse.

But some of those nicks came directly from church. Altar call was an emotional part of the service when the pastor invited worshippers to come forward and confess their sins or make prayer requests. In the meantime, everyone sang slow-moving hymns like "Just As I Am" and "I Surrender All." As the scents of Dentyne gum and Final Net hairspray re-circulated through the central air conditioner, many in the congregation twitched and wailed and reached toward heaven, begging forgiveness and exalting His majesty. Occasionally someone was moved by the Holy Spirit and started ranting in tongues.

Immediately, the organ died down and everyone stopped singing, closed their eyes, and bowed their heads. Everyone except me, that is. I was up on tiptoes, stretching to see over all the dark polyester suit jackets. While the mouthpiece of God spoke in tongues, the pastor reached up to the three gilded crosses hanging behind the choir and chanted in Hebrew: "*Adonai Elohim,* Hallelujah, Hallelujah, Hallelujah," over and over. Others prayed aloud: "Thank you, Jesus" and "Praise Jesus."

After a minute or two, the person speaking in tongues was released by the Holy Spirit and collapsed into the hands of a neighbor. On cue, another person in the congregation became a vessel for the Holy Spirit and interpreted the message, every time an acknowledgment of our pain and suffering and a reminder of His love. All we had to do was love Him back and do His will.

At the faintly mustachioed age of twelve, I decided I was ready to accept the divinely offered, grace-given rebirth of my soul and become a born-again Christian. In our church, this event was best demonstrated by being baptized; that is, being completely submerged in a small pool of water at the front of the auditorium.

The angelic, white baptismal gown I wore over my T-shirt and swimming trunks was supposed to make me look like a clean, new creature before God, but I thought it made me look more like a ghost. It resembled a death shroud (which, in a certain mystical way, it was), and I felt very nervous. After leading us in prayer, our pastor motioned for me to come up to the pulpit. From there he took my hand and led me down into the waist-deep baptismal font until we were at eye level with the congregation. The water was warm and made me want to pee.

"Son, as you know, Jesus is the Son of God. He was sent to this earth, born of a virgin," the pastor said, projecting his voice for the congregation, "and when He grew up, He became a carpenter and then a healer and a teacher. He was the *perfect* blood offering, Who was sacrificed on the cross for *your* sins," his voice now boomed, "and for *everyone's* sins, for *all time!* Can you say amen?"

The congregation answered, "Amen!"

"Amen," I said.

"And after lying there in that tomb for three days, our Savior *rose again*! And He *ascended* unto heaven!" Flecks of the pastor's saliva sprayed my cheek as he bounced up and down in the pool.

In a moment, he raised the handkerchief in his left hand high over my head and placed his right hand on my shoulder. "Let us pray." He squeezed his eyes shut. "Dear Heavenly Father, You have assured us that if we trust in you with all our heart and lean not on our own understanding that *You will* make our paths straight!" Many in the congregation said amen and grunted approval. "So we ask of you now, Father, come into this young man's life, make his paths straight before him, and prepare for him a place in your Kingdom." He closed by quoting John 3:16. "For God so loved the world that He gave His only begotten son, that whosoever shall believeth in Him shall not perish, but have eternal life.

"And everyone said, amen."

The pastor looked down at me and asked in a solemn voice, "Son, do you believe Jesus died and rose from the dead for you?"

I couldn't help it. I started to pee. "Yes, sir?"

"Then by the powers vested in me, I baptize you in the name of the Father, and of the son, and of the Holy Spirit!"

He cupped the handkerchief over my mouth and nose, plunged me back into the water, and immediately pulled me out again. I sputtered chlorinated water and beamed at the congragation with my white buck teeth I was still growing into. The organ piped "Bless the Lord, O My Soul," and I splashed my way out of the pool. I saw my parents. They looked so proud.

Soon afterward, my dad felt it was time I learn how the world's religions stacked up. He said that we, the Assemblies of God church—together with the Baptists, as he'd been raised—occupied the topmost rung on the ladder of godliness. We were most correct. After us came the Anglicans and the Methodists. Farther down were the Episcopalians, Lutherans, and Presbyterians. Seventh Day Adventists and the like were mixed in there somewhere toward the bottom. That was about it—unless you included the Catholics. In my father's opinion, the veracity of the Roman Catholic church was dubious at best, and Catholicism was barely visible above the cutoff line for all Christians (Vatican II events notwithstanding). After all, Catholics decorated their churches with graven images of saints, which smacked of idol worship. Not only that, he said, but they actually drank *real wine* during communion *and* practiced the baptism of infants, well before a person has a chance to understand what baptism is all about.

Any group lower than the Catholics was definitely out of luck. They were the "unsaved" and therefore did not receive a get-into-heaven-free pass when they died. This meant the Jews (especially the Jews, since they had killed Jesus) and everyone else in the world would end up simmering in some hellish netherworld for all eternity. At the time, I didn't know who "everyone else" was, but I guessed there couldn't be too many people that fell into that category; maybe a few primitive tribes in the jungle and, of course, atheists, devil worshipers, and communists.

However, as I headed into my teens I learned that "everyone else" included Muslims, Hindus, Buddhists, Taoists, Jains, and many others. They were, in fact, most of the people who had ever lived—the immoral majority, as it were—all going to hell in a handbasket. It sounded senseless, even brutal, and because of it some Christians thought God surely judged "everyone else" differently, perhaps under a divine exception clause. Maybe they could earn merits once in heaven and eventually even become full-fledged saints? Though there was no biblical support for such conjecture, and I wondered: If Jesus was *the only way*, how could there be *any other way*?

In the meantime, it felt good to put my fifty cents in the tithing envelope at church and check the box on the reverse side that read "African Missions." Maybe we could Christianize the heathen Africans, save their souls, and teach them about right and wrong. My dad smiled when he passed the faux-gilded collection plate down our pew and saw my donation. It made me think my mom might be right; maybe I should go into the mission field to help save some of those lost souls. Like Jesus said in Matthew 4:19, *Follow me and I will make you fishers of men.*

One Saturday when I was fourteen years old, I was home by myself. My parents were in town, and my sister was at her friend's house working on a 4-H project. A friend of mine invited me to go bowling with him that evening. His mom said she would drive us into town.

An autumn thunderstorm was rolling in, so I grabbed a

light jacket. I wrote a note for my parents and left it on the kitchen table. While I waited at the back door, the phone rang again. Something had come up; my friend said his mom couldn't drive us anymore. Maybe we could go another time.

I was disappointed and went to get the note I had left for my parents. But before I tossed it into the trash, I had an idea. I would leave the note out, hide in the hall closet, and spy on everyone. Later, I'd jump out and scare them all to death. It would be a great joke.

Thunder rumbled across the countryside, and it started to rain. Electrical power to the house flickered off and on and made me nervous, so I was glad when my mom and dad came home. Quickly, I went to hide deep in the closet between the winter coats and boxes of Christmas ornaments. My parents were strangely quiet when they came in and hard to hear over the storm. When my mother read the note I had left out, she started to cry. My muscles stiffened. My father's voice gradually rose until I could make out what he was saying. I clamped my eyes shut and held my breath. I stayed as quiet as a church mouse.

"Don't be foolish!" he shouted.

My mother sniffed.

"Do you want me to stay or not?"

"Oh . . ."

"So you'll do whatever I want? Whatever I say?"

"Yes."

My father huffed. He sounded unconvinced. He stomped off to the refrigerator, then into the living room to the couch and turned on the TV. My mother disappeared.

After a while, the thunder grew distant and the rain eased. When it got dark outside, I sneaked into my room, jumped out my bedroom window, and ran barefoot across a field of wet alfalfa. I stopped when I reached the county road. My knees buckled. I fell down in the middle of the road and curled onto my side. The tar-chip surface was wet but warm from the day, and it comforted me as my tears blended with the rain. A whip-poor-will echoed my cries.

My father moved out a few months later, and for several years we did not see or speak to each other, though rumors trickled back. My Christian father, the author of my morals, beliefs, and the one whom I had idolized, now slept with women he hardly knew. I also heard he had pulled a gun on a man in a bar. (Did it matter that it was only a starter pistol, made to shoot blanks?) I suppose he had his own dragons to slay.

My mother came unglued. I often woke up in the middle of the night to the sound of her sobbing into the phone in the kitchen. I couldn't tell who she talked to, pleaded with, but it had to be my father or one of his girlfriends.

After a long, drawn-out separation, my parents divorced when I was eighteen. My mom found a job working for minimum wage at a commercial greenhouse. She and my sister had many private conversations in those days, but she left me alone. She needed me to be strong, which suited me fine; strong, aloof, closed off.

The three of us went to church less and less often. Even so, I still got down on my knees beside my trundle bed every night and begged Jesus for guidance and mercy and for a way to make sense of what had happened. The Christian foundation I had kneeled on all those years had shifted under me. Hairline fissures had appeared where there had once been solid footing, evidence of its man-made architecture. Like any true believer, my first reaction was not to dive deep or climb high in comprehending my situation, but to repair and restore my world to its original condition. In this way, I thought, I could go on living life as I always had.

As one might expect, the consequences were disastrous.

CHAPTER 2

The Writing on the Wall

TIFFANY AND I were little more than kids when we married at ages nineteen and twenty-four. She was a cute, bubbly young woman who came from a family of blue-collar Christians like my own, though in their case they were devout Baptists. With their encouragement, I dusted off my faith, joined a Bible study group, and listened to contemporary Christian music by artists like Amy Grant and Michael W. Smith.

I also read the Bible, cover to cover. But I didn't do it because I felt I was somehow responsible for my parents' divorce and should seek absolution. Neither did I do it to find Scriptures to blame them for the choices they had made. Rather, I studied God's word so I could build my own, more perfect marriage and replace their ending with a happy one. If I could do that, I thought, I would feel better about what I believed in and about the Bible itself.

Tiffany and I were prayer-warriors for God. We beseeched Him to bless us and protect our marriage, perhaps because we sensed how different we really were. She wanted children; I wasn't so sure. She wanted to be a latter-day June Cleaver and her husband's biblical helpmate; I was still in college and had only a part-time job, which meant she had to work outside the home. I had bizarre urges to climb mountains and fantasized about homesteading in the wilderness; she liked it fine in our Midwestern oil refinery town, right down the street from her parents' house and the Dunkin' Donuts.

I graduated from college a few months after we were married. As the first in my family to hold a bachelor's degree, relatives assumed I would drive an expensive, American-made car and live in a suburban home that consumed far more resources than necessary. Tiffany and her family had counted on a similar bed of roses. Such were the privileges and expectations of the American dream, or at least its white, middle-class rendering.

However, that kind of lifestyle had never appealed to me. Almost immediately, our marriage felt like a recurring nightmare, like something I had been through before and now I must go through again. No matter how sincerely Tiffany and I prayed, the gap between us grew until it was too great for our religion to bridge.

After the divorce was final, I was too embarrassed to talk about it with family or friends. Instead I sealed it up, shaved my head (in penance, before letting my hair grow long), and dove into graduate work in geography, the subject I would soon teach in Tanzania. I also found comfort by going to Sunday morning services at Campus Crusade for Christ. Publically, I held my hands up to Jesus and begged for an understanding of why my marriage—the cornerstone of my Christian faith—had not worked out according to plan.

The only other place I found relief was in the mountains. On semester breaks, I traveled west to climb in the Sierras of California, the Wind Rivers of Wyoming, and several ranges in Colorado. For reasons I could not yet comprehend, struggling to the top of a mountain not only healed old wounds but incubated new life.

I was back at school after one of these trips, studying for a test in the student commons. I had to get to class, so I packed my bag to leave. On my way out, I saw a bulletin board littered with spring break ads. It was hard not to notice all the flashy colors, the subtropical getaways, and photos of women in bikinis. Still, to me they seemed fake and frivolous.

My gaze fell to the bottom of the display. A flyer for South Padre Island, Texas, showed a photo of three tanned girls holding cans of Bud Light. Half hidden underneath this flyer was a booklet of perforated postcards. I was curious, so I stooped down, reached under the Padre flyer, and tore off one of the cards. Across the top, it read, "Peace Corps. The toughest job you'll ever love!" Next to the blurb were tiny images of people teaching children, digging pit latrines, and testing water samples.

I had heard of the Peace Corps but knew nothing about it. Even so, as I held the card in my hand I felt a light go on inside me. The work looked meaningful and gritty and, like a plaster cast over a broken bone, it promised a protected space where I could knit back together a life that was shattered. Plus, the thought of travel tempted me. My grandfathers had been in the Navy, which had enabled them to visit points in the Mediterranean and the Pacific. Otherwise, no one in my family had lived far from home since my ancestors had sailed to America from northwestern Europe to become coal miners, steel workers, and pipe fitters: the salt of the earth. Now I had that chance.

I told myself a white lie: The Peace Corps would also let me serve as an unofficial ambassador for Christ. During off-hours, I imagined preaching the Gospel to heathen hearts and minds. I still believed primitive, native peoples were damned to hell for not knowing or accepting the name of Jesus, though I had started to wonder how God could live with Himself for setting things up that way.

Six months later, the Peace Corps called to tell me I'd been assigned to volunteer in Tanzania. I was thrilled and told my mother first. She tried to be supportive, though it was hard for her. She was genuinely afraid for me. I called my dad next. We'd had only sporadic contact for years, but when we talked on the phone I could tell he was concerned. He was also perplexed as to why I wanted to give two years of my life to the primitive Negroes. As for my grandmother— my dad's mom—she was beside herself. She was convinced I would bring home an African wife who, in her words, would "have a bone in her nose." I calmed her down by saying I would serve as God's instrument in darkest Africa and teach a less fortunate (at the time, my euphemism for "less intelligent") people how to help themselves.

Frankly, I had no idea what to expect. In April 1994 I phoned the Peace Corps headquarters in Washington, D.C., for the latest on rumors of a "situation" developing in Rwanda. I didn't know it then, but in a few short months I would be stationed in the northwest corner of Tanzania, a mere eighty miles from the border of Rwanda, where the 1994 tribal bloodbath claimed an estimated 800,000 lives.

My friends, however, razzed me about the Peace Corps being a "hippie party" and a two-year vacation. Soon, they said, I'd be kickin' back in a grass-roofed tiki hut on a tropical beach, drinkin' local brews, smokin' funny cigarettes, and lovin' the nights away with *National Geographic* centerfold girls. To me, their jokes only served to underscore my indoctrination against sins of the flesh, especially "interracial commingling."

But deep down, I knew living in Africa would be far more

meaningful than any of the conventional reasons I could think of for going. It was a nameless ambition that lurked on the edge of my consciousness like a seraph coiled in the shade of a tree. I could make out its contours but not its motive. If trustworthy, it would show me the way to save myself. If not, it would turn on me before I could escape.

That day back in the student commons, I had taken the humble Peace Corps card and zipped it into my pack as if it were a sign from God. And maybe it was. Like a rite of passage, the Peace Corps would pitch me into territories wilder than anything I could imagine in my insulated corner of the world. In the process, my understanding of reality would be shaken and ultimately fail. Block by block, it would be brought low until nothing remained—nothing, that is, but God.

CHAPTER 3

Threshold

THE KENYAN SUN blazed directly overhead, and the air was so hot I thought my short-sleeved shirt would melt into my green vinyl bus seat. From the window of our Toyota minibus, I saw a black man up ahead. He wore a three-piece suit that was half a shade darker than his skin and buttoned to the nape of his celluloid collar. As our bus approached, I glimpsed his face. It was streaked with sweat. Squinting into the heat, he pushed a bicycle along the ragged edge of the shoulderless desert highway, and could have been a Catholic clergyman on his way to pray over a dying child in Nairobi's slums. Yellow dust and oily exhaust coated him each time a lorry, land cruiser, speed taxi, or minibus like ours screamed past.

The country that blurred past my window was leaner and bonier than any I had ever seen. It looked like Mars and brought to mind the opening scenes from *2001: A Space Odyssey*. The wildlife, however, reminded me more of *The Lion King*, or *Jurassic Park*, or maybe Busch Gardens in Florida. We saw several zebras and had to stop once for a herd of giraffe galumphing its way across the highway. But this was no zoo, and no beer hut waited for us around the corner.

In the border town of Namanga, we pulled up next to a

homely customs office that was conspicuous among the cinder block buildings because of its vinyl siding. I scanned our minibus and counted twenty-two of us. Getting everyone's luggage checked and passport stamped could have taken hours, but our mop-headed, forty-something director, David, had a better plan. He collected our passports and took them into the customs office to acquire all the necessary documentation for us while we waited in the bus. It was much more efficient, but I wondered if he had to pay a bribe.

Meanwhile, dozens of men, women, and children besieged our bus. They stood several rows deep and strained to push all kinds of wooden trinkets, jewelry, and cloth goods through the windows into our young, muddled faces. Not surprisingly, none of us spoke Swahili, the regional lingua franca, though a few had been smart enough to bring travel dictionaries.

Rolf was the first one of us to assemble a short sentence. He shouted it to a woman who presented him with a small, wooden rhino. Simultaneously, she pressed her bare breasts into the lower, closed portion of his window.

Brad, the guy in the seat in front of me, noticed, too. "Nothin' like a little local charm!"

I was transfixed. Her breasts were wrinkled and sagging, and her nipples, each of which was the size of my thumb, stuck to the window and dragged behind the greater flaps of flesh. God, I thought, that had to hurt.

"*Hapana asante, mama! Hapana asante!*" Rolf repeated the phrase over and over, firmly but with a smile on his clean-cut, bespectacled face. His wife, Cynthia, snickered next to him.

I shouted over the clamor, "What are you saying?"

"It means 'No, thank you.'"

I squinted and cupped a hand behind an ear.

"It means, 'No, thank you,' I think!"

I nodded and turned to the young man at my window. He wore a red-checkered sheet wrapped around him like a toga, and each of his pierced earlobes was stretched out around a black film canister. He held up a necklace of geometrically shaped pieces of tin for me to see.

"*Hapana asante!*" I said.

He looked confused, and I felt bad, but none of us in the group yet owned a single shilling, a unit of currency adopted during the days of colonial British East Africa. And while any of the hawkers around the bus would have accepted U.S. dollars, we had no clue as to the relative value of anything. Did a cute, handcrafted trinket go for fifty cents or fifty dollars? We had no idea. For the next half hour, *hapana asante* became our mantra.

David finally returned, and with some relief we left the excitement of our first encounter with the natives. I had seen movies with African themes like *The Power of One*, and so I assumed most Africans must be witch doctors and keepers of black magic. Their job was to lead young initiates through rituals that would break them down and make them vulnerable. But when we approached the border fence, I revised my notion—men clad in dusty green fatigues skulked about with Kalashnikovs slung over their shoulders. Each one smoked a Sweet Menthol cigarette and peered out from underneath his beret with sidelong suspicion.

Once through the Kenyan border gate, we drove through a literal no-man's land of a hundred yards or so to the gate on the Tanzanian side. As we crossed over, a flash of realization hit—I had left my past behind, and an entire planet of unknowns was about to open before me. I stared at the burnt, crusted ground slipping by and fingered the gold cross around my neck. Reassured, my breathing eased and my gaze blurred.

After we crossed the border, we were back on the high desert road heading south to Arusha, one of the largest cities in Tanzania. For the next ten weeks, Arusha would be our base camp. During the day we would learn the rudiments of Swahili at the Peace Corps training site. At night, we would lodge with separate host families. Along with Swahili, our syllabus would cover safe sex (local populations varied in degrees of HIV infection from 10 to 50 percent), current affairs and controversies (government corruption and female circumcision/genital mutilation), teaching methods and recalibration of our grading structure (A = 80–100%, B = 60–79%, etc.), and the major do's and don'ts of East African cultures. For instance, men wear long pants, women wear dresses, and only children wear shorts; people are summoned with the right hand only, palm facing down as the fingers are curled in; livestock are summoned in the same manner but with the palm facing up; never sit with a leg crossed over a knee with the sole of the foot facing someone (big insult!); and never give to or take from the hand of another using the left hand (bigger insult!). Surviving this, we would be commissioned as teachers at schools dotting the Tanzanian countryside.

But on that first day on the bus, none of us knew any of that. It was still hours before we would reach Arusha. In the meantime, I watched the shadow of our bus race along the ground, freakishly out of proportion to the bus's actual size. I checked my watch. It was 5:30 P.M. In the front seat, David leaned forward over the partition and talked to the driver. The driver straightened, cocked an ear back, nodded, and pointed ahead. In a few moments we pulled off the left side of the road—the driving side—and stopped.

David stood up and addressed us. "Hope everybody's doing okay. We should get into Arusha in about an hour or so," he said as he glanced down at his bulky, Navy Seal–style wristwatch. "It'll be dark by then, so we'll go to the Impala Hotel for dinner.

"And I know you guys are wiped out from traveling, but as long as we're here, I thought you might like to see something special." He bent to look southeast through the bus windows. "So if you look out thataway," he pointed, "you can barely make out Kilimanjaro, the world's biggest free-standing mountain." Everyone turned and focused bloodshot eyes.

"Oh, there. See it?" Cynthia said. We followed her pointing finger and soon everyone squinted and nodded.

"If you want," David said, "you can get out here and stretch your legs, take some photos. But let's make it quick. Five minutes."

I grabbed my camera and stepped outside. The dark massif on the horizon drew me from the inside out, as if it were a magnetic pole and I was cast in iron. The little-boy's ego in me desired only to climb it, plant the flag, and reduce it to yet another medal on my chest. In this way, I was like most men who are fascinated with guns, knives, and other phallic symbols of masculine insecurity. Anything deeper was still far beyond my grasp.

I squinted into the evening light. The mountain's long, slender profile arced heavenward, barely distinguishable from the earth and sky orbiting around it. It exuded both majesty and menace. My experiences in the Rockies had taught me how mountains had a special talent for drawing emotions of deep candor up from my very core, and I sensed this mountain and I would get to know each other much better.

We were soon on the road again, and a sparse collection of trees began to appear. Sometimes called umbrella trees, acacias have flat crowns and three-inch thorns that poke out from their limbs. Acacias are icons of the African savanna that are stamped on everything from T-shirts to shampoo bottles. Here, however, they were dwarfed by baobab trees. Like holy pillars that prop up the enormous dome of the African sky, baobabs reach up to a hundred feet in height and have trunks that can grow to over a hundred feet in circumference. Determining a baobab tree's age is difficult since it does not produce growth rings, but carbon dating has shown that some very large individual trees may be over 5,000 years old. This makes them contenders for the world's oldest living things and adds credence to their nickname, the Tree of Life.

The sun sank below the salt grass fringing the horizon. As the air cooled, we saw another mountain behemoth come into view ahead—Mount Meru. Before long, more trees appeared: eucalyptus and some species of pine, all planted in long, neat rows. I saw succulents, too, similar to agaves only much bigger. I later learned these were sisal plants, a nine-teenth-century import from Mexico and a refugee in colonial Tanganyika. Sisal plantations once covered huge swaths of East Africa. However, during World War II the invention of nylon replaced sisal being marketed for use in cordage.

As we neared Arusha, tiny, one-stalled kiosks popped up along the highway. The glow from oil lanterns and charcoal fires lit their interiors and gave us glimpses of canned goods, boxes stacked on shelves, and faces.

And the trash! Torn bags, old flip-flops, ruined chairs, and a thousand other bits of unidentifiable crap was strewn along the roadside. I could only imagine the armies of rats breeding under so much filth. "What a total dump," I said. Luckily no one else heard me, but what I had thought was more along the lines of, *I can't believe these people live like this! I sure am glad I'm not one of them—not black!*

I was convinced that since I had spent years in multiethnic colleges, I no longer harbored the bigoted views I'd grown up around, but the truth is that not so deep inside me lurked arrogance, prejudice, and fear. I have to confess, my pride liked it that way. I liked feeling superior and entitled and set apart, chosen, even though I would never have admitted that to myself in a million years.

Pretending to be open-minded, I reminded myself about the reading I had done in preparation for living in Africa. I recalled how most of the continent had no public waste-disposal system, and that people used things until they were completely used up. For example, after a shirt was no longer wearable it became a head-cushion for carrying water buckets, and then a rag for washing floors. Finally, it was thrown to the pigs, or just "thrown out." Using a thing until it was wholly consumed was the definition of *ultimate materialism.*

A waxing gibbous moon had replaced the glow of sunset with a pallid mien, and the air became quite cool. Darkness spilled down the slopes of Mount Meru, and the windows of the bus were snapped shut, one by one. I drew my arms into my sides to keep warm and wanted to kick myself for leaving my jacket stored in my bag, now lashed to the roof of the bus. Unusual smells began to seep in, too. They were odors acrid and sweet, of wood smoke and meat cooking over fires, of urine and things I couldn't place.

We would arrive in Arusha soon. As we bounded along that equatorial tarmac, I looked at the folder in my lap. Schedules, agendas, and photographs of faraway places filled its interior. The slogan on the front cover—"Peace Corps. The toughest job you'll ever love!"—reminded me of the challenge I had accepted.

I breathed deeply. More wood smoke. Fires kindled.

CHAPTER 4

An Omnivore's Dilemma

MEAT. STEWED BANANAS and nettles. Rice and beans simmered in a chunky tomato and cabbage broth. Chapati fry breads. A scrambled egg or two. And more meat.

Dinners revolved around these staples, although a certain side dish deserves honorable mention. *Ugali* is a cooked blend of water and corn flour. (Sorghum, millet, or cassava are used instead of corn in areas where those crops were more widely grown.) The common practice is to take a portion of *ugali* about the size of a baseball and mold it into a shape suitable for sopping up bean juice or stewed nettles. *Ugali* felt like a warm lump of Play-Doh, and it was fun to clutch and squeeze and work in the palm of my hand. Most folks loved it, though I usually passed—the taste of *ugali* brought back distant memories of Play-Doh, too.

However, the freshly baked breads were divine, especially one sold at a downtown bakery in Arusha with a label that boasted it was "Enriched! With Fat and Sugar!" It reminded me of angel food cake, and I sometimes polished off an entire loaf of its spongy goodness in just one sitting.

But the main vehicle for each meal was meat. At the time, I was not a vegetarian—not even close. Throughout the ten-week training period in Arusha, it was the great pleasure and personal mission of my host family mother, Mama Suzan, to serve meat at each of my breakfasts and dinners. (Lunches were served at the Peace Corps training site.) Bear in mind, this meat was no prime rib or steak or even ground round. Most of it was marbled gristle that had the consistency of a greasy, rubber shoe sole and required considerable determination to render chunks small enough to permit swallowing.

Nevertheless, I enjoyed most of the food, especially the breads, the chapatis, the teas, and the myriad cooking bananas. Rice dishes were wonderful, too, as long as I watched for tiny, hidden stones. Harvested and dried out in the sun on the ground, the rice often contained bits of local geology before it made its way onto market tables. One or another sorting technique could be employed to help preserve dental fillings, but none were foolproof. After a few minor events, I learned to chew much more thoughtfully.

Coffee, thank God, was another story. Until I arrived in Africa, I'd never had much use for the unsavory bean on which the fate of empires has turned. Every few years throughout my childhood, some relative would encourage a sampling of the opaque extract, usually accompanied with a devious grin. With such bitter memories, I had long since given up on coffee.

However, when Mama Suzan brought breakfast to my room my first morning in Arusha, I felt I had no choice but to partake. The tray was set with fried eggs, strips of fried meat, toast spread with Blue Band margarine, and a cup of coffee. More than a little skeptical, I pursed my lips to the rim of the tin mug and braced myself. When I tasted it, my eyes brightened, and while the acrid bite was still detectable, the greater measure of it was mild and creamy, and produced a candied, caffeinated drink that was perfectly, wickedly rich. As my coffee cooled, the top congealed into a chewy skin that kept the liquid part hot underneath and stuck to my lips as I drank every drop.

Africafe is a coarsely granulated, instant mix farmed and packed in northwestern Tanzania. Mama Suzan had prepared it for me using boiled whole milk straight from the cow that very morning. She had also stirred in a few heaping teaspoons of sugar culled from the cane plantations south of Lake Victoria.

I was the latest in a series of five Peace Corps Volunteers to have been hosted by the Mollels. I considered them a good, Christian family who helped their own by helping people like me. Mama Suzan was the matriarch. I guessed she was in her midsixties, and she took great pride in how she dressed. Each day she wrapped herself in floral cocoons of primary colors made from free-flowing, traditional *kanga* cloth. She preferred to keep her graying hair cropped quite short, almost bald, though she was careful to don a voluminous turban of material whenever she went to market or to church. As for her voice, she always spoke to me in puckered, high-pitched little notes. It was not quite baby talk but sounded like the speech reserved for small children, even toddlers, which is essentially what I was. I think she liked me and enjoyed my company, perhaps since I shared the Christian name of her late husband, William. This was how she and her family referred to me. She had given it a try, but could not manage to pronounce the name Bill. It had instead come out more like "Blulla" or "Ballilla," so I let it go at William, which when they said it sounded like "Weelyum."

The centerpiece of the Mollel property was its courtyard, and in the center of the courtyard was a hand-operated well pump. The yard was bordered by the house and several pink hydrangeas on one side and by a row of outdoor latrines and showers on the other. None had running water. For bathing,

I half filled a five-gallon bucket with cold water from the pump and topped it off with a pot of boiling water Mama Suzan was always kind enough to heat for me. I carried the bucket of warm water to a shower stall along with a bar of Dial soap and a bottle of Pert Plus I'd bought at a shop in town. After lathering up, I dipped steaming water from the bucket with an empty food tin to rinse off.

For the privy, I filled the same bucket with well-water and carried it to a latrine. A four-gallon, metal jerry can and cup were stationed inside each latrine next to a hole in the concrete floor. After doing my business, I performed a sort of manual bidet: I used my right hand to hold the cup of water while *only my left hand* washed my bottom. (Hence, the dirty left hand is socially proscribed.) I flushed by pouring the water I had carried from the well into the basin-hole. Last but not least, I carefully scrubbed my hands, fingers, and nails.

One afternoon, on the way home from the market, Mama Suzan said she needed to mail a letter to her relatives who lived near Kilimanjaro. As we neared the post office, we saw that the line to buy stamps wound into the street. At the rate the line moved, it could easily take thirty minutes before we made it to the clerk behind the iron window grille. Luckily a policeman standing guard at the door saw us. He smiled and waved for us to come over.

He said something cheery to me, but my Swahili was infantile so I deferred to Mama Suzan. She chuckled and nodded that it was okay. The policeman looked relieved. He led us to the front of the line in the lobby, where we interrupted a customer at the window in mid-transaction. The customer stepped aside for us and no one objected.

We thanked the officer, but I was puzzled. I searched Mama Suzan's face. She chuckled again, grabbed my forearm, and pinched my skin.

"Oh, white!" I said, and I smiled.

I had been taught that white was the color of cleanliness, godliness, purity, and all things proper. Certainly in Africa, white made me special and put me at the front of the line. I accepted this judgment without qualms—though I was no racist, I reminded myself. I was a Christian.

The main entrance to the Mollels' yard was situated in a gap of thirty feet or so between the bathroom stalls and the house. From here a wide path led to the Peace Corps training site. After leaving the Mollels', the path went by Father Alexi's little Catholic church, which was shaped like a geodesic dome but was barely twenty feet in diameter. Past the church, the path came to a rough-hewn kiosk, where I liked to buy Cadbury Milk Crunch chocolate bars or Fanta sodas in bottles. A little farther, it crossed over a paved road that led into town. From this point, Mount Meru filled the northern panorama—and my imagination.

Mount Meru is a dormant volcano that reaches 15,000 feet into the sky. I had heard that during the long rainy season from March to May a thin web of snow could sometimes be seen high above tree line. Arusha is nestled at about 4,500 feet on the southern slopes of the mountain. Due to the town's altitude, daytime temperatures seldom climbed above 85° F. Still, it was warm enough to host stands of brilliant, flame-red bottlebrush trees and white-blossomed tamarind along all the main thoroughfares. Purple jacaranda and pink-blossomed oleander, too, made it feel like Easter morning every day of the year.

By the time I passed the paved road into town, I started to meet other volunteers on their way to morning classes. The walk to class was a time when we could catch up with one another's latest adventures in local cuisine, or spring a new Kiswahili word into action. (In Bantu languages, each noun falls into one of several noun classes. In its own class, the word "Swahili" receives the Ki prefix.)

Each weekday morning at 8:00, twenty-two of us convened in the main house at the training site. There we settled into folding chairs on the screened-in porch of the classroom area. One of our first lessons taught us that 8:00 is read as 2:00 on the Swahili dial. This method of telling time is common among equatorial peoples worldwide. Because sunrise and sunset occurs at roughly the same time each day year round, these times are considered 12:00 in Swahili time. In other words, think of the clock turned upside down and backward, so that by 10:00 A.M. (4:00 Swahili time), we had struggled through sufficient classwork to earn a "spot" of midmorning *chai* served with *maandazi* cakes and *biskuti* (biscotti).

We numbered eighteen men and four women. Josh was the youngest, at twenty-one. Rich was the eldest, at thirty-four. (I secretly pitied Rich for having ended up in a country of such severe poverty, where assumptions about his financial state might be made based on his shortened first name alone.) Like me, Josh and Rich were geographers. Another volunteer I connected with was named Brad. He had hiked and camped in the Sierras while living in California, which gave us plenty to talk about over games of hacky sack. I also got to know Rolf and Cynthia. They were a newlywed couple in their late twenties who had invested time in the outdoors, too. I had a sneaking suspicion I would spend meaningful time with each of these people.

From the beginning, no one in the group knew which school they would be assigned to. After six weeks, in mid-July, our instructors finally made their decisions and presented us with our fates. When it came to me, the instructor named Kiobya said, "*Bwana* William, it is true! You yourself will be going to my home area near Bukoba. You will be teaching A-level geography at Rugambwa Girls' Secondary School. It is a splendid area that I think you will find most enjoyable."

As he spoke, I remembered Kiobya had told us about a fishing village he was from on the western side of Lake Victoria. He had said when he was very young his father had taken him hunting. While his father hunted, Kiobya had stopped to rest beneath a *mwarobaini* tree and drifted off to sleep. Silently, a python slithered down and wrapped itself around his body. As the snake tightened its grip, Kiobya awakened and screamed. His father sprinted back and killed the snake with his machete but accidentally nicked his son. To illustrate his story, Kiobya had brought his fingers across his forehead with a slicing sound and indicated the diagonal scar.

In spite of his story about large, malicious serpents, Kiobya sounded encouraging, and I was glad to finally know where I would settle and teach. Yet I was also disappointed. I had hoped to be stationed at a school closer to Mount Meru or Kilimanjaro, or even the Uluguru Mountains in the east. I was still a novice mountaineer, but I felt driven to climb and go as high as I dared. I would discover that such impulses came from deep within my psyche. Their intent was to push me to the brink of death in order to ritually "kill" me and collapse my reality.

After we received our assignments, we learned we would each be traveling alone to visit our school during the next week. That afternoon, everyone tromped off to buy bus tickets or make taxi reservations—everyone except me and Josh, that is. Since my school was in Bukoba and Josh's was in Mwanza—another town in the northwest—we would need plane tickets to the deep interior of East Africa.

CHAPTER 5

The Tree of
Good and Evil

AS A RULE, public transportation in Africa is unreliable, to
say the least. On the morning Josh and I were scheduled to
leave Arusha, all flights from the two closest airports were
canceled. Because our schools were so far away, our site visits
were likewise canceled. So instead of khakis and penny loaf-
ers, we pulled on jeans and Vibram-soled boots, and stuffed
our packs with gear fit for surviving the jungled steeps of
Mount Meru.

Arusha National Park surrounded the mountain and
offered a guided trail service that began at the park headquarters. Sleeping huts were also positioned along the way
to the summit. The official legal approach, however, required
a fee. Being relatively young, poor, and ambitious, Josh and I
had no intention of climbing in the conventional manner. We
were confident we could find a "back door" to the mountain
that was free of charge and offered greater adventure.

We had no portable stove, so we precooked a pot of rice
and beans. We also packed oranges, peanuts, chapatis, several chocolate bars, and some rusk biscuits. (In East Africa,
as in Britain, "biscuits" mean cookies, "crisps" mean chips,

and "chips" are fries.) I also whipped up a batch of no-bake peanut butter dough—a sweetly caloric amalgam of peanut butter, powdered milk, and honey my mom used to make for me when I was a kid.

To the outside of my pack I strapped four metal clips, called carabiners, and some daisy-chained lengths of nylon webbing. I had a climbing rope, but it was heavy. For this trip I decided instead to take a coil of nylon cord I had purchased in town. I didn't think we would run into any serious climbing, and I took this gear only because I thought it looked rugged and manly jangling around on my pack. Curiously, the one item we did not have was a map. But no matter; I was well-versed in matters of blind faith, and I was fairly confident all we needed to do was hike uphill.

The morning was cloudy and cool as we marched through town. Our packs weighed between thirty and forty pounds apiece. We got directions from people along the way, and before long we left the blaring kiosk music, hagglers, and mobs of street kids behind. The green living things began to outnumber the gray built ones.

By noon the sky broke into a mosaic of blues, whites, and grays. We glimpsed higher slopes and valleys. The dirt road we had been hiking on turned into a wide, sandy path, and our attention focused on avoiding frequent spatters of cow dung. Maggots and flies busily bored holes into every cow pie with the singular mission of turning it into more maggots and flies. Ficus and ironwood trees cradled the path. Their dark green crowns were ponderous and thick and tattled with liana vines that reached to the ground. Hanging mosses danced spookily in the slightest breeze. The damp quiet was occasionally split by the raucous, throaty barks of collobus monkeys. Long black-and-white hair covered their body from head to tail and accentuated their gymnastic leaps through the trees. The magnitude of the valleys paralleling our ascent overwhelmed us. Gorges plunged thousands of feet almost vertically, yet remained dense with vegetation and dripping with moisture. From the depths, swatches of clouds rose quickly to meet us.

By mid-afternoon, we came upon a sparkling mountain stream. Only a few inches deep, it trickled and darted over a bed of rounded stones and black volcanic silt. We had been hiking hard for the better part of a day, so it was the perfect place to take a break. I had finished the water in one of my bottles, and I went to refill it. Since the water was clear, I decided not to look for my iodine tablets or ask Josh for his water filter.

As I crouched to dip my bottle into the cool, free-flowing water, a herd of cows trundled up the trail and marched straight through the brook and onto the far bank as if Josh and I weren't even there. Black mud sucked at their dripping hooves. A few wore bells around their necks. One of the last cows to cross was a large though gaunt gray bull with an alarming six-foot span of horns. When it reached the middle of the stream, it stopped and proceeded to piss out a great, curdled gush of blood—dark red and frothy.

I jerked the water bottle out of the stream. Josh chuckled and pointed at me and shook his head.

"Got that filter, Josh?"

His laughter trailed off as he turned to dig into his pack.

Josh was from Kentucky. He'd given it his best shot but was unsuccessful tutoring the rest of us in the correct pronunciation of his hometown, Louisville, as "Luwuhvuh." Both he and I had recently graduated with degrees in geography, but neither of us had much experience teaching. Many of our anxious chats around the training site concerned how we planned to teach African geography to Africans. Of average height and build, Josh was a constant cutup who found semi-arid humor in almost anything. One of his recent witticisms was in fashioning an alternate meaning for the Swahili words for "two breads," or two loaves of bread. On the chalkboard at the training site, he had written "*mikate miwili*" (me-KAH-tay me-WEE-lee) in quotes, and waggishly forged Lorena Bobbitt's signature below.

The cows left us amid a tardy cocoon of dust. The herd's pastor next appeared wearing tattered shorts that were too big and a winter coat that was too small. He had no shirt or shoes. Most conspicuous was a blue woolen cap that sat perched atop his head like that of a magician, only in miniature. He was an ancient-looking fellow, white-haired and short, and ambled along on cracked and crusted bare feet. He held onto a rope tied around the last cow's neck and tapped its rump with a stick.

Josh and I offered the customary greeting for an elder: "*Shikamoo*." This is a term of respect that survives from the old Arabic, which makes up about one third of the Swahili language. Its literal translation is, "I hold your feet." When the old man heard us, he brightened and pulled tight on the sisal rope looped around his cow's neck. His white-stubbled smile was absent of all but two or three stained teeth in his lower jaw. "*Marahaba!*" he said, which means "As it should be." He then brought his quavering, leathery hands together before his bowed head, though not so much in humiliation as in agreement.

In broken Swahili, Josh asked if he knew the best way to climb the mountain while I fished the dictionary out of my pack. The old man's smile relaxed as he listened. That's when I noticed a thick, fibrous sclera covering both his eyes. I suspected he navigated this terrain from a long familiarity with its twists and turns and perhaps by following his cows and hanging onto the last one's rope, like a seeing-eye cow.

When we finished asking our questions, the old man closed his eyes. A minute passed before he breathed and opened them as though he had awakened from a dream. He pointed at the trail with his stick and described a path that bent through the undergrowth and led to a forest of bamboo. As he spoke and gestured, I scribbled down what he said so I could look it up later. What I discovered was that he said the trail through the bamboo was obvious since it had been carved by forest elephants. After leaving the bamboo forest we would see a certain tree, and this tree signaled a turning point. From that point on, he didn't know. He had never gone beyond the place where the trees grow short and the cold becomes sharp.

We gave him a Cadbury Milk Crunch bar for the information, and he seemed grateful. He bowed to us several times with praying hands. He went back to his cow, swatted it on the rump, and dissolved into the foliage. We heard cowbells in the forest for some time after that.

"Well, I reckon the ol' boy knows his shit. You get all that, Hatch?" Josh asked. He turned to look over my notepad.

I shook my head. "Something about turning right, and a tree—with rocks. He said rocks, didn't he?"

Josh smiled and scratched under his floppy-brimmed hat. "Well, shit."

Before long we entered a maze of bamboo. We followed elephant tracks through a corridor that could only have been made by a four-ton pachyderm. Each track was as big as my chest. The trees on the other side of the bamboo forest were shorter and stumpier, so it was noticeable when we came upon an evergreen tree of considerable girth. Known as a *Podocarpus*, or Yellowwood tree, it grew at an unusually high altitude for its kind. Its roots bulked up above the ground, and its twisted, gnarled branches were festooned with all manner of mosses and creepers. A damp, acrid smell hung about the place, too. It coated our nostrils and lungs and reminded me of decayed coffee grounds and cat pee.

Many paths intersected at the tree. Most of the herbaceous forbs and undergrowth had been stamped out from years of foot, paw, and hoof traffic, and we thought this had to be the tree the old man had told us about. Opposite from us the ground ramped up into a rocky, moss-strewn buttress. From here we were supposed to continue on the right-most path that turned north.

Intuition told me this was a very special place. Local tribes might even have considered it a sacred place, despite the fact that everyone I had met in town was either Catholic or Lutheran. My host brother, Patrick, was Catholic, and even though I was a Protestant I had recently attended Mass with him in Arusha. I hadn't understood a word of the priest's liturgy or the lyrics to any of the songs, yet it was comforting to be in a sturdily built house of the Lord all the same.

This place, however, was completely different. The smells and the twisted vines were light-years away from what I knew to be upright and holy. This alone told me it was evil. I could almost feel the cold paganism radiate from the tree, and I half expected Lucifer himself to slither down the trunk.

I remembered reading textbooks published by Bob Jones University Press and A Beka Press that described Satan's grip on Africa. In general, the A Beka textbooks placed the blame for Africa's disease, poverty, and lack of progress on its own populace. The African peoples' miseries, these books said, were due to their pernicious indulgence in idolatry, superstition, and witchcraft. According to the fifth-grade text, "In countries where the people are still held in fear by witchcraft and spirit worship, [postcolonial] self-government soon turned into dictatorship." And in a senior-high text, "For over a thousand years, there was no clear Christian witness in the vast heartland of Africa; the fear, idolatry, superstition, and witchcraft associated with animism (the belief that natural objects and forces are inhabited by mostly malignant spirits) prevented most Africans from learning how to use nature for man's benefit and thus develop a high culture. . . ."

Bob Jones' seventh-grade text clearly explained the spiritual error of traditional African religions: "The strong influence of magic and demonism on African religion made much of African life unhappy and savage. Satan's strong hold on these people kept them worshipping him rather than the true God."

I understood Africans were religiously uninformed before Europeans arrived in the nineteenth century. Still, it was hard for me to see that they were more naïve or gullible to Satan's whims than anyone else simply because they were Africans.

I saw the glint of bigotry embedded in my circular reasoning, and I calmed down. People had always created a central place around which to meet and pray and reaffirm life. It was a universal human trait. I looked at the tree again and decided it was probably not Satanic. I decided it was instead an aging example of an interesting, albeit primitive, religious ceremonial place where people worshipped what they knew. But if this were the case, a question arose: Were the values of right and wrong rigid and absolute, or were they fluid and multifaceted?

I was nervous again. I prayed silently. *Dear God, what is this place? Is it good or evil? Please, Father, I need your help. I'm listening.*

Just then a flash of violet fluttered across my face. I jerked my head back to see a butterfly. Its wings were iridescent and lined in inky black. Flitting down the path, the butterfly came to rest in the boughs of the holy rood. It was then I noticed dozens of green cocoons hanging like pregnant emeralds high among the leaves and smaller branches.

"Guess we take this one," Josh said as he pointed up the path. "Look right to you, Hatch?"

But my thoughts were still nestled between the cocoons.

"Hatch!"

I shook off the daydream. "What?"

"You hatchin' a plan, Hatch? Or an egg or somethin'?"

He had struck a chord, and I was embarrassed. I blinked up at the weather and down at my wristwatch, still set to "normal time."

"Five o'clock," I said. "Better move. Get as high as we can on this ridge before dark."

Josh nodded.

I waded into the wet grass to where the higher trail started but stopped to glance back. The little fleck of violet hurried into the gathering mist below.

CHAPTER 6

Serpentine

WE GAINED ALMOST 9,000 vertical feet on the first day, so I slept like a rock that night. My only dream came just before dawn.

The day is sunny and bright. I am standing in a dirt road, and I see Tanzanians walking around. My Peace Corps friends are here, too. We are talking and laughing the way we always do . . . when gunshots erupt! It's the police! They have automatic rifles. They're spraying bullets at everyone. And they have dogs! Big black ones with sharp teeth, leaping through glass-less windows in tall, white buildings. Everyone is screaming and falling, being run down. Butchered!

My watch alarm startled me awake. I sat up in my sleeping bag. The hood was cinched down so tightly on my face it left only a small circle through which I could breathe. I was blind, and for a moment I didn't remember where I was. Verging on panic, I breathed in hard. The cold, sharp air immediately brought me around and I fumbled for the zipper.

Since we had no tent, Josh and I had slept out in the open, and when I unzipped my sleeping bag I was gripped by the lean, icy air. I pressed the Indiglo button on my watch; 5:00

A.M. I heard Josh move around in his bag, but I couldn't see him. I couldn't see anything. It reminded me of visiting Mammoth Cave in Kentucky when I was a boy and the tour leader had shut off the lights to demonstrate total darkness. The blackness was stagnant, solid, though without form. I had held more air in my lungs than normal just in case it was all gone.

I groped around for my headlamp, found it, and clicked it on. My eyes winked shut in the sudden whiteout. All around us the grasses and stumpy trees glistened in an armor of pure, silvery beaded light, as if we had awoken in a cavern lined with crystals or diamonds. But instead of silica or carbon, these gems had grown from condensation to produce a heavy frost. We pulled on more layers and shook the crusty cold from our gear, powdering ourselves with a crystalline film in the process.

"Damn! Cold as a witch's tit!" Josh said. "Thought we were in Africa!"

We loaded our daypacks, stashed our backpacks, and moved up the ridge. Along the way, we encountered the dark, contorted profiles of the last remaining trees. From the edge of my tunnel vision, lighted by my headlamp, they resembled ogres reaching out for my coat, or my arm, or an eye.

The grasses under our lug soles soon transformed into the hard clap of rock. Some parts were clean and smooth, while others were littered with shattered, ball bearing–sized stones. House-sized boulders punctuated the landscape, too—dark-complexioned and anywhere from glassy to pocked in texture. We scrambled up the forty-degree slope and reached the crater rim by mid-morning. From there we crept on all fours over to the edge, where a rocky, phallus-shaped gendarme stood erect over the lip of one of the highest rock faces on the planet. We peered into the matriarchal crater, 5,000 feet deep. The opposite, eastern half of the crater wall had been blasted away long ago, and a low deck of clouds spilled out all the way to Kilimanjaro, some eighty miles to the east.

We backed away from the edge and picked our way over the crumbly rim toward the summit. We had been out of water since we left camp that morning but came across a boulder draped with icicles. Carefully, we braced our bottles under the drips and prayed to cash in on a few sips of water when we returned.

The sun was high overhead when we finally approached a pyroclastic mass we had so far referred to as "the block." Behemoth in scale and attribute, it was perhaps sixty feet high, one hundred feet wide, and of indeterminate length. Deeply incised gorges fell 1,500 feet on the outslope side, and a sheer wall plunged nearly a mile into the crater on the other.

"Yo, Haji," Josh said, referring to the long-sleeved shirt wrapped around my head.

"Yeah."

Josh scratched under his chin and sat down on a flattish rock. I sensed a lack of faith in his movements. As soon as he got comfortable, he told me that he had come far enough and was ready to head down.

Quietly, I opened my daypack, pulled out the climbing gear, and began fashioning a sit-harness from a length of two-inch, tubular webbing. An anxious power had taken control of the gears in my head. Mountains symbolized a psychological vault in which my soul had been locked away, and I sensed that climbing them was the way—or at least part of the way—to break out.

"Dude!" I said, mustering conviction in my voice. "I've done this lots of times. Here." I handed him the harness. "Put this on."

"What, are you high? With a *clothesline*?"

"Aw, it's fine. I won't fall. Now when I get to the top, I'll set an anchor, a good one, and belay you up. Sound good?"

Josh's brow furrowed in the shade of his safari hat. He exhaled and brought a hand up like a salute to shield his eyes from the midday sun. After a moment, he nodded and stood up. "*Bwana,* I may be dry as a dog bone, but I ain't afraida no shit-pile of rocks. Game on!"

We pulled on the improvised sit-harnesses I'd thrown together with spare webbing. To this, we tied into a six-millimeter yellow cord that might not have supported a blanket hung out to dry on a pretty spring day. Four carabiners connected our harnesses to the "rope." We also had one keychain carabiner with the words NOT LOAD BEARING microscopically embossed along its spine. I used this one on my harness. Since we had no pitons or other protective gear, I would climb free solo—that is, if I fell I would be badly injured, or worse. At the base of the block I looped a massive, horn-shaped boulder with a webbing sling for Josh to use as a bottom anchor while he belayed. In this way, he'd be out of the system while I climbed. I knew if I came off, the system would likely fail, and I wanted to make certain I did not take him with me into some very deep air.

I taught him the basic climbing commands and prepared to climb.

"All right, on belay?" I asked, checking both our harnesses and tie-ins.

"Belay is on."

I turned and looked up at the block. "Climbing."

"Up . . . climb—what was it?"

"It's 'climb on.'"

"Gotcha. Climb on!"

A waft of thin air blew across my face. I swallowed a hard lump of fear and whispered to myself, "Please, God," and started climbing.

I judged the rock wall to be about sixty feet high. In a quiet place in the back of my mind, I began to convert metric to English. The clothesline I had picked up at a shop in Arusha was twenty meters long. That's what the price tag had said.

I mumbled to myself, "One meter, a little over three feet, like thirty-nine inches, so twenty times three—" A rock peeled off from under my left hand. All my weight fell onto my right arm and right leg. I yelled down, *"Rock!"* Josh was now thirty feet below. He danced to his left. The rock shattered and the fragments skipped over the edge of the crater.

I breathed hard and found another handhold. In a moment, I composed myself and shouted, "Climbing again!"

"Climb on!"

I exhaled through pursed lips. "Twenty meters times three, sixty, add a little more, like sixty-five . . ." A hot flash of fear shot through me. My palms prickled with sweat—not good for grip. I realized I may not have enough line to reach the top. I would have to convince Josh to . . . let go of the rope.

But I couldn't think about that now. And I certainly couldn't think about downclimbing this pile of crap. It was too late. Never mind how we would get down later.

I did not expect to reach the top, but the rope kept coming. In another minute I slapped a hand on top and smeared the rock with a film of sweat that instantly evaporated. My heart relaxed and my palms dried. I didn't know how much line was left and I didn't want to stand up and risk being jerked back from the edge, so I rolled onto the rough surface, faceup. I closed my eyes. The thump in my chest eased off. My lungs filled with drafts of thin, dry air and I opened my eyes to a bottomless sea of blue. Then I felt a gentle, almost imperceptible tug on my waist harness. I peered down over the edge of the block.

"Hey, Hatch!" Josh shouted. His free hand was cupped around his mouth. "I'm out of line down here!"

"No problem!" I lied. "Give me a minute to set up, then I'll—I'll tell you what to do!"

I scanned around for a boulder, a rock horn, or a projection, anything I could tie myself to, but there was nothing. Instead, I took a deep breath and braced my feet against the crusty lip of tuff at the edge of the block. I untied myself from the line and wrapped it low around my back. I was going to give Josh a classic hip belay; not the most desirable method in the world, but what every mountaineer had done before the invention of modern gear. In this way, I could help him if he started to lose his balance, but he couldn't completely slip and fall or we'd both go for a ride.

While Josh tied into his harness, I looked around and became even more unsettled. Over my left shoulder, a pennant flapped in the breeze on a pole at the top of a little cairn of rocks. It marked the summit—and it was nowhere near the volcanic block we were climbing. The flag was perhaps twenty feet higher and several hundred yards farther around the rim.

"Hatch! You on belay?"

I bent forward to look over the edge. "On belay, Josh!" I shouted it quickly and with energy, trying to transfer confidence through the line.

"Climbing!"

"Climb on!"

I adjusted in my seated, braced position, and began feeling for slack to take in from the yellow cord running around my hips. Each time he made a move, I brought up the line. I kept only enough tension on the line to give him a sense of security, but not so much as to destabilize him and pull him off balance.

I leaned forward where I could see him. "Dude! How's it going?"

Josh laughed his slow, Louisville laugh and grinned at me. "Shit." He was almost halfway up. Most of the climbing below him barely qualified for class five on a scale known as the Yosemite Decimal System (YDS). The YDS subjectively describes the threshold of what is termed "technical climbing." Few climbers normally rope up for anything less than class five, although a fall on lower-angle, class four terrain could certainly be deadly. Class five is an open-ended decimal scale where "moderate" climbs begin at 5.8. The so-called difficult end of the scale begins at 5.11 or 5.12 and evaporates past 5.14.

Josh had rested for a minute on a narrow ledge at the midpoint. The climbing above the ledge was more demanding, perhaps 5.3, a lot crumblier, and provoked him to make comments like "Dadgumit!" or "Bastard!" But he never slipped. He never came off. He never even weighted the line, which was a very good thing.

When Josh topped out, I made room and gave him my hand for the last move. Relief broke out across his face. "Shiiit!"

"Nice job, bud. Let's get you untied." I loosened the well-cinched, though unweighted double granny knot from his harness.

"So this is the—" The last word caught in his throat as his gaze locked on the pennant. It was too far away for us to make out the lettering on its fabric.

Still wearing harnesses, we shouldered our daypacks and ambled the fifty feet or so over to the other side of the block. From there we studied the castellated rimrock that separated us from our goal. We discussed water, distance, and the hour of the day, but our young, male egos reminded us how far we had come. The end was in sight. Even Josh's earlier voice of reason fell silent before the rush of achievement.

The descent on the other side of the block was class three. We had no problem downclimbing it. The rest was simply a matter of picking our way over a bulwark of stone palings and frozen shards of volcanic jetsam. The threshold to ultimate reality was ever-present.

A metal pole rose six feet from a pile of rocks at the summit. At the top of the pole a sun-bleached, light blue pennant was printed with the word "Konica," after the film company. We guessed they had sponsored a climbing party.

At the base of the summit cairn was a metallic box about ten inches square by two inches deep. Painted silver and bolted onto the rock, it read: REGISTER PLACED BY THE SIERRA CLUB— 1957—MOUNT MERU. PLEASE CLOSE LID CORRECTLY. The date on the lid declared it a relic from the colonial period, a time when this land had been under British hegemony and was called Tanganyika. I opened the hinged lid on the box and inside was a tablet that recorded the names of those who had climbed and summited before us. The dates went back to the 1970s. A nubbin of pencil had been left in the box, too. I signed the tablet, handed it to Josh, and stood up to take in the view.

In all my life I had never seen anything so boundless, so breathtaking. The Serengeti Plains stretched away to the western horizon and were interrupted only by the volcanic peaks of Monduli and Ol Doinyo Lengai. Like Mount Meru, the Maasai people considered them holy mountains.

I turned and saw a little trail that descended around the north and east sides of Meru's crater. Most if not all climbers came by that way. Past the forests, the view to the east was dominated by Kilimanjaro—or just "Kili" for climbers in the know. The composite scene was magnificent, and I thanked God for helping us get there.

But something was missing.

All during our climb, but especially after we broke through the tree line, I had sensed a thirst and a yearning ooze up my spine like hot mercury in a thermometer. My expectations had been high. I was only semi-conscious of my need to discover a holy grail of some kind waiting for me at the top, a chalice I could drink from that would fill me and make me whole. Instead all I found was ether.

"Hatch," Josh said. He had cut an orange in two and held half of it out to me.

We were out of water and most of our food was gone, so I took it. The pulp was sweet and moist, which I needed, but the soft white rind was tasty, too, and I dug it out with my bottom front teeth. Just then the juicy peel slipped from my fingers and landed in the rubble at my feet. As I reached to get it, my eyes adjusted into a shadowy nook and caught a spark of light glancing off a rock. I took the small stone and held it up to the sun. Olive-green and lustrous, it sparkled with a thousand microscopic facets of light. It was a mineral called serpentine—not rare, but certainly not common on this mountain. Serpentine is high in magnesium and iron and is found in very dark, igneous rocks. It has even been found on the moon, Mars, and in comet debris. In its purest form, it assumes a marble-like quality and was once known as chrysolite, the totemic stone of the Israelite Tribe of Asher in the Old Testament. Purported to prevent fever and madness, chrysolite was also said to make one disposed toward repentance.

I curled my fingers around its mint green moxie. It was cold. I squeezed harder, trying to absorb my own belief in its Mosaic powers. Then I unzipped a pocket and slipped it in.

"You ready?" I asked Josh.

Lounging next to the summit cairn, Josh grunted and

hoisted himself into a yawning stretch. "Think we'll make it back before dark?"

"You mean our packs?"

He nodded.

I glanced at the sun and shook my head. "We'd better move."

After packing up, we scrambled across the serrated ridge toward the block. Climbing the north side of the block was not bad, but the south side required us to rappel halfway down to where the climbing eased off. We precariously downclimbed the rest and set out in dusky half-light around the crater rim. One or two sips of water had collected in each of our bottles since that morning. It was well after midnight before we found the top of our ridge, then our backpacks, and eventually a tree that showed us the way.

The entire climb took three full days. We had no water for much of it. But greater than my thirst for water was a beguiling need to know more about the sylvan shrine we had come across, strung with its rosary of cocoons. On the hike down, I fantasized about what ceremonies may have been held at the tree and I imagined Africans in trances, dancing, maybe having orgies and worshipping false gods. My Christian friends would say those people were possessed by demons, and the tree itself was an outpost for Satan. I understood what they were saying, but perhaps the Africans worshipped nothing more dangerous than their own fears and ignorance. This seemed reasonable to me.

Part of me wanted to forget about it and just focus on my job: being a good geography teacher. End of story. But minute by minute, my questions were dividing, configuring, growing. And like the shell of a reptilian egg come to term, cracks had opened in all the old answers.

CHAPTER 7

Circumcision

MY PEACE CORPS friends had returned from visiting their teaching assignments, and on the first day back at the training site we focused on tales of travel that related everything from the whimsical to the shocking.

We heard how several people had gotten sick on bumpy bus rides, and one person had been puked on by a nearby passenger. Another guy told how he had been riding in the seat behind the driver and glanced up as his bus was drifting into the passing lane. The driver had dozed off in spite of the bag of coffee beans he'd been munching his way through. Our friend lunged forward and grabbed the wheel as the bus had torn into a roadside path, pedestrians diving for cover.

Another friend told how he'd taken a videocoach bus that had shown a Jean-Claude Van Damme film. At one point the bus careened headlong toward a one-lane bridge at the bottom of a hill. Simultaneously, a fuel-tanker truck plummeted from the opposite direction toward the same bridge. The truck driver gave it all he had, vying to get to the bridge first. The bus driver floored it, determined to beat the truck. Meanwhile, music from a fight scene on the bus's overhead movie monitor had risen to match the drama. Staccato strings and brass exploded in triple forte.

In a millisecond, the truck driver locked up his brakes and the bus flew across the bridge and past the truck on the other side. Great, bright smiles of relief had erupted across the passengers' faces. Some even applauded, as if their favorite soccer team had scored the winning goal. Meanwhile, our friend had slumped into his seat with a pale expression, even for a *mzungu*, a white person. He glanced up at the video monitor. Jean-Claude was okay, too.

Folks in our group hooted and clapped their hands. The story was certainly fun to hear, but it also carried a message we were beginning to perceive. In the past two months, we had discovered how people here valued life in ways that were often difficult for us to fathom. They were ways that ran the gamut from irreverent to grossly comic to revolting.

Privately, I loved it. I knew it was probably inappropriate, but I thrived on social mores that to me seemed so completely illogical and absurd. Living where everything I knew about life was suddenly up for grabs meant I could let go and detach. After all, I was a white guy, so locals expected me to be weird by nature. It was liberating. I could back away from everything I had ever identified with and take a long, hard look at what I thought was right and wrong, true and false. From this new vantage, I could see if the absolutes I'd always trusted and built my reality around were as impeccable as I had believed.

Rich's travel story was interesting, too. He had taken a bus to Dar es Salaam, the main coastal port, on his way to visit his teaching assignment. He had spent the night in Dar before making his way back to the bus station the next morning to continue traveling south. (Rich would be discouraged by faculty he met during his initial school visit and opted for an alternative. He ended up teaching at a school close to mine in Bukoba.)

Like me, Rich was a geographer. He was an inch or two

taller than I and made a habit of wearing a moss green canvass jacket, a satchel slung across his chest, and a safari hat fashioned halfway between a cowboy hat and an Indiana Jones fedora. He was six years older than I and resembled the intrepid geographer I aspired to be.

Dar es Salaam's downtown mosaic had pulsed around him with black foreheads shining in the sun and whiffs of lavender and sooty exhaust fumes. The city's architecture blended Islamic points and parabolas with dusty, Victorian pastels and blocky, Soviet-era buildings. And no matter the style, most everything gleamed from whitewash or sweat under the oppressive tropical heat of the coast.

A gap opened in the crowd and two men approached Rich. One was a midget and shouted, "*Mzungu, nipe pesa!*" *White guy, give me money!*

Confused and overwhelmed, Rich shook his head no and answered in tired Swahili, "*Hapana, bwana. Hapana.*" *No, sir. No.*

The taller of the two men was shocked. In response, he had taken his fist and repeatedly popped his midget sidekick on top of the head. After each pop, the midget had bleated, "*Hapana! Hapana!*" as if he was a cash drawer being totaled to ring.

Rich had backed away from the bizarre scene to re-examine a slip of paper on which his connecting bus information was written.

An Indian cab driver mired in the flux leaned out at Rich. "Hey, you guy!" he shouted in English. "Needa leeftee?" *Need a lift?* The cab was a cramped white Peugeot. Its interior was adorned with red felt lace and a spring-action doll of the goddess Kali, wiggling and stuck to the dashboard. A photo of Rambo holding a grenade launcher was pinned above the rear-view mirror.

After considering the cabby's offer and the gridlocked traffic, Rich declined and waved the driver on. *"Hapana asante,"* *No thank you,* he said.

The crowd suddenly parted behind him. He was grateful for the space and the illusion of moving air, but then he heard the snickers and the jeers. He turned to witness a grown man, dirty and completely naked, masturbating and shouting at an imaginary legion of demons arrayed before him.

Rich could take no more. He turned back to the cabby, pulled a 1,000 shilling note from his pocket, and said, in plain English, "I am going to the bus station."

All of us enjoyed the stories and the laughter that morning. But when it came to me and Josh, we brought our hands up empty. Instead of going on site visits, we had hung out with host families, hand-washed our clothes with All-Detergent Vim, and gotten to know the town a little better—and we had climbed Mount Meru.

Energy in the room popped with chatter. "Whoa!" "Dude!" "No way!" Rolf was an avid backpacker and climber. He demanded to know every detail—a description of the route, time involved, wildlife encountered, provisions taken, and so on. The instructors allowed us to spin our yarn for a minute or two, they themselves intrigued, but Meru was a different kind of story. The unabridged version would have to wait until *chai*—with milk and sugar—was served later that morning.

Six young men in our volunteer group actually hiked up the mountain the following weekend. They took the route Josh and I described. They made good time and climbed as far as the rim. However, one of them tumbled down a rocky scree field. His forehead was lacerated, but he survived and everyone made it down okay.

Their adventure, like ours, stressed the physical challenges involved in climbing a mountain. While such stories may not mention the terrain of the soul in so many words, it is implicit and metaphorical, even if the adventurer is unaware. I wondered if the reason for our adventures was to quench a latent, spiritual thirst. Or as it says in Psalm 78:15, "He split the rocks in the wilderness and gave them water as abundant as the seas."

The word "wilderness" means something different to each person. A Hadza hunter-gatherer who lives on the Tanzanian savanna might believe she has glimpsed the technological wizardry of the First World if she goes on safari in a land rover. On the other hand, a suburbanite from St. Louis, Missouri, would likely consider the same trip a fantastic, wilderness adventure.

Wilderness, therefore, is a difficult concept to pin down, but its etymology provides a starting point. According to Roderick Nash's landmark text, *Wilderness and the American Mind*, the root of the word comes from the Old Norse-Teutonic vernacular. The term depicts a place having the quality of "will," that is, being willful and uncontrollable. The adjective "wild" is derived from "willed" and describes a state of being lost and confused. Later, "wild" was added to the Old English "deor," a word that refers to dangerous beasts that killed and ate people. Finally, the English suffix "ness" denotes a quality or condition. The result is a word that signifies a dreaded place populated with wild beasts.

The terms "desert," "waste," and "wilderness" are often used in the Hebrew Bible to indicate a cursed land where God dealt out punishment on sinful people. By the same token, these are places where one can be humbled, purified, and made ready for a promised land. The prophets Elijah, Moses, and John the Baptist went into wilderness to experience physical privations, where they received inspiration and guidance from God. Matthew 4:1 tells us that after being baptized, "Jesus was led up by the Spirit into the wilderness to be tempted by the devil." He fasted there for forty days, endured a spiritual catharsis, and returned to civilization prepared to speak for God.

The Book of Job tells of a behemoth that dwelled on the wild, eastern steppes, and a leviathan that lurked in the western deeps. Several times throughout the Bible, the evil armies of Gog and Magog are described as being camped in a wilderness north of the Eurasian homelands. And in another holy book, the Quran's Sūrat al-Jinn mentions creatures called jinn made of "scorching fire" who inhabited the great southern desert (the Sahara). Likewise, for many Eurasian polytheists of the first millennium, mountain wildernesses were a fifth cardinal direction and an abode of gods and devils, trolls and chimeras.

Consequently, wilderness adventure has long been regarded as praiseworthy due to its legendary challenges. "Where there was wildness," wrote the late Henry Middleton, "there was possibility, chance, genuine life full of promise and risks and perplexing uncertainty." One's mortality is exposed in the face such uncertainty. Wilderness has the power to bridle the ego, goad the soul, and open portals to the eternal.

Wilderness can also reflect functions of the human psyche. In this way, it is a metaphor for the soul. Early twentieth-century psychologist Carl Jung explored this concept with the terms "collective unconscious" and "archetype." For Jung, the collective unconscious is part of the unconscious mind. This psychological realm is inherited and shared by all humans and is the psychic structure that organizes experience. Archetypes are the images that populate the collective unconscious. Archetypes occur in only a few, original motifs at birth, yet they evolve into myriad, unique forms as each individual moves through life. These motifs seek to be lived out in the conscious mind, but because they are unconscious they can only be discerned indirectly in our behaviors, in our art, and in our religious customs and myths. They are also the images seen in dreams that take such forms as a wise old man, a hero, a serpent, a red cave, or a white room.

Or a mountain.

We practiced our teaching skills for the next couple of weeks. Model school teaching was a time for everyone in the group to put their nascent instructional abilities to the test. Our instructors arranged for us to do this in actual classroom settings at Ilboru, a nearby boys' secondary school.

As a rookie teacher, I was lucky my students were patient. For example, when I taught plate tectonics, I cut a tabletop-sized sheet of cardboard into a jigsaw puzzle that represented continental tectonic plates. On class day, I asked the students to assemble the continental pieces to form the ancient super-continent, Pangaea. They finished it in about the time it takes to tie one's shoes. I then asked them to disassemble the puzzle in the fashion that Pangaea would have broken apart during the so-called Mesozoic Era, 225 million years ago. In this way, they proceeded to form Laurasia and Gondwanaland, and finally the individual land masses as we know them today.

I was amazed at how advanced fifteen and sixteen-year-old Tanzanian students could be. But I shouldn't have been. Part of my misconception of Tanzanian youth, and of Africa in general, was based on my own experiences at their age—

driver's ed, football games, and girls. The conception of "darkest Africa" that I had grown up with was based on grainy, black-and-white Johnny Weissmuller reruns and H. Rider Haggard's *King Solomon's Mines.* I recalled some of my high school peers thinking Africa was a country located somewhere in South America.

In Tanzania, most young men and women who studied at the secondary (high school) level took what equated with college-level physics, chemistry, and calculus in the United States. To my dismay, I learned I'd be playing scholastic catch-up for a while. One of my greatest classroom struggles would be to challenge and actually teach my students worthwhile information.

That said, I remained an idealist at heart. I hoped to inspire my students. I wanted them to look past the rote memorization of facts and figures and develop interests that would stir in them a fresh curiosity about life. I wanted them to see their place in the world with new eyes, discover for themselves what was true, and break through their myths and become whole.

People were abuzz the last day at the training site. Everyone hustled around, anxious to get back to their host families and pack up to leave the next morning. We'd been vaccinated, we were stocked with Mefloquin pills (a malarial prophylactic), and we had bathed our mosquito bed-nets in tubs of high-potency DEET. Culturally, we were armed with a battery of nouns, verbs, adjectives, and scruples. Training had taken ten weeks, and we were anxious to move out and start our new jobs. The only remaining business was the road trip to Dar es Salaam and the Peace Corps swearing-in ceremony at the U.S. ambassador's home. Departure from the training site was set for 6:00 A.M., so we were advised to pack that evening. The drive, we were told, should take about nine hours.

After we adjourned, I jogged home. When I reached the path that turned into the Mollel property, I saw Mama Suzan across the courtyard. She was shaking out laundry and pinning it up to the line. I waved and shouted, "*Habari yako, mama?*" *How are you, mama?* She waved and burped a chuckle. She knew that the shy American kid with shaggy brown hair and a first name like her late husband's was about to travel to Dar and then Bukoba.

I was grateful for the Mollels' hospitality, yet I was ready to move on. I headed straight to my room and flew into packing. I grabbed my JanSport pack out from under the bed and stuffed it with my things—clothes, radio-cassette player and tapes, Walkman, journal, multivitamins, and the colored chalk I'd brought from the States.

Over the rustled sounds of packing, I almost missed Patrick's voice across the yard. He spoke with Mama Suzan. I listened as I held my climbing gear. I remembered the tree on Meru and that I had meant to ask him about it. My watch said it was almost 6:00. Per the customary East African schedule, dinner wouldn't be ready for two or three hours. I could finish packing and find Patrick. He'd probably invite me into his room, or I could invite him to mine. It didn't matter, as long as I got him away from Mama Suzan and the others. I wanted to see what he knew about the old pagan ways, and I did not want either of us to feel self-conscious.

In Arusha, I had learned that Tanzanians were struggling to modernize and acquire all the baggage that came with it. Colonial Eurocentrism had assured them such bags were filled with money, prestige, and happiness. Townsfolk I met roundly disparaged pre-colonial beliefs and lifestyles. Most preferred nice, Western-styled clothing, and a tiny percentage of them owned BMWs or Mercedes. They esteemed all things Western—that is, from the U.S. and Europe.

However, a few ethnic groups had taken a different path. Groups like the Hadza and the Maasai had maintained their traditional ways of hunting and gathering or pastoring cattle and goats. At best, they were ignored by the urbanites. At worst, they were taken "legal" advantage of. The Arusha and Meru peoples had already lost significant parcels of land around Arusha town to new subdivisions. In Kenya, the Kikuyu and Maasai who were within range of Nairobi's sprawl had suffered a similar fate. In both places, foreign companies had built greenhouses to grow flowers for European markets. Other giant agricultural businesses were consuming the space needed by indigenous groups to grow their food and water their cattle. In their wake, the old ways were being forgotten as quickly and as piously as possible.

I finished packing in ten minutes. I set my pack next to the door, took out my little Gideon Bible that had white covers, and found a passage I remembered, John 15:7: "If you remain in me and my words remain in you, ask whatever you wish and it will be done for you." It made me feel better. With those words in mind, I kneeled at the side of my bed as I had since I was a kid and prayed. *Dear God, I feel like I've distanced myself from you recently. I don't know why, but especially on Mount Meru. Please, bring me back, God. Speak to my heart through Patrick and help me again, Father. In Jesus' name I pray, Amen.*

With renewed confidence, I went to my bedroom door and cracked it open. The yard was empty. Patrick's room was two doors down, and like all the rooms in the house his had an exterior door that opened onto the courtyard. As I walked over, I heard a punctilious British accent coming from his

radio: "This has been the BBC News, Radio Free Africa."
At once, the announcer's voice was replaced with the grainy
recording of a marching band playing the program's theme. I
shouted over the music.

"*Hodi, hodi!*" *Can I come in?*

The radio music went dead. "Eh, yes. Who is there?" Patrick called from inside, in English. He pretended not to recognize my voice.

"It's me, William."

"Oh, yes, yes, William," he said as he opened the door.
"Please, come in. Do you want to say in the English, or for
practicing the Kiswahili?" He knew I had been trying to
speak Swahili as often as possible.

"English is fine today. My brain is tired."

Patrick chuckled from beneath his wispy mustache. He
was a few years younger than I, in his early twenties. I followed him in and he pointed to a chair. "Please, William, sit."

Patrick still had on his work clothes, the ones he wore to
manage his little beer and soda kiosk that was five minutes'
walk from the house. His shoes were buffed brown leather
wingtips, which complemented his khaki dress slacks. His
shirt was long-sleeved and had white and green pinstripes
with buttoned-down collars. In this uniform, he invoked the
air of an up-and-coming entrepreneur—suave, confident, and
a little arrogant. This was necessary for a young man making
his mark in a volatile economy. But today he looked weary,
and he softened his workday persona with a smile.

As I sat, I assembled my thoughts. I had learned when
speaking with Tanzanians in English to separate my words
and speak in a distinct, almost blocky fashion. "You know, I
leave tomorrow for Dar es Salaam."

"Yes, yes," Patrick said. He plopped himself into the chair
opposite mine. "We can be very sad to see you go."

"Of course, I will come to visit, maybe at Christmas." I felt slightly self-conscious and fidgety. "But before I go, there is something I have been meaning to ask you. Something I saw on Mount Meru."

Patrick smiled and shook his head and waggled a finger at me. "You, William! You are a climber of this mountains! Eh, eh, eh . . ." He finished off his descending tones of disbelief with a click of his tongue. I thought I detected a note of local brew waft through the air between us.

I nodded. "Yes, it was a difficult climb. My friend, Josh—you know, Joshua?"

"From Peace Corpse," he said innocently, as in a dead body, again pointing at me.

"Yes, Peace Corps. When we were climbing Meru; we met an old man in the forest. He told us the way to climb the mountain and said to look for a—a certain tree, like a special tree."

I needed to say no more. Patrick's eyes leveled, and his face grew somber. He rubbed his jaw and cleared his throat. "Yes, sometimes I remember this certain place. I was somehow going there with my father, but not since I was very young. There is a very great tree with many hangings—" He looked at me for help, holding his arms out like wings.

"Branches?"

"Yes, yes, *branches*," he said, relieved, and settled back into his chair. "This tree, with some *branches*, it can be very special." He stopped and rubbed his jaw again as if remembering and focusing his thoughts, as if considering how much information he wanted to divulge. "My family, they can take this milks, or beers, or sometimes this goats. Because this can be the place our ancestors, they come to visit."

"You mean, spirits? The spirits of your ancestors?"

"Yes, yes, this spirits, ghosts. And they can talk for us to

God. Especially when no rains are coming, or poor crops, or items are troublesome, they can go there and beg for us help."

Since he was relaxed and talkative, I decided to probe further. "So when was the last time you were there, at that place?"

"Oh, very young. And sometimes there can be many, how do you say?" He looked around the room for a clue, then back to me, quite serious. "This skins! From the man's—" He pointed both his hands at his crotch.

"Foreskins?" I said, also searching for the word. "They take their—foreskins?"

"Yes, yes. Of course, when they are boys, they *cut* them, and leave them their skins on this tree. These items, they are for our ancestors." He relaxed back into his chair and absentmindedly began picking his nose, the way all locals did in public.

I was delighted he did not seem to mind talking about the subject with me. I had seen how a couple sips of 75-proof Konyagi could grease the wheels of conversation, but here was a guy who called himself a Christian—he and his whole family—so I was surprised by his unrepentant candor. What Patrick had just described would never fly with any mainstream church practices I knew of. They sounded like pagan rites, and in my mind they were not far from the stories I'd heard of mutilated cows and orgiastic sex cults.

Nevertheless, Patrick did not say they had worshipped Satan but rather God, only in a different way. The classwork I had done in anthropology reminded me that tribal religions were part of an entire way of being that included marriage, birth, stories, work, and a thousand other dimensions of life. The people who had worshipped at the tree had surely loved one another, and I suspected they had also had their differences, even warfare, just like everyone else.

I thought about asking Patrick more about his faith, but I didn't want our conversation to sound like an interrogation. Besides, I needed time to think, time to pray about it and turn it over to Jesus.

Patrick looked away and squinted, as if replaying a seldom-visited memory. "I do not remember many items about this place on Meru, but I can be asking my mother for additional details. She can give to you this additional details."

I nodded, thankful, distracted by my own thoughts.

"I am only wishing my grandfather could somehow be telling you," he went on. "Long ago, he has gone to our ancestors, but he was keeping so many cows, there on Meru, even when his eyes, they have become stopped." Patrick chuckled and raised a hand to the top of his head and patted it. "He was very much enjoying to wear this small blue hat."

CHAPTER 8

Common Ancestors

A ROOSTER CROWED in the feedlot out back, but it was still dark. I got up and dressed quickly. After I took down my mosquito net, I brushed my teeth with treated water and put my backpack on. Mama Suzan waited for me in the courtyard with a sack breakfast. I was actually relieved Patrick hadn't brought up the sacred tree business at dinner the night before. Maybe he had been drunk on Konyagi and forgot, but I was not going to bring it up myself. In any case, it made it easier for me to say good-bye knowing Mama Suzan's sadness at seeing me go was probably sincere.

The rooster crowed again. Under the glare of a bare bulb hanging from a wire stretched over the yard, Mama Suzan hugged me and handed me the paper sack. We exchanged a few sleepy words of thanks and I promised to visit. We hugged again, and then I stepped into the cool black of predawn carrying all my worldly possessions on my back.

I had grown accustomed to the path to the training site so I didn't need to use my headlamp. Instead, I navigated by starlight and a deep blue glow swelling in the east. The neighborhood was eerily quiet. For the first time, I heard my footsteps on the hard-packed earth echo off gated courtyards along the way. Iron prongs jutted up like spears from the top edge of every gate, and multicolored shards of broken bottles were cemented into the upper lips of every wall. Everyone in our group had been warmly received by people around town, so we were baffled by the fortifications they lived in. I thanked Jesus we did not live like this back home—or did we, only in a different way?

As I walked through the chilly darkness, dogs routinely thundered up to the inside of the gated compounds, leaving little doubt trespassers would be ripped to shreds. These were the same dogs that, by day, were so timid and abused by everyone, especially their masters. Children regularly threw rocks at these sore-ridden, fly-infested curs. But not at night. At night, dogs banded together and formed alliances and none dared approach them. The metamorphosis baffled me.

Our bus for the day had undergone a metamorphosis or two of its own. Snub-nosed and stocky, it looked like a relic from someone's 1970s trans-Africa tour. It was barely long enough to seat all twenty-two of us plus a few of the staff, and every inch of it had been brush-painted in the funkiest shade of deep-ocean azure. After we lashed our luggage to the top frame, we climbed aboard and left Arusha, grooving to the driver's cassette tape of Bob Marley & the Wailers. Time travel was complete with classics like "No Woman, No Cry" and "Redemption Song."

The early morning air was cool and fresh, so the windows on the bus were shut, but before long the sun was high and the windows came down. The green smells of Africa blew in like a warm breath. A magnificent swath of rich, volcanic soils between Meru and Kilimanjaro supported peanut, corn, and coffee plantations.

Now and then I looked outside, but I mostly kept my nose buried in my new reading material.

"What you reading there, bro?" Brad asked. He and Cynthia and Rolf were playing cards in the seats across from me.

"New Testament. It's in Swahili," I said, slightly proud of myself. All three of them stopped what they were doing. "So I have to guess sometimes, but I remember a lot of the verses, so that helps."

Brad nodded. "You Christian?"

"Oh, yeah."

They smiled. Brad nodded again, and they went back to their game.

I went back to translating, but in a moment Josh broke my concentration. "Yo, Hatch!" He pointed out the window. "Check it!"

I glanced out at a billboard we were passing. Very few billboards were erected along any stretch of African highway. This one was written in English and touted local wood carvings and basketry it assured the discriminating tourist had been *made by handcrafted people*. Everyone on the bus cracked up, but I found it religiously accurate, if rationally flawed.

Moshi is a town on the southern slopes of Kilimanjaro. From here I had hoped to get a close-up view of the mountain and its fabled, hanging glaciers, but true to form it had donned a thick cloak of moisture. It wasn't long before we passed through town and turned south. The Usambara Mountains stood to the east. The Usambaras are a range of low yet dramatic fault-block mountains that top out at close to 8,000 feet. On our west stretched the wide-open Maasai Steppe. By mid-afternoon, we arrived at a highway junction and turned southeast toward the coast. We had been descending all day, and inversely to our drop in altitude, temperatures had been steadily rising. More windows came down. Most of us on the bus stared out and watched the landscape evolve from acacia and candelabra-tree savanna into waxy-leaved miombo woodland.

Isolated mud and grass huts gave way to cinder-block shacks with corrugated iron roofs. These, in turn, gave way to bigger concrete buildings subsumed in a bigger, smellier, noisier human landscape. People on bicycles hauled vegetables or sacks of grain or fish peppered with flies—sure sign we were closing in on the coast. Radios in hardscrabble kiosks were turned up all the way, which distorted their galloping, electric guitar tunes and lent a quasi-circus mood to the chaos. More cars, trucks, and taxis crowded onto the highway, but the videocoaches grabbed my attention the most. Their air horns blasted out the first dozen notes from some pop tune, and slogans like "Mama's Fresh Milk" and "Jesus Makes Love" were painted on the back. Here and there, half-clothed kids kicked soccer balls fashioned from wads of plastic bags. Buildings, buses, and kiosks advertised Pepsi and Coke on dusty signs. Men peed behind bushes in alleys.

We were coming into Dar es Salaam, Tanzania's largest city and its capital city, before the capital was moved inland to Dodoma. The name, Dar es Salaam (or "Dar is a slum," as we facetiously called it), is an archaic form of Arabic. It is usually translated to mean "Harbor of Peace," and the city itself is a matrix of cultural and historical contrasts. Long before it acquired its present name, Dar was a Bantu fishing village. Eventually it became an Arab port that traded in slaves and ivory, then a Portuguese slave port, then Arab again, then German, and then British. In 1961, Dar, along with the remainder of mainland Tanganyika, became independent from Great Britain, and socialist. (Tanganyika was the Bantu aggregate of the words for "sail," or "sailcloth," and "plains." Therefore, both its inland and coastal geographies were reflected in its name.)

In 1964, the nearby island of Zanzibar, plus the smaller islands of Pemba and Mafia, formed a political union with Tanganyika. Tanzania became the nation's new, compressed moniker. Over 120 ethnic groups are contained within Tanzania. Each speaks a different language and has different customs. In spite of it, Tanzania achieved relative peace, albeit abject poverty, under the stewardship of its much-loved founding father, Julius Nyerere, "The Teacher."

Road weary, we pulled into the Peace Corps office in Dar late that afternoon. After a brief tour of the grounds, we unloaded our luggage and stored it under lock and key in the main house. We lodged at the Palm Beach Hotel across town. Real bathrooms with showers and flush toilets seemed decadent. The Palm Beach Hotel was not downtown but close enough that we could walk to the shops and restaurants and the Sheraton Hotel (with the upside-down S). Town was fun, but our group spent more time at the beach watching moonrises over the Indian Ocean, rippling out from the shore, primordial and pregnant.

On our first day at the office, each of us was scheduled to have a final, private interview with David, our Peace Corps Tanzania country director. As we had seen him before on the bus to Arusha, David wore a floral-design shirt, shorts, and flip-flops. Toward the end of my interview, he leaned forward from the sofa he was reclining on, teacup in hand.

"I think you'll do great," he said. "Just relax. Have fun." He stood, and as I got up to shake his hand, he looked over my right shoulder.

"And as long as you're here, I'd like you to meet someone. Bill, this is Dr. Jane Goodall. She'll be at the party tomorrow night at my place. And Jane, this is Bill Hatcher, one of our newest volunteers."

I turned to see an older woman of sixty or so. She was

small and slight of build, and she had tied her long gray hair back into a ponytail.

"Hi, nice to meet you," I said.

"Likewise," she said. We shook hands.

I turned to David. "So, should I send the next one up?"

David looked as though he wanted to explain something. Instead, he only smiled and nodded. "Yes, Bill. That would be great."

As I trotted down the stairs, I felt as though I had met the older woman somewhere before. David said she was a doctor, and her name sounded familiar. I wondered if she had given our group vaccinations before we left the States. I couldn't remember.

I reached for the door to go outside, and I heard them talking. "Oh, not to worry," the lady said in a soft yet authoritative British accent. "Keeps me humble, you know."

My question was answered at the party on the following evening. It was there that I learned Dr. Jane Goodall is one of the twentieth century's preeminent researchers in primatology, and an internationally recognized advocate for community-based environmental programs in Africa.

David's home was in a neighborhood that faced the Indian Ocean. The briny smell of mangroves at high tide bathed his backyard, which was only a hundred yards from the beach. It was the ideal spot for a party. Rice pilaf, coconut bean soup, and octopus—spiced with saffron, cloves, and pomegranate—were welcome changes to our up-country diets. Some of the volunteers drank Tusker lagers, while others like me sampled the usual cadre of soft drinks. Music preferences shifted between Hootie & the Blowfish, Indigo Girls, and Alanis Morissette.

The sun had been down for a while when David turned
the music off and tapped a spoon against his glass. He introduced Dr. Jane Goodall. Applause flared up, and I mentally
kicked myself for so blankly greeting her and walking away
the day before.

Dr. Goodall first spoke of the research she had done with
chimpanzees in Gombe, Tanzania, since 1960, and her work
with Dr. Louis Leakey and the Leakey family of Kenya. In
Tanzania, she said, plundering, poaching, and the AIDS epi-
demic had created great challenges for wildlife conservation
and antiquities preservation. One of the most positive actions
we as Peace Corps volunteers could take to stem these problems was to educate the people—not only academically but
about social issues as well.

She was careful to make the point that human beings are
animals, too. Chimpanzees and humans share a common
ancestor who lived six million years ago. From that ancient
primate we inherited our tendencies toward wars and killing
as well as our capacity for love and compassion, traits which
are also found in chimpanzees. She said our brains are fully
capable of controlling our behaviors, though we haven't been
very good at using them.

We all laughed lightly and shook our heads. Dr. Goodall
went on to talk about Roots & Shoots, a community-based
environmental program she had recently started in western
Tanzania. But I couldn't help but consider what she had said
a moment earlier. Here was a brilliant, sophisticated woman,
reporting that we were all merely animals. She said chimps
and humans were 98.7 percent genetically identical. We had
simply evolved onto different branches of the primate tree.

I meandered to the back of the yard behind everyone else
and leaned against a chain-link fence. I took another sip of
my Stoney Tangawizi, a carbonated ginger soda. Dr. Good-

all claimed to be a Christian, although most people I knew would label her stance on evolution (and religious pluralism) nothing less than blasphemy. It was an old story—science versus religion—and what Dr. Goodall suggested about humans and apes made me cringe.

I had been taught people were created in the beginning by the hand of God quite separately from the animals. Church fathers had declared it an act of fiat creation, *ex nihilo*, that occurred between six and ten thousand years ago. At the same time, I had memorized the geologic ages from a Golden Guide book on fossils when I was a kid. The Golden Guide said the earth itself was estimated to be 4.5 billion years old, and the universe, first generated with the Big Bang, was 14 billion years old.

Recognizing my penchant for science, my ex-wife and her Christian parents had persuaded me to subscribe to periodicals published by the Institute for Creation Research. I had also listened to radio programs like Dr. James Dobson's *Focus on the Family*, broadcast from over 3,000 radio stations worldwide. People like Dr. Dobson, Pat Robertson, and Jerry Falwell said their scientific panel could prove the earth was only a few thousand years old. The earth's present-day condition, they said, was a direct result of events that had occurred during the Great Flood of Noah. They preached that evolution was a pernicious lie, a trap planted by Satan to aid in his singular mission of turning people away from God.

The tenets of Young Earth creationism were, perhaps, the most rigid and literal of all creationist stances. However, a breakaway school of thought called Old Earth creationism (OEC) accepted that God had created the earth billions of years ago. Many spinoffs of OEC developed. One was called Gap creationism. In this view, the earth is very old. Many ages of prehistoric life have come and gone, but the earth was barren when God restarted life as explained in Genesis. A related school of thought was Day-Age creationism. Here, God created life in six of His own "God days" each of which could have lasted for eons. This position had much in common with theistic evolution and Progressive creationism, which believed that God worked out His creation *through* evolution. Humans, however, had been spared from that vulgar process and were uniquely created in His most noble image.

Out on the fringe were people like Dr. Goodall. They believed that humans had, in fact, evolved just like everything else. The only difference was that God started the whole project spinning billions of years ago because, as I was told as a child, He was lonely—a curiously human affliction, if you asked me. Nevertheless, He bestowed souls upon early humans when He deemed them well-enough evolved to deserve and appreciate eternal salvation.

I had learned that material creation could be interpreted in dozens, perhaps hundreds, of ways, each of which was impossible to prove or disprove. But why now? Why was I again debating the old arguments of science versus religion? Was it because I esteemed Dr. Goodall, a Christian and famous scientist, and I saw that her outlook clashed with mine, a nobody? Or was it because Creationism persistently went so far out of its way to "prove" science wrong that it had started to sound like they "doth protest too much"? Or was it because I wanted to throw out anything associated with my father and what he had professed?

My dad would have pointed a finger at me and told me I was getting too big for my britches. Maybe I *was* getting too big—too big for a confined view of reality about to break wide open. I could agree with that much.

I could also tell it was going to hurt like hell.

BOOK TWO
Burial

CHAPTER 9

Meeting the Goddess

THE EARLY MORNING rain tapped a sleepy rhythm on the deck outside our cabin door. My eyes were still closed as I lay in my bunk, and I let the rain lull me in and out of cool semi-consciousness.

After a while, I got up and peeked outside. The light was dim and it was hard to see, but I could make out whorls of bruised clouds leaning stacked and fallen like Gothic ruins. A stiff breeze boiled whitecaps on the surface of the lake, and the ship bounded as if we cruised the open sea.

The night before, Rich and I had wished Josh the best of luck at his school in Mwanza before we boarded the M.V. (Merchant Vessel) *Victoria*. We had a first-class cabin, but it was nothing fancy. The room was a metal-studded cell hung with two berths. It was painted eggshell white, and its only perk was a mirror bolted onto a wall over a sink that had no running water.

Second-class rooms were about the same, except there were six berths to a room and there was no sink/mirror combination. Passengers with third-class tickets had no accommodations, so they slept out on deck, maybe on benches, or in luggage racks in the bar. If they were lucky, they staked their claim in the ship's cargo hold and huddled around sacks of grain and mountains of green bunch-bananas piled higher than a man's head. And if they were very lucky, they might find a Land Rover or a Land Cruiser parked in the hold with the doors left unlocked, where seats and floorboards made good beds.

The M.V. *Victoria* was one of three colonial-era steamers that plied the waters of Lake Victoria. All three ships were equipped with fine, brass-fitted mahogany railing and had been kept in more or less seaworthy condition over the decades. Each one made regularly scheduled stops in Bukoba, Tanzania, in the west; Kampala, Uganda, in the north; and Kisumu, Kenya, on the northeastern shore. Mwanza was the south shore port. The other two steamers that made runs out of Mwanza were the M.V. *Bukoba* and the M.V. *Serengeti*. The former was a passenger liner like the *Victoria* and the latter mostly a cargo ship, though there was always room for third-class passengers.

All trips across the lake boarded in the evenings and departed by 9:00 or 10:00 P.M. The *Victoria*, with capacity for 600 passengers, was the biggest and the fastest and was able to cross the distance between Mwanza and Bukoba in about eight hours. The *Victoria* even had a cozy bar in the aft section of the promenade reminiscent of Bogart's favorite hangout in *Casablanca*—minus the piano.

Rich and I were hungry, so we rooted around in our luggage for the box of Marie Tea Biscuits and jar of pineapple jam we'd packed. After breakfast, we pulled on our jackets and went out on deck to see the ship had turned to face a thin line of trees on the lake's horizon. Temperatures were in the upper fifties, and an eight-knot breeze that smelled like zinc and cold fish splashed over the bow.

Other passengers started to come out on deck, too. Many leaned against the rail and studied the dark, expanding shoreline, now off the ship's port bow. But on the starboard side, facing east, a mute line of men scrubbed their arms and faces and necks in tubs of water. As chilly as it was, they wore only a swaddle of linen wrapped around their hips like diapers. After drying off, they passed around a jar of Vaseline. Each of them scooped out a fingerfull of translucent jelly and applied a transparent sheen to every exposed part of their body. Their skin was certainly dark, though it glowed with an admixture of ginger-brown and henna, not quite the swarthy, buffed black of most others on board. Their hair was not as tightly curled, either, even wavy.

I later learned that Arabs and Indians had come to East Africa in several waves over the past 1,200 years. In Tanzania, these groups had mostly gathered into enclaves of Sikhs, Hindus, and Muslims. The gentlemen I saw washing themselves that morning were African Muslims. They were performing their ablutions, or *wudu*, in preparation for devotional morning prayers, known as *Fajr*. When finished, each one donned either a simple tunic or a long, bright white *galabiyya* gown. Then they kneeled onto a small rug and prayed the first of five daily prayers to Allah.

Almost everyone on board was startled when the big-throated horn of the ship split the air. Three long blasts followed by three short ones announced our arrival at the port of Bukoba. Rich and I scanned the expanding terrain. The shore was velvety green and lush. It leaped up from the harbor like a sea serpent to form a line of bluffs plaited with hanging vines and trees all plump and curvy. The town itself was nestled in a valley a mile north of the harbor.

As our ship docked, we scanned the pier for representatives from each of our schools. Two men picked us out from the darker faces on board and waved. We smiled and waved back and made our way in line down the gangplank to meet our contacts who had driven to the port in school-owned Land Rovers.

"Meesta Hatcha?" asked a man through a jovial grin. His build was rotund for a Tanzanian, although average for an adult, American male.

I answered in Swahili. "Yes. My name is Mr. Bill Hatcher."

"Oh! *Sawa sawa*," *Okay*, "Meesta Beel. I say! Your Kiswahili, it is very good!" he said in English. Like all Tanzanians I'd met, he replaced his *i*'s with long *e*'s and randomly exchanged his *l*'s and *d*'s for rolled *r*'s. This practice resulted in bread being turned into "bled," sorry into "soddy," hit into "heat," and playing into "praying," and vice versa.

"*Asante.*" *Thanks.* "But I am only learning. And your name, *bwana*?"

"Oh! Sorry, sorry. Me myself, I am Rugambwa's second master. My name is Mr. Rwelengera," he said, very slowly, having experienced the difficulty his name caused foreigners.

We shook hands. "I am happy to meet you Mister—"

"Rwe-len-ge-ra," we said together, as he coached me through each syllable.

"Oh, very good! Here, let me help you." He took my JanSport and heaved it into the back of the Land Rover.

I waved good-bye to Rich across the crowded landing. He was off to teach A-level geography at Ihungo, an all-boys' boarding school on the north side of town. I was on my way to Rugambwa, an all-girls' boarding school just south of town. The two schools were separated by several miles and the valley in which the town of Bukoba rested.

Mr. Rwelengera and I climbed into the white, mud-splattered Land Rover with several other people and set off over a road that smelled like damp rust. He drove with one hand on the wheel while he picked his nose with the other. At the same time, he chatted in Kihaya, the local dialect, with the other passengers, whose presence confused me—were they also going to the school? In a few minutes, we turned onto a muddy lane posted with a white sign that read RUGAMBWA SHULE YA SEKONDARI. He stopped the truck and let out the half-dozen folks who had hitched a ride up the hill. "Getting a leeftee" was the code of the road in East Africa, and one I would exercise many times.

Rugambwa Secondary School was named in honor of Laurian Rugambwa, a Bukoba native and the first ordained African Catholic Bishop. It was established in 1960 as an all-girls' boarding school for both O-Level (Ordinary, or high school) and A-Level (Advanced, or college-preparatory) students. When I arrived in August 1994, Rugambwa employed fourteen faculty and several staff, and had a student population close to 650. Built of brick and concrete by a British missionary organization, the campus included an administration block, a library, and two main classroom buildings. All were two- and three-story structures. Single-story buildings included an agriculture classroom and a kitchen/dining hall. Students were housed in a two-story dormitory adorned with cross-shaped windows.

In 1971, Rugambwa and all other properties in the country were nationalized by the Tanzanian government. School administrators, shopkeepers, and farmers across the land woke up to discover their land belonged to the newly independent republic. However, in a conciliatory move the government promulgated ninety-nine-year lease options to all former property owners.

Rugambwa had once been a bastion of education for young women, though decades of underfunding had taken its toll. Few windows were still fitted with panes of glass, so that birds and bats nested above chalkboards and crapped on bookshelves. Usable desks and chairs were in short supply, so when the bell rang students often carried their chairs from class to class. Wooden classroom doors were full of holes and swung knobless in the winds that breathed in and out across the lake each day.

Although Rugambwa boarded its students, the school could afford to offer only one serving of rice and beans each day. This meal was sometimes supplemented with *ugali*, shucked and milled from the school's little patch of corn out back. *Chai* was served without milk or sugar at mid-morning teatime.

Students who were unable to buy supplements for this meager diet suffered lapses in focus and attention and were generally more lethargic. But in addition to their studies, the girls were also charged with maintaining the entire school grounds. One form, or grade level, was responsible for cutting the grass on campus using handheld scythes. Another form level swept and mopped classroom floors. Since the school's plumbing had been defunct for many years, students fetched water for the kitchen from a nearby stream using five-gallon buckets. No plumbing also meant the flush-basin privies no longer flushed. Therefore, a revolving student detail had the task of shoveling out the mounds of human waste that regularly piled up over the toilet seats.

In the spirit of its British colonial legacy, the students, faculty, and staff did their level best to hold things together and take care of what remained. Rather than being fatalistic, people toiled with the unswerving faith that things would be okay, that life would go on—even when it didn't—*Mungu akipenda,* God willing.

*   *   *

A dozen brick houses, roofed with corrugated iron, dotted the lakeward perimeter of campus. They were home to many of the school's teachers and their extended families. A unique arrangement of floriculture surrounded each house, but the mainstays were hibiscus and frangipani trees—crowned with pink flowers that bloomed each night and smelled of honey wine.

Several other volunteer teachers lived at Rugambwa. One was Chris, a Peace Corps woman from an earlier group who taught biology; three British VSO (Volunteer Service Overseas) volunteers who taught math and English; and Saito, a Japanese man working for JVS (Japanese Volunteer Service), who taught chemistry. No other houses were vacant when I arrived, so I shared a home with him for my first semester. Saito was habitually clad in round glasses, khaki slacks, and a buttoned-down shirt that he somehow managed to keep immaculately iron-pressed. Incredibly, he was learning to speak Swahili, *and* English, *and* how to teach chemistry for the first time.

On the day following my inaugural pizza party with the other volunteers, Saito offered to take me to town and give me a tour. Peace Corps issued each of its volunteers a Trek bicycle and helmet, but it forbade us from piloting any sort of motorized craft. The Japanese Volunteer Service, however, supplied their volunteers with medium-sized Kawasaki motorcycles, and there was no prohibition against my accepting rides as a passenger. I needed to find out where the market and stores were located, and open a bank account, so I accepted Saito's invitation.

After we left campus, we passed a whitewashed Catholic church. A little farther down the hill we passed the home of an American missionary family who coordinated provisions shipped to refugee camps on the Rwandan border. Finally we came out at an intersection in view of the lake. Turning right led to the port; turning left led to town.

Taking the town road, we paralleled the beach and saw several people wading thigh-deep in the lake. They were bathing, and they were completely naked. A flock of wary cormorants bunched together a little farther out. The birds, however, needn't have worried; the Tanzanians I met were seldom keen about getting too far out into open water. Very few cared to learn how to swim, even fishermen, but wading was okay for most. The group of men I saw had soaped up into industrious froths of foam conspicuous against their dark skin. Women, too, in a separate group a little ways off, but I tried not to look.

The day was sunny and fresh and about eighty-five degrees. Bukoba sits at 4,000 feet above sea level and is doused with lake-effect rains nearly every morning. Most afternoons are clear. Rainfall averages eighty inches annually, which is plenty for cultivating sugarcane, tea, and coffee in the leached-out, ferralitic soils. In fact, the Africafe coffee mill was located on the lakeshore next to the port, churning out the root cause of my most recent addiction.

However, the dietary mainstay of the region was bananas. I was told that over twenty varieties of the fruit grew around Bukoba. The most common types included sweet, finger-sized bananas, "normal" bananas (the kind you find in an American grocery store), plantains for cooking, and finally, a kind the size of a grown man's forearm used to make *rubisi*, or banana beer. Banana trees grew in almost every direction, so I was amazed to find they weren't even native to Africa. Instead, all the world's bananas originated in Southeast Asia and were introduced to Africa in the eighth century by Arab seafarers.

As we turned and crossed a short bridge into town, the road became tarmacked. Saito slowed down, lifted his visor, and turned his head so I could hear him. He pointed to an inn on our right that had a wraparound veranda. "Over there, that is Lake Hotel and restaurant. Good foods," he said. His smile was contorted by the foam padding in his helmet. He closed his visor and sped up. The air felt balmy and pleasant on my bare arms as we cruised under a canopy of tall shade trees. Dozens of people either rode bicycles or walked along the sides of the road carrying plastic bags from the market. At the end of the corridor of the trees we emerged into the full light of Bukoba. Saito pulled into a gravel parking lot and stopped.

"Here is our bank. You can do banking here. But first, we walk to market and I show you the shops—the shopping."

"Great. Hey, you hungry? Want to get some lunch?" I said, a little too fast.

He beamed a blank smile as if waiting for more information. Then his eyes brightened, and he laughed. "Oh, yes. Hungry!" he said, rubbing his stomach. "Okay. Let's eat."

We grabbed our daypacks and walked across a dirt street that fed into Jamhuri Road, the only paved road in town. The streets were wide and bright and bustled with people who were wafted aside by the occasional taxi or Land Rover. Most Bukoba natives were darker and rounder in face than people in Arusha, and medium-short in height. At five feet eleven inches, I was taller than most.

"Okay. This restaurant is Rose Café. Maybe we get something here?"

"Sounds good."

We pushed aside the sheer muslin cloths that hung in the doorway and entered a room painted navy blue and decorated with World Cup soccer calendars. After being out in the bright sun, this interior was dark but also cool and inviting. Across the room, we came to a glass counter that displayed an assortment of the morning's samosas and chapatis.

A small blackboard hung on the wall behind it with a menu written in chalk.

Saito waved and greeted the attendant in Swahili. After going through all the selections on the menu, we discovered only one offering was available that day—banana soup with tomato and cabbage. We also bought a couple leftover samosas and two Pepsis. While we waited for our orders to come up we took a seat on white lawn chairs arranged around a table spread with a plastic tablecloth. The tablecloth was transparent, except for several aquatic images. It reminded me of a shower curtain.

The server brought the soup, samosas, and sodas. I had never eaten cooking bananas before, but they were mild and potatoey. Spiced with cardamom, cumin, and a touch of ginger, they had a definite Indian zest. I was surprised with how well they met the acrid plumpness of tomato and the hearty bite of cabbage in the soup. The samosas were warm and oily yet flaky and salted just enough to make my mouth water profusely. I washed all of it down with a warm Pepsi. Between the two of them, I thought, Pepsi and Coke must own the world.

"So have you traveled around the area much?" I asked Saito. I drew helpful circles on the table with my finger.

"Hmm. Near Bukoba . . ." Saito said, chomping his way through a samosa. "Yes, I went to see River Kagera, which is north, maybe, ahh, fifty kilometers? I don't know. To see lake and beach. There is very nice beach called Uganda Beach. And there is river going to Lake Victoria." His smile faded.

I swallowed my bite. "What . . ."

"There were peoples, many peoples, not living. They, ahh, floating in river from Rwanda. You know Rwanda? It has problem. Very bad problem." He stopped eating and stared at his food.

"Yes, I know. It's a very bad thing," I said, not clear on the details. I was more curious that he and I were new friends, commiserating over a bloodbath, while in another war our own grandfathers had been bent on each other's mutual annihilation.

After we finished our meal, we walked to the open-air market. The streets out front were lined with boys buffing the shoes of men seated and hidden behind the latest news. A wheeled cart heaped with cassette tapes was parked half a block down. Its PA system was so loud no one dared approach, even though it played the all-Africa favorite, Bob Marley, singing "Buffalo Soldier." A line of men and women sat across the street. They cadenced their feet to the reggae rhythm as they treadled their antique Singer sewing machines, all black and chrome.

We hopped over the open-sewer ditch that formed a moat around the market. Once inside we encountered a menagerie of hagglers and hucksters and bare-backed men shouldering eighty-pound bags of grain. Many of the vendors were bent from polio or afflicted with softball-sized goiters, but they seemed unconcerned. They patrolled tables mounded high with white flour, or beans, or peanuts. On other tables, fruits and vegetables were arranged into neatly balanced piles of four. The rear of the market opened into a line of stalls. Skinned and gutted cows and goats dangled from lintels and made the stalls look like execution chambers. The carcasses hung stiff and headless in the afternoon sun, nibbled and shat upon by happy swarms of flies.

I decided against buying meat that day, and most days after that. I instead bought onions, peppers, tomatoes, bananas, two kilos of rice and beans, and a two-foot-long bar of soap I could later cut into usable chunks. And, feeling bold, I tried an intimidating-looking fruit called a jackfruit. Although it was shaped like a spiky football and smelled like a men's locker room, the inner flesh turned out to be a creamy confection, tasting like mango, banana, and pineapple. It was well worth the trouble.

After leaving the market, we walked past another café, a bookstore, a mosque painted blue, a Hindu temple, several churches and, best of all, an ice cream parlor. While the churches were either Lutheran or Catholic, I suspected the ice cream parlor was non-denominational.

Prompted by all the holy ground, I dumbly asked Saito if he was a churchgoer. "Oh, no, no. I am Buddhist," he said. "But not very good Buddhist!" He held up a bag of fish wrapped in newspaper he had just bought. We chuckled and kept walking.

"You are Christian?" he asked and pointed to my cross necklace.

I smiled as I reached up to touch it. "Yeah, except I haven't seen any churches around here like the ones I went to in America."

"Oh," he said, but I could tell he didn't get it.

"See, in America I went to a Baptist church or an Assemblies of God. But I haven't seen those *kinds* of churches around here. Does that make sense?"

"Hmm." He nodded. "What will you do?"

"I don't know. Guess I'll pray at home by myself."

As I answered him, Saito was startled and stopped. He looked past me. "Oh!"

I stopped, too, and I smelled it before I turned around. Several tons of rat-infested garbage was heaped to the side of the road next to a stream that ran through town. Most startling was a young man who was dressed in rags and reclining on top of it. Oblivious to us, he gnawed through the remains of what looked like the leg of a kid goat.

The bizarre scene derailed our conversation, though I was uncomfortable with how I had answered Saito and didn't feel like the issue had been resolved. I knew I could always sit in on a local church service, a Lutheran one if I had to. I remembered the Catholic service in Arusha I had attended with Patrick. The sermon had been delivered in Swahili, which was fine, but that was two months earlier, and I hadn't darkened the door of a church since.

Maybe I was just overwhelmed with new experiences and I needed to settle in first. Or maybe it was something else. Whatever it was, I pushed it out of my mind and invited the affairs of the busy streets, clean and unclean, to come in and distract me.

Days passed and I was teaching. I was glad to finally be doing my job, though the work was demanding and I realized I would learn far more as a teacher than I ever had as a student. Every night I was up late with three or four textbooks spread out on the dining room table, grading papers and designing lesson plans.

I taught two classes each day. Both had close to forty-five students. My first class was Form Five Geography, which met from 7:30 to 10:00 in the morning. These young ladies were in their mid- to late teens, and the subject matter prescribed for them by the Ministry of Education was physical geography. Topics included meteorology, glaciology, plate tectonics, soil science, geology, and surveying—my strong suits.

After this class, I had a break until noon and took an early lunch at home. Then I walked the hundred yards back to school to teach human geography to my Form Six students. Material for this class focused on regional demographics, historical geography, and economic geography—not my strong suits. My Form Six students averaged nineteen or twenty years of age, though two of them were Catholic sisters who were in their thirties. They were a little older, a little bolder, and much more apt than my Form Fives to challenge me on topics I knew scant more—or oftentimes less—than they.

Form Five and Form Six students were expected to be proficient in English. I was happy to oblige this mandate, although it contributed to my students' eyes glazing over during lectures. Some teachers threw erasers or sticks of chalk at students who dozed. However, I preferred to make subjects more interesting by switching to Swahili, or even bits of Kihaya I had picked up. This tactic always brought my students around and elicited a few giggles, probably at my expense, which was fine.

Less than 10 percent of all Tanzanian children expected to do well enough, and have sufficient family funds, to advance to this level of college-preparatory education. National examinations were held each year for certain grade levels. If a student passed, he or she was invited to begin the next level. If not, their educational career was finished. They received no second chances and returned to the *shamba*, the farm, to till the ground. If the student was female, she would marry and bear as many children as biologically possible to help gather firewood, carry water, harvest food, and care for younger siblings and elders.

Since Rugambwa was a government boarding school, the students wore uniforms—a white, short-sleeved blouse, a gray woolen skirt, and black shoes. Most also owned a black cross-tie or a men's necktie for special occasions like graduations. And no matter their age or rank, all students were expected to keep their hair cropped short or woven back into cornrows if it was longer.

After classes and chores for the day were finished, the girls often sat together on the grass in little groups. They laughed and leaned against one another and played with each other's hair. I wondered what they gossiped about. Seeing how they interacted comforted me and made me miss something I hadn't known in a long time, if ever: deep friendship and communion.

However, Mr. Rwelengera told me that while most students were from Tanzania, several hailed from Rwanda. Some were Tutsis, others were Hutus. Each had to be housed in separate dorms. Housing them together, he said, could cause trouble following the recently attempted genocide in the country to our west.

I was unable to tell where any of the girls came from based on their last names. Nevertheless, I was fairly good at remembering their first names, especially the more unusual, odd-sounding ones. Seeing this as an advantage, I made an effort to learn all of them as quickly as I could. My students were impressed, but I could tell it was hard for them, especially the Form Six girls, to take me very seriously. I was too thin, too youthful, and too easygoing to garner much in the way of true respect. For that, it seemed, a teacher needed to be old, fat, and carry a big stick. I preferred to have fun and get them outside for fieldwork. We also started a geography club and went to visit national parks, airports, and hydroelectric dams.

For those interested, I set up top-rope climbs on the quartzite cliffs near campus. It was a fun diversion, and a few of the girls were pretty good at it. The climbs were on the easy side, going 5.0 to 5.5, but what amazed me most was how they chose to climb in their bare feet. Although, who could blame them for keeping their only pair of shoes stored safely on level ground?

One of my Form Five students challenged me in many

ways, made me laugh, and never ceased to amaze me with her irreverent poise. Her name was Farida. She was nearly as tall as I, very slender, and strong—all useful talents in the game of climbing. On our first school rock- climbing trip, she took issue with my shirt.

"I say! Mr. Bill! What is this meaning, 'Belay Slave'? You are wearing a profanity!"

I craned my neck around to see what was printed on the back of my green T-shirt. I had gotten the shirt at a climbing competition in Illinois. "No, that's just slang for a person who belays everybody else and never gets to climb. Like me, now," I said, waving my arms at all the students waiting to take a turn.

One of Farida's friends leaned into her face. "See, I tell you," she said, concluding a debate they must have had about it.

Farida persisted. "So! This offends me," she said and folded her arms.

I flashed back to my xenophobic upbringing and suddenly felt guilty. "Well, I won't wear it anymore if—"

"Oh, Mr. Bill! I am only joking at you. I like it okay-fine." Farida gave a wry snort and poked a finger at her friend.

"Yeah, well, double the belt on your harness, kiddo, if you want to climb next." I pointed at her climbing harness in an attempt to redirect my embarrassment.

"*Abey?*" *What?* she asked, unfamiliar with my American accent.

I reached down to her waist-harness and doubled the belt through the buckle—a standard safety procedure. She obligingly held her arms up out of the way and studied my face. I focused hard. I was barely able to overcome the pleasant distractions of her athletic figure and skin that glowed like an African plum dipped in honey.

"Mr. Bill, why is this?"

I cleared my throat. "It's so you won't come out, just in case."

"In—"

"In case. You know, like in the unlikely event it happens."

"Just . . . in . . . case," she said, tasting the shape of the words.

I noticed her full lips, darker one above, lighter one below. I finished buckling her harness. Just then Farida's eyes bounced open and fixed on the front of my Trek helmet. "*Sho!*"

I crossed my eyes and spotted a blade-thin shadow at the brim but felt nothing. "What . . .?"

As Farida pointed, something violet-colored fluttered away from my helmet and alighted onto a shaded rock. Farida tsked her tongue in delight. I exhaled in relief.

"Mr. Bill. What do you call this one?"

"That is a but-ter-fly, Farida."

"But-ter-fly."

"Yes. Good. How do you say it in Kiswahili?"

"It is called *kipepeo*."

"Ki-pe-*pe*-o."

"Yes! Very good, Mr. Bill!"

Farida liked to climb and came along on all the Geography Club outings, but her test scores were never outstanding. She studied for tests and turned in her assignments on time. Yet what she really liked to do, what she looked forward to most, was getting outside to see and touch things and *become part of* the geography. In this way she reminded me of myself. I also sensed she learned for the sheer joy of it—learned what interested her and was fun for her, anyway. Maybe she came from a well-off family and did not care how well she performed in school. Maybe it would not matter to her if she was accepted to a university or not. At any rate, she was curious and quick to smile, and her nonchalance infected the rest of the girls. And I was glad for it.

Farida was from the coast. She was Muslim, and her complexion hinted at South Asian ingredients. Because of this I found it curious how well she got along with her classmates, most of whom were devout Christians. And I was glad for this, too.

While I liked all my students, Farida was the only one I truly befriended. But on account of my position as her white, American teacher, eleven years her senior, I distrusted my emerging feelings for her, or hers for me if, in fact, she might have any. Due to this, and the fact that she was black and Muslim, I kept my distance—for a while, anyway. In spite of it, she and I were on a collision course to becoming friends in a way that was completely different from any I had ever known. And for this, I would be glad most of all.

I was home between classes, eating leftover spaghetti for lunch. It suddenly became eerily quiet outside, and I stopped eating. I sat still. I heard my heartbeat.

A compression wave shook the air. Birds panicked and flew. I ran to the front door and looked toward town in the direction of the blast, but heard nothing more. Chickens clucked out back. A lorry drove down the road.

I found out what happened later that day. Refugees fleeing Rwanda often carried weapons when escaping their homeland hell. After they reached the relative safety of Tanzania, they discarded their weapons, because if the police caught them in possession of contraband, an equally terrible retribution was guaranteed.

A grenade had been ditched near town and was later discovered by children at play. The explosion claimed several young lives.

CHAPTER 10

Crossing the River Styx

PLASMODIUM FALCIPARUM WAS the verdict; one of the more lethal strains of malarial parasites. My mild fever had grown warmer over the previous several days, and it was accompanied with aches and pains in every joint of my body, and lethargy, too. When the simple acts of breathing and blinking my eyes became laborious, I knew I had more than an ordinary flu bug.

Saito gave me a lift to the hospital, where a Tanzanian lab tech drew a blood sample and confirmed my suspicions. I had probably been infected in Dar when we were sworn in. Zillions of Anopheles mosquitoes fed on the high human populations at the coast, and now the parasites had matured in my veins. Apparently our weekly dose of Mefloquine hadn't done the trick. At any rate, I swallowed a more potent pill called Fansidar that the Peace Corps had given us for just such an emergency. I felt better within a day.

Peace Corps had given its volunteers an anti-malarial drug called Chloroquin for years but had recently replaced it with a newer one called Mefloquine, the trade name for Larium. The switch was due to the evolution of resistant strains of malarial parasites. Still, I felt skeptical about the little red pills we were supposed take once each week. They were alleged to be very powerful, but their side effects were not completely known. In a class session on malaria at the Arusha training site, Rolf had said he'd heard that some physicians advised travelers not to take Mefloquine for more than six weeks at a time. They said it was hard on the liver as well as the psyche. Several people in our group had already complained of having strange dreams and feeling moody, and months later Josh took a few swings at a guy in Mwanza for no apparent reason. He blamed it on the drug, but folks from Kentucky do tend to have a wild spirit, for example, Jim Bowie, Kit Carson, and Daniel Boone. (Josh granted me permission to cite this incident, possibly because my mother's side of the family is from Kentucky.)

I fully recovered in a few days, and since we had a three-day weekend coming up—for an Islamic holiday, the Prophet Mohammed's birthday—I decided to explore the countryside and get a feel for the land. I asked Mr. Rwelengera about it, and he said I might be interested in some ancient pictographs painted in a rock shelter not far away. He also said there were some interesting caves to the north, but other than marking an approximate "X" on my map, his description remained curiously vague.

I took this as good news. Maybe there were no nearby mountains to climb, but the thought of investigating prime-val rock art and exploring the underworld certainly grabbed my attention. I wasn't sure why. I knew it would expand my understanding of the geography and history of the area, but this was only a placebo that masked a deeper, unspoken desire. On Mount Meru I had taken a kind of drug laced with new information. My response to it had weakened an inner adversary, a parasite. Now I was ready for my next dose.

Chris loaned me her Peace Corps issue tent, and Saito said

I could borrow his machete—for protection, I thought. I packed my bike fore and aft until the frame was in danger of blowing its welds, and I set off from campus.

The terrain rose and fell every few miles, and I soon learned how to shift gears on my Trek 830 in the most economical way possible. Even so, teenaged boys riding heavy, one-speed Raleigh bicycles routinely cruised by, ringing their bike bells. I could imagine the stories they'd tell about the white guy they had beaten on a fancy "sport" bike.

But children were entertained the most. As I pedaled, they often ran alongside and laughed and shouted as long as they could before stopping to pant and point. But to the littlest ones, three and four years old, I was a ghoulish freak. To them the mere sight of me elicited screams and gasps of terror as they clutched at their mother's sides.

Up and down and up and down again. Some hills were too steep to climb on the uphill side, and I was forced to dismount and push. Of course, the downhill sides were easy and refreshing. Many of the intervening valleys were quite flat and lush with tea or sugarcane, but some were too wet and marshy for crops and remained as wetland enclaves.

Physiographically, these frozen waves that rippled across the landscape are called *cuestas*, or hogbacks, and were formed the East African Plate drafting eastward behind the India Plate. These tectonic forces created Kilimanjaro, Mount Kenya, and Mount Meru, and all the lakes in the Great Lakes region of East Africa. Perhaps the most expansive feature is the Great Rift Valley itself. Farther west, the amplitude of the terrain increases until the border of Rwanda and the Democratic Republic of Congo is reached. Here, the terrain leaps up to form the Ruwenzori-Virunga Mountains. The jungles that surround these highlands were popularized by Dian Fossey and her book *Gorillas in the Mist*.

The labyrinth of underlying faults and tectonics go largely unnoticed and are easily overlooked by all but the discerning eye. Nevertheless, the release of their pent-up pressures has created a wonderfully confusing terrain—terms that described my subconscious state to a tee.

Late that afternoon, I stopped on a ridge crest to consult my 1:50,000 topographical map. Mr. Rwelengera had indicated the pictographs by drawing a pencil mark next to a rather blank spot on the map south of the Kagera River. I looked up from my chart. The broad, sweeping valley below me reached thirty miles north to the river. Shadows drained into the valley's soft spots, and I imagined how bands of early humans might have scanned this panorama for herds of giraffe, gazelle, and even mammoth.

"*Habari, bwana?*" *How are you, sir?* The familiar greeting jerked me out of my prehistoric daydream. I turned to see a young man standing in the road.

"*Nzuri*," *Good*, I answered reflexively.

He judged from my face I was a few years older than he, so he followed with the respectful "*Shikamoo.*"

"*Marahaba*," I replied. I was still uncomfortable with being on the receiving end of this custom.

The young man wore a white, buttoned-down shirt, long black pants, and pink flip-flops, and he looked as though he could have been a student at a secondary school. He introduced himself as Pascali, and said he lived nearby with his wife and children. Yes, he had attended a nearby day school through Standard Seven (more or less sixth grade), but had not passed his exams for admittance to O-Level. He returned to his family's *shamba* to farm bananas, coffee, and a few vegetables. He said they also kept chickens.

I pointed to the map and stitched up my best Swahili to ask him about the rock shelter. Without hesitation he nodded and said "Mugana," which was the name of the place. He said he knew where it was and pointed down over the escarpment, and if I wanted to he could take me there now. Sensing him to be a sincere young man and probably Christian, I agreed. With Pascali as my guide, I pushed my bike with all my baggage into the steep, snarling bush.

In a few minutes we rounded the edge of a cliff. When I saw the overhangs, I stashed my bike and we climbed over a tumble of boulders toward a concave area, perhaps twenty feet deep. A tremor shot through me when I thought about wild animals that might inhabit the place. I had left my machete on my bike.

Vines covered the entrance of the rock shelter like beaded curtains, and we pushed them aside to climb in. The light inside was low. We stayed crouched on the floor. I listened and watched, but nothing moved. Not until my eyes adjusted, when I spotted an entire rock mural of fish, an elephant (or a mammoth?), and several human-like stick figures bleeding dots of red. Whole herds of giraffes were depicted, and in one corner was the image of a dugout canoe. All of the art had been painted onto the light-colored rock in red ocher.

The moment was meditative. I felt fortunate to stand where a family of early humans had once huddled around campfires and gazed out across the valley below, planning, dreaming, praying. I had read about petroglyphs (drawings etched into rock) and pictographs (paintings on rock) in the lakes region of East Africa. No one knew their age. However, archaeologists who had dated the fat residues in ocher paint mixtures, as well as the sooty carbon deposits in the hearths, said they must be at least 15,000 years old. Others who had studied the stone tools gave dates of up to 70,000 years based on knapping techniques, though it was impossible to say whether the paintings were drawn at the same time the tools were made.

I only sensed the deep antiquity of the place. I felt like

an eyeball standing in the socket of a neolithic skull, and I wished I could peer back in time and see who or what those ancient people had worshipped and what they considered truth. I was positive it was worlds away from my Christian truth—the One Authentic Truth.

I took some photos and accepted Pascali's invitation to visit his home and meet his family. That evening I camped behind their hut and studied my map. It showed a road at an intersection I had traveled through earlier that day. The road went north from the intersection in the direction of Kashozi and the caves, my next objective. I decided I would backtrack to that point, which was called Gera, and go from there. The next morning, I thanked Pascali and his wife, Asha, for their hospitality, gave them a bag of peanuts, and was on my way.

In a few hours I arrived at the busy crossroads. Dozens of people moved about with bags strapped on bicycles and firewood balanced on heads. As usual, my bicycle and I attracted a surplus of attention. When I stopped to consult my map, several men approached me and asked where I was headed and how they could help. Hoping yesterday's guided scenario might repeat itself, I gave them my name and told them I needed to travel to Kashozi. Immediately, they huddled to discuss the matter and began pointing in wildly different directions. The pitch of their voices climbed and their faces grew taut. The debate drew even more attention. Other men, women, children, and even a few goats and chickens crowded around. Everyone scribbled maps in the dirt as they tried to absorb some of the action.

Just then an old, white Land Cruiser rolled into the intersection. It was spattered with mud and missing both headlights. Its driver squealed its aging brake pads to a stop and several people extracted themselves from the human knot within.

The commotion around me stopped. Paused in mid-gesture,

one of the men in the group raised a hand and shouted to the driver and pointed at me. From his seat, the driver shouted back and pointed through the windshield. The man who had hailed the driver then turned to me and explained in patient Swahili that this vehicle was on its way *toward* Kashozi, though not *to* Kashozi. In any event, I should get in. At a certain place, he said, I could get out and travel the rest of the way on foot. He said it would be his great pleasure to escort me.

I pushed my bicycle over to the Land Cruiser. The driver got out and strapped my bike and all its gear to the hood using strips of old bike tube rubber. I climbed in to find a seat. In the intervening minutes, the truck had become repacked with no fewer than fifteen people, some of whom were tiny kids who were frightened and squirmed at the sight of me. My self-appointed guide stood on the rear bumper and held onto the roof. As far as I could tell, he wore only a long, black raincoat buttoned up to the collar. He wore no shoes.

The Land Rover was packed to the brim with passengers. There was no more room; or so I thought. A woman and her baby managed to squeeze in at the last minute. I was about to give up my seat for her when she handed me her infant, who was wrapped in a *kanga*. Not a word was exchanged, though the mother's smile communicated her request for me to hold the child on my lap. The baby was fat and cute. I smiled and nodded at the mother. The woman wriggled into a stooped position between a wheel well and a seatback. I was not sure I could have fit into that spot anyway.

The countryside was spectacular. Lush, forested slopes were matted with milicea and parinari trees, and valleys were terraced with fields of cassava, rice, and beans. The road was rain-gullied and rutted, and as we bounced along I thought it must be completely impassable during the rainy seasons. Meanwhile, my bike was lashed to the hood like a trophy kill.

After an hour of bouncing side to side nearly as much as we had been moving forward, my chaperone banged on the roof and shouted for the driver to stop. I looked around. I saw no other roads or even a mud hut, and I wondered what he had in mind. I handed off my infant charge to a man seated next to me—motioning the switch to the mother—squeezed through all the damp flesh, and paid the driver for myself and my guide. After we unlashed my bike and gear, my new friend pointed to a path alongside the road. I blinked and looked again. To me it resembled a rabbit run that disappeared into the jungle, but this was the way, he said, to cross over to Kashozi Road and the lake. It wasn't far.

I pushed my bicycle and he led the way, and it was all I could do to keep up. He just kept going and going, and it wasn't long before my dehydrated brain thought of him as the Eveready Battery Man. I had been out of drinking water for an hour, and we had not stopped for any kind of lunch, though it probably wasn't anything out of the ordinary for this guy. I had learned it was common for people in the villages to have sugarless tea for breakfast, no lunch, and plantains or beans and rice for dinner—every day.

In a little while, the undergrowth turned into long blades of papyrus and *ishanga* grass. The ground became spongy and wet. Kingfishers whizzed by, and occasionally we spooked an ibis or a whole flock that flapped and squawked. They sounded irritated to be roused from their roosts.

Before long, we were knee-deep in muck the color of pitch and the smell of sewer. I recalled Humphrey Bogart in *The African Queen*. I thought of the leeches that had suckled themselves onto his body as he waded through a similar swamp, not to mention the crocs. But on we went, and the water became deeper, hip-deep, and I pictured the parts of my body that leeches now had access to. By that time, I had hoisted the crates containing my gear onto my shoulders and my guide had balanced my bike horizontally on his head.

We finally came to the edge of a turbid river where the water was deep and open. The opposite bank was a hundred yards away. I felt sure it would be difficult to swim, probably dangerous, and impossible with all my things. Luckily, a man was poling his dugout canoe in the middle of the river. Eveready and I waved and shouted. The man saw us almost immediately and changed tack to come up alongside us. After negotiating passage, we handed him my bike and gear. I struggled over a gunwale and thudded onto the rough-hewn floor. Eveready was more graceful.

As we poled across, the owner of the canoe pointed downstream into a thicket of papyrus. He chuckled and said something in Kihaya. Translating to Kiswahili, my guide indicated a family of crocodiles that were studying our progress. He explained that only a month earlier a woman who had been washing clothes at the bank was seized and dragged into the river. Her body was never recovered. The man said attacks were not common, but it was still much better to use a canoe. I could not have agreed more.

After we reached the far shore we unloaded everything, I re-packed the bike, then I paid the ferryman. Once again, the Eveready Man and I were off. The path that left the riverside was steep, and the sun was now high overhead. I wasn't sure how my guide was doing, but we had been on a frenzied sprint over hill and dale, and I was parched.

I was feeling dizzy, when the path we were on opened onto a dirt road. Eveready paused. "*Barabara ya Kashozi*," *Kashozi Road*, he said, waving an open hand at the road. He again zipped ahead, and I obediently followed. While in full stride, he also announced "*Ziwa Nyanza*," *Lake Victoria*, and pooched his lips out to his right. Tanzanians often pointed with their lips. I looked but saw only a twinkle of blue sparkling through breaks in the trees. It mocked my thirst, but I knew the lake was surely cool and would afford a refreshing soak later on.

Then I spotted it. Ahead and to the side of the road crouched a small, unassuming kiosk fashioned of sticks and grass. The familiar red, white, and blue "wave" logo of a sun-bleached Pepsi sign hung over the counter window. The banner mystically declared, "*Chaguo Ni Lako.*" *The Choice Is Yours.*

The only choice I cared to make at that moment was soda. Nearing the kiosk, I called for my man to hold up. I dashed to the counter. Two young girls sat inside, one brushing out the other's unruly shock of hair. Maybe they could see the despair clotted into the sweaty streaks of dirt lining my face, but they dispensed with formalities and awaited my request. I ordered a Fanta orange soda. I asked Eveready if he wanted one, too, but he preferred Pepsi, and so it was. Mine was sweet, syrupy, and at ambient air temperature, and I finished it off in less than ten seconds. I ordered a second and then a third.

Rehydrated and riding a sucrose buzz, I thanked my guide and told him I understood that he needed to get back to Gera. I told him I could make it on my own from here. I handed him five hundred-shilling notes—almost a dollar. He looked surprised. He delicately grasped the wrinkled papers in one hand, his Pepsi in the other, and was overcome with gratitude. He bowed, thanked me, and then spun around and disappeared down the road. His rubber raincoat flapped back and forth around his bare shins. As I watched him go, I marveled at the kindness of people I had met. Poor beyond comprehension, they never lacked in sincerity, courtesy, and simple humanity.

I wondered what would happen if all of those who had all the gadgets, money, and power—people like me, I supposed—were as selfless and giving as this shoeless man? Or like Pascali and his wife, Asha? I shook my head and took another drink from my fourth Fanta. I knew exactly what they'd say: "Then we wouldn't have all the gadgets, money, and power! Now would we?"

Maybe. And maybe it wouldn't matter. It made me question who the truly poor ones were and what true poverty was. On the one hand, people like this guy had so little. They lived in nothing more than wattle-and-daub homes. The Maasai lived in mud-dung *boma* huts. Even more extreme were the Hadza hunter-gatherers, who lived with no roofs or walls at all. On the other hand, there were people like me who consumed as much as humanly possible and lived in concentric, polymer boxes that began and ended with the omniscient, all-powerful TV.

The gulf between their lifestyle and ours was becoming clearer than I had ever known before. Many of us who lived in the global North had so many material possessions and seemed so fearful of losing them, as if we were possessed by our possessions. Perhaps they supplied us with our inflated sense of ourselves; that we were better than Africans because we had *stuff* that they, through whatever personal, moral, or biblical failings we accused them of having, didn't.

I handed my empty bottle to the girls behind the counter and thanked them. Cautious of the weirdo, they took it and slotted it into a blue plastic crate to return to the bottling company for reuse. "*Karibu, bwana,*" you're welcome, sir, they said, curtsying.

I took my bike by the handlebars and glanced down the road behind me once more. Eveready Man was gone. I'd probably never see him again, though it was awfully kind of him to help me out like that, a complete stranger.

I didn't even get his name.

CHAPTER 11

Sanctum Sanctorum

THAT EVENING I descended a mossy cleft in the escarpment and camped on a dazzling, white beach. My map called it Mukerenge Bay. I was tired, and sitting in the sand next to the water relaxed me. I scooped out a hole in the sand for no reason.

I set up my tent close to the water so I could hear the gentle waves, and for dinner I had my last chapati and a dollop of peanut butter. I watched several kingfishers hovering off-shore while I ate. They were almost motionless, suspended twenty feet or so above the surface. When one spotted a potential meal, it knifed into the water. In a couple of seconds, it resurfaced with a *dagaa*, a fish similar to an anchovy, bent double in its bill like a pencil-thin mustache. Having scored a meal, the kingfisher flitted off toward the cliffs and the trees, perhaps to donate its catch to a brood of straining, hungry beaks.

Six dark blobs sat on the beach a few hundred yards away. They were paunchy yet serpentine and stood out against the light-colored sand. Perhaps they saw me because two of them slinked down to the water's edge and slipped under. At first I thought they were crocodiles, and I knew I'd have to move my camp away from shore, but their shape wasn't right. Their heads were too small, and none could have been more than five or six feet long. Shuffling through memories of PBS documentaries, I realized they were actually monitor lizards, Nile monitors, to be exact. Legend has it they kept watch and alerted people whenever crocodiles came near and periodically stood on their hind legs to "monitor" their surroundings. Monitor lizards' venom is unexpectedly weak. However, the most curious point I remembered is they were capable of parthenogenesis—meaning that females can lay viable, "immaculately conceived" eggs without ever having been fertilized by a male. It was a humbling thought.

I watched them until evening shadows eased out onto the lake, which is what the monitor lizards were doing, too. They may have been helpful to people in the past, but I only waded up to my knees for that much-needed dip.

As soon as the sun went down, I crawled into my tent and listened to the rhythm of the waves until they rocked me to sleep. Later that night, the waves slapped against the door and soaked the floor of the tent. Splashing out into the night, I grabbed hold of the self-standing tent and dragged it and my bike onto some grassy tussocks on higher ground. I had forgotten how large lakes can muster a tidal effect similar to that of an ocean.

The next morning, I awoke to a library of hushed mutterings outside, and when I unzipped the door I stood up in the Lilliputian company of fifteen or twenty children. All of them were barefoot and wrapped in tattered shirts or shorts, though not many wore both.

I scaled myself down and gave a miniature wave. "*Habari za asubuhi, watoto,*" *Good morning, children,* I said. My eyes smarted into the sunrise over the lake.

"*Nzuri. Shikamoo,*" *Good, we respect you,* they replied in unison and curtsied, even the boys.

"Marahaba." *As it should be.*

Fresh out of things to talk about, we stood there for a moment and evaluated one another. The children were extremely bashful and whispered to one another behind tiny, curled hands. Several chewed on blades of grass they spat out once the fibers had become mealy. It reminded me of breakfast. I had filled my bottles with lake water the night before and treated them with iodine, but I had nothing left to eat. Reality sank in, and I knew I had to find food if I was going to make it to the caves.

According to my map, Kashozi was only three miles north. As I packed my gear and loaded my bike, the children watched and whispered. They were unable to hold their laughter, however, when I brushed my teeth and frothed at the mouth like a rabid dog. I couldn't resist giving them each a squirt of Colgate, and soon we were all brushing our teeth. They used their index fingers like toothbrushes as they laughed and spat and ran around in silly circles.

I almost decided to stay and visit with them, but I had a higher calling. I waved good-bye, waded through the grassy sand, and hauled my bike up to the road. It wasn't long before I came to a bend in the road, where a handful of concrete buildings stood vacant and crumbling. The place matched up with the location of Kashozi on my map, and a dozen people milled around in the road, kids mostly, carrying bundles of firewood on their head. Others clustered near a cinder-block kiosk about twenty feet long by twenty feet wide. Music thumped from a stereo-system hitched up to a truck battery in the kiosk, where the Ace of Base pop favorite "The Sign" erupted at top notch.

I walked my bike over to the shop counter. The shelves inside were stacked with staples as well as luxuries: Tan Band margarine, Cadbury chocolates, Kasuku shortening, bags of sugar and tea, eggs, matches, hurricane lanterns, tins of kerosene, and bottles of soda. And centered above it all hung the ubiquitous portrait of Tanzania's president, Ali Hassan Mwinyi.

The silhouette of a man picking his nose sat behind a table inside the darkened shop. When I leaned over the counter, he scooted the chair out behind him on the dirt floor and came to his feet. About six feet tall, he was a solid, powerfully built fellow whom I guessed to be around forty. I felt a twinge of intimidation. This had been my general reaction toward black people since I was a child, but especially strong-looking black men.

Oddly enough, he looked nervous, too. He reached up and squelched the music. "Having good commodities. You wanting?" he asked in English.

He relaxed when I answered in Swahili and told him my name.

"Eh?"

"Bill . . . William," I said, adding the more common name. His smile expanded around two rows of square teeth like white shower tiles.

"Beel?"

"Yes. Bill."

"Like Beel Cleentone. President of U.S.A.!" he added in Swahili.

"Uh, yes. Same name, but we are not related."

Hearing this, he and those gathered around broke into uproarious laughter. They swatted their thighs and slapped me on the shoulder as if I were, indeed, a celebrity. I couldn't help but laugh, too. In a matter of seconds, I had gone from a complete outsider to the center of approval.

As the chuckles relaxed, the shopkeeper extended his hand, and in the spiel of any good peddler introduced himself as

Gosbert Mushema. He seemed friendly, and I wondered if he could help me find the caves. I bought three Cadbury Dairy Milk bars from him and ate them while I told him my story. His smile dissolved when I mentioned the caves.

He was quiet and thought for a moment before he answered. "Yes, we can go," he said, "but you must know there can be leopards and large snakes in these caves."

I thought he was testing me, so I reached around to my bike and patted the machete tied to the rear crate. I told him I'd be just fine.

Gosbert's smile returned. He shouted in Kihaya to three of the older boys and in a flash they sped off on foot. He explained to me in Swahili that for the first cave, we would need a very long, very strong rope. He had sent the children to a nearby fishing village to find one, but I would need to cough up the cash to buy it.

"How much money do you have?" he asked.

I was running low. "How much it will it cost?"

"It depends on the rope, but it is made from grass, so it should be doubled when we use it."

"Grass?"

Gosbert chuckled. "Yes, *Bwana* Bill. Grass rope, it is very strong!" he said, as he pretended to pull at either end of a length of rope.

We locked up my bike and gear in his shop, and soon the boys returned with a great coil of rope. It was made of three thick cords of braided grasses, which brought its overall thickness to about two inches. I grossly measured its length by uncoiling it in spans between my open arms and counted fifteen spans, or about nintey feet. It seemed incredibly strong.

Gosbert also tested it and gave his approval. Having no idea how much a rope like this cost, I once more found myself at the mercy of a local person's good graces. I could not hide the fact that I was white, and it was commonly thought that all white people, especially white men, were foolishly rich. After all, I had traveled all the way to Tanzania to become employed in teaching, the earlier profession of their nation's founding father. None of the people here would ever have the means necessary to travel to the United States. Still, the fact remained I was not carrying much money, and way out here in the bush, letters like *A*, *T*, and *M* were merely three, unrelated runes in the alphabet.

Gosbert could tell I was no ordinary, rich *mzungu*. But neither was he going to rip off an artisan in a neighboring village who had *absolutely* no money and who had spent days, maybe weeks, harvesting and weaving this rope. "Three thousand shillings," he said in a deadpan tone that belied decades of haggling.

I leaned in close to his ear and told him that, sorry to say, I had only 2,500 shillings, or about four bucks, on me. "What can I do? Cut the rope?" I asked.

Once again, I was transparent as a bottle of Konyagi. He whispered that if I put up my 2,500 he would front the remainder. I could pay him back another time. He was being generous, I understood, but I also sensed he really wanted to see the caves. I reached into my pocket for the paperclip I used as a money clip and pulled off five 500-shilling notes, each printed with an image of a giraffe and a zebra. My teacher's ID card was now the only item in my paperclip.

We handed the boys more cash than they had seen in their entire lives, yet there was no doubt they would deliver it to the rope-makers. The tight weave of the social fabric here amazed me. Gosbert coiled the rope and handed it to another young man to caddy. I grabbed my daypack, and we started off through the fields behind his shop to find a cave mysteriously known as *Kalyabagole*—The Cave That Ate the Bride.

However, we weren't alone. The event had drawn a lot of attention, what with plans of descending into a leopard's lair and all. A dozen men and a horde of children buzzed with chatter as they followed us into fields of russet grass that stood nearly chest high. Grasses like these were used to thatch roofs and floors, line bed mattresses, and coil into donut-shaped head cushions for carrying anything heavy. They could even be woven into ropes like the one that would soon lower me and Gosbert into the earth.

We walked along a narrow path for about a mile until we approached a slight depression in the terrain. The sunken area was about twenty yards across. Gnarled trees clustered near the low point. As we entered the depression, Gosbert told the story. He said that long ago, a betrothed woman had been out in the fields catching *senene*, or katydids. They were a local delicacy commonly served as an appetizer at wedding feasts. Paying little attention to her footing, she ran across the opening to the cave and plummeted to her untimely death. That was the official legend, but there were others.

Not long before Europeans arrived in the nineteenth century, local people sought refuge in caves when the kingdom of Buganda carried out raids. On at least one such raid, Bugandan warriors discovered locals hiding in one of these caves and besieged it. Because there were so many caves, Gosbert couldn't recall which one it was, but he said the warriors set fire to heaps of grass and threw them into the cave. Everyone inside was either asphyxiated or burned alive. He said nowadays on certain occasions, elders met at that cave to perform ceremonies.

We came to a tangle of spinach green bushes in the depression. In the center was a hole five feet across, nearly circular, and dark as the pupil of an eye. I crouched over it. I strained to pick up variations in color or texture, but the sun soared high overhead and my eyes could not adjust. I could, however, feel the dank, cool lens of air press against my face. The air smelled like rotten wood and moldy cement. It reminded me of my grandparents' basement, and I thought I could hear water dripping, too. I pitched a stone into the void and it hit bottom in a few seconds. It couldn't be that deep.

Gosbert and I did not trust the bushy trees at the opening to hold our weight. Since there was enough manpower available, we decided it would be better if each of us was lowered into the cave and hauled out again later. We doubled the rope and tied the ends together to form a loop. We also tied a knot every three feet or so along the topside length that should, in theory, give our human anchors a better grip. Once doubled and knotted, the total length of the rope shrank to thirty-five or forty feet. This concerned me, but after I tossed another rock into the hole and heard it swiftly land, I was convinced the cave couldn't be that deep, and if I was wrong they could pull me up again.

I made sure I had my water bottle, my camera, and my mini Mag flashlight in my daypack. I also made sure Saito's machete was securely zipped in with only the handle sticking out, in case the stories about wild animals had any veracity. Meanwhile, Gosbert lined up the strongest roster of men and gave them instructions. He spoke in Kihaya, which I didn't understand much, so I hoped it wasn't something like, "Let the white guy down over the edge. I'll count to three, then everybody let go. We'll go home, sell his bicycle, and buy lots of beer!" Or something biblically approximate to the prophet Jeremiah, who was cast into a similar pit.

I sat down and dangled my legs over the edge. I reached for the rope, put my feet in the loop, and rolled onto my stomach. I immediately saw a problem. I would have to let go of the rope above the hole and juggle my hands onto a section below the edge as I was being lowered. All this had to happen while I balanced my feet in the loop. It was tricky, but like usual I was playing it by ear, making things up as I went along, and most of the time everything worked out just fine. Most of the time.

Gosbert kneeled next to the edge. "Ready?" he asked.

"Ready!"

He turned and shouted to the gang of belayers and motioned for them to begin paying out rope. They reminded me of a tug-of-war team slowly losing its battle. Gosbert chuckled and shook his head at the crazy white guy.

Right away, the rope cut into the soft ground at the top of the hole, knocking all manner of dirt and debris and pieces of rock into the pit below me and onto me. The softball-sized chunks of sandstone and quartzite were considerably harder than my skull. "Please, God," I prayed. If only I had worn my bike helmet instead of my wide-brimmed safari hat. I peeked out below but saw nothing, only bottomless black. The analytical calculator in my head ran the numbers and predicted I would soon arrive at the end of my rope.

The men lowered me for nearly a minute. Suddenly it was like someone had flipped on an old fifteen-watt light bulb. A red mound of earth surrounded by black, spongy goop materialized below. Gosbert yelled down, "Can you see?" He told me the belayers were nearly out of rope. I knew they'd be stacking up tighter around the anchor loop as their faces popped blisters of sweat.

"Yes! I see it!" I shouted, startled by my own voice rebounding off the walls. Since I was close, I called for them to hold tight while I jumped off. The distance was little more than a step, three or four feet at most, and I was down. I brushed grains of dirt from my shoulders and hat, and I shouted to

Gosbert that I was okay. He said to find someplace safe off to the side. He had seen how the rope had sliced into the edge, so he wanted to climb down under his own power.

I moved over to one of the cave walls and in the process flushed up a screeching covey of bats. I closed my eyes and covered my head. Once they cleared out, I opened my eyes and took inventory. I heard no animal sounds or threatening growls, only the flutter of bat wings and the dripping and tinkling of water. Regardless, the place stank like rotting flesh and loose stools. I put my hand out to lean against the rock wall. It felt cold and waxy, corpse-like, not at all welcoming. I brushed off my hand on my shirt.

My eyes were adjusting, and I determined this was no ordinary, limestone cave. Rather, heavy rainwater had seeped in and dissolved the silica cementing agents in quartzite, the primary basement rock in this area. The floor of the main room was perhaps thirty feet below the surface and twenty feet from side to side. A large pyramid of bat guano was heaped just off-center. Continuing my survey revealed a dark side passage about five feet in diameter. I was still trying to focus when I noticed something out of place. I blinked. In front of the side-passage was a large clay pot, broken at its base and awash in a sludge of ash. The pot lay in a three-stone hearth.

I blinked again, and my mouth fell open. Next to the pot, as if tending dinner over the fire, sat the blank, open sockets of the permanent resident of this tomb. I stepped closer and bent down. A human skull lay on the floor, but only the anterior portion. The mandible was detached and lay a few inches in front of it. All the front teeth and a chunk of the maxilla were missing. Several long bones and vertebrae had been scattered about, probably the result of scavenger damage. I had entered some sort of burial chamber, and I felt thrilled and nervous at the same time. The skin on my neck prickled.

Gosbert grunted his way down the rope using only his arms. He would be down in few seconds. What would he say? Would he be angry? Maybe he'd leave me here as a sacrifice? But too late, he was down.

He shook out his arms, pumped from the descent, and turned to me with a wide smile of accomplishment. But when he focused past me his eyes narrowed and then grew large. "Oh, oh, oh, oh," he said in a descending scale of awe and reverence.

Gosbert bowed his head and squatted. He steadied himself by placing his left hand on the floor. He closed his eyes, crossed himself with his right hand as though he was at church communion, and then mumbled something in Kihaya. His shook his head from time to time. It was awkward, and I felt like I was in the way, so I tiptoed away from the skeleton. I squatted and bowed my head as Gosbert had, but I kept my eyes open and watched him for the next cue.

After a minute, he stopped mumbling but stayed squatted with his head down. My gaze drifted back to the bones and the cooking hearth. I was amazed; me, a Christian, in the nave of a pagan shrine. What would my family and the folks at Brown Street Baptist Church say if they could see me now? Would they be intrigued, appalled, or mute? My skin tingled, and I was strangely pleased at the thought. Then I remembered history lectures that described the grisly fate of Christians sacrificed in tribal Africa. I swallowed hard.

Gosbert raised his head and stood up. I stood up, too. "*Bwana* Bill," he said softly, "this one is my ancestor from the Chwezi people. They died long ago. There is no problem. We are welcome, but we cannot stay long."

I looked at the skeleton and then into the dark cavern.

I asked Gosbert if he wanted to come with me and take a look, but he shook his head, smiling, almost embarrassed. He said he had come far enough and would stand guard under the rope. "But be careful," he said. "Watch for leopards and snakes!"

My eyes had fully adjusted to the dim, gray light, but the passageway was pitch black, so I clicked on my flashlight. I bowed my head to the skeleton in case Gosbert was watching, and then I crouched into the wet, dripping cavern. The mineral-rich water eroded the soil beneath my feet and made the ground soggy. The darkness became heavier and the walls closed in until I had to crawl on all fours. I put the mini Mag in my mouth. I passed a smaller side channel on my right and made a mental note, hoping I wouldn't become lost in this catacomb.

The cavern became so tight, I was forced to shimmy along on my stomach. Then it abruptly turned upwards so I could stand, though it was still closed in all around. I couldn't raise my arms from my sides.

As soon as I stood, the beam from my mini Mag flashed across a glistening black blob directly overhead. I snapped my head up. My light illuminated a writhing colony of spiders. I gasped around the mini Mag. The spiders flexed and stiffened. I had no idea if they were poisonous or not, but they certainly did not look friendly. Each was as big as a silver dollar. Their legs were like shiny black needles and made suction sounds against the massive, shimmering web.

I held my breath, stooped low, and kept the light on them. Luckily, they didn't move. I backtracked until I found the side channel I had passed earlier. I went in and again had to undulate like a snake in order to make progress.

Without warning, my left arm plunged into water. At the same time, the ceiling sloped down nearly to the water's surface. I poked my flashlight through the gap and saw a chamber on the other side. I held my breath and slid into the water.

I came up quickly on the other side into the dank air of a small cave. It was about ten feet across but only four or five feet high. I climbed out of the water, crouched, and realized how repulsive the place was. Black and green and red fungus coated the walls and hung down from the ceiling in strandy globs. I poked at one with my machete but decided it best to leave it alone. The smell was stale, and the left hemisphere of my brain reminded me of *The Hot Zone* by Richard Preston. In that author's account, the origins of some of the more malignant, flesh-eating diseases such as Ebola had been traced to certain caves in Africa. I breathed shallow, careful breaths.

As I knelt there, an oddly familiar sense of claustrophobia squeezed down. It felt like the room had focused on me with an attention that was staunch, pigheaded, and disapproving. A chill seeped into my bones, and I wanted to run.

I had to get out. When I snapped my flashlight around to leave, the beam glanced off a dark yet symmetrical object on the wall to my left. I refocused and saw a horizontal crack running the length of the stone wall. I looked closer. A pipe lay in the crack. I reached over and picked it up. There was no doubt; it was a smoking pipe made of dark-colored clay. Its bowl was cone-shaped, and at its base was an upwardly inclined tube through which smoke could be drawn. I tried to imagine who in their right mind would have come to this place to light one up. But perhaps, I thought, the pipe was once used during rites of passage.

I hadn't thought about it in a long time, but my dad had smoked a pipe when I was very young. I missed the fragrance, but not the smoke.

Gosbert's distant voice echoed through the cavern. He

asked if I was okay and if I would please come soon. He sounded anxious to leave. I put the pipe back on the wall and slid back down into the water. Gosbert gave out a chuckle of relief when I sloshed back into the main chamber. He signaled up to the crew and instructed me to go first. He told me to stand with my feet in the loop and to not look up in case a rock came loose from the edge. I did as he directed, and he shouted to the others. They lifted me into the air in starts and stops. As I twisted around, I looked down at the guano, the potsherds, and the skull. It watched me until its eye sockets grew faint and dusky.

At the top, a strong, straight arm came down to my face with the palm wide open. I grabbed on and was borne onto the lip of the pit. I crawled out into long, green grass, shot through with beams of blue sunlight. The air was warmer here and a breeze floated through with the smells of cooking fires and of the lake beyond. It had been less than an hour, but I was relieved to see and smell so much color and life.

I had found a piece to a puzzle down in the caves. I did not know what it was or where it fit, or even what the puzzle looked like. I only knew there were other pieces to be found, and I needed to gather them as soon as possible. For now, that meant I had to find the second cave.

CHAPTER 12

Belly of the Beast

ON OUR WAY back to Kashozi, Gosbert told me that descending into the cave reminded him of adventures from his youth, and he went on and on about his travels to Kampala and other places. He said he had served in the Tanzania People's Defense Force (TPDF) in 1978 when Idi Amin invaded from Uganda. Amin had attempted to annex a portion of Tanzania's Kagera Region, then called West Lake region. The TPDF succeeded in driving Amin's army out, though many Tanzanians died and the financial costs to the country were high. Gosbert also told me how people in all the local villages had performed dances and ceremonies nonstop during the war. They had petitioned the ancestors for help, especially at the Cave of God.

"You know, *Bwana* Bill, this other cave, it is not far," he said. "If you want, I myself can take you there." Gosbert added there was a chance we'd be invited to the New Moon Ceremony, held each month, to commune with the ancient ones. The ceremony, he said, was scheduled to happen that night at the cave. He could ask the elders in charge if it would be all right for me to come along and watch. "Besides," he said, grinning, "you have now met one of the ancestors."

When we arrived back at his shop, I strapped the grass

rope on top of the crates behind my bike seat and checked my watch. It was already mid-afternoon. I needed to get home, get cleaned up, eat, and prep for classes the next morning, and according to my map Kashozi was more than twenty rutted miles from Bukoba. I estimated it would take me at least three hours to reach the north side of Bukoba Valley and another half hour to ride through town and up the other side to Rugambwa. Plus, I had told Saito I'd be home before dark on Sunday. If I left right now I'd be pushing it.

However, I didn't know when I'd be able to return to Kashozi, let alone have another chance to see a New Moon Ceremony. If I didn't go to the second cave now I'd not only miss a rare, cultural opportunity, but I'd also risk losing a spiritual momentum that was still tenuous and mostly unconscious.

"*Bwana* Gosbert, how far to the Cave of God?"

"Oh, not far, *bwana*. Almost we can see it," he said. He pointed north, opposite the direction to Bukoba. Gosbert locked the shop door, grabbed his heavy steel bicycle, and we pedaled north to the Cave of God.

Before long, we coasted onto an open, grassy plain, where the road tipped away in front of us. A cool breeze began to dry my soaked jeans. It fluttered under my shirt and dried the sweat from my chest and back. We were nearing the north end of Rubafu Point, and I saw how the peninsula was bordered on three sides by the wide-open lake.

Gosbert motioned to a side road that split off to the right. We took it and soon came to the edge of an escarpment that overlooked a small village of grass huts. We found the top of a narrow path and walked our bikes down into a dense forest of lichen-speckled *mwarobaini*, or neem trees, which are similar to mahogany. As the ground leveled out, these broad-leafed evergreens gave way to the bunched symmetry of coffee plantations. Clusters of red and green coffee beans hung in the caffeinated shade.

At the edge of the treed area, we came into a yard of hard-packed dirt. A mud-brick house sat in the middle of the yard, thatched with grasses that resembled blond bangs of hair. A woman worked in front of the house. Barefoot and bent over a homemade hand broom, she swatted debris toward the periphery of the yard with a rhythmic *shwsh-shwsh! Shwsh-shwsh!*

"*Hodi hapa?*" *May we come in?* Gosbert shouted, announcing our arrival. The woman stood and squinted to identify her visitors. She adjusted her faded *kitenge* wrap. Her tightly crinkled hair was mostly white and cut short over a wizened face that made me assume she was in her seventies. Her posture and build, however, suggested she was a decade or two younger.

"*Shikamoo, mama,*" Gosbert and I shouted.

"*Marahaba,*" the elder croaked. She recognized an old acquaintance accompanied by an odd-looking stranger. As we approached the house, Gosbert chatted with the woman in Kihaya. He then turned to introduce me in Swahili.

"This one, he is called *Beel,*" he said, squeezing emphasis onto the unfamiliar name.

"*Beedee?*" the woman asked. Her cheeks and eyes stretched thin like she'd just witnessed a bicycle accident.

"Bill-*William,*" I said.

"Ahaa! Weelyum!" Her face relaxed, and she smiled.

Gosbert then introduced Sofia. He explained that she and her husband, Silvanus, lived here and farmed coffee, mostly. Her weathered eyes were steady and intense, though they softened with a cozy smile as she held my right hand.

Gosbert again spoke in Kihaya. Talk became low and somber, and I sensed the topic of the cave had been broached.

When Gosbert said the word *Kalyabagole*—the cave we had explored earlier—Sofia's tired eyes dilated with long-lost memories, and she brought a hand to her mouth. Gosbert shook with excitement as he told the story. Sofia waggled my hand in a friendly way and exclaimed, "Oh! I say!" with a hint of incredulity. But then she became small and spoke in a contrite manner.

Gosbert said that Sofia was very happy we had met an ancestor, but the New Moon Ceremony had been held the night before. We were too late. My hopes sank a notch. Seeing my disappointment, she welcomed us inside to rest and to meet her husband.

Like most homes in rural Africa, theirs had no furniture except a three-legged wooden footstool stuffed into a corner. Since I was the guest, they invited me to sit on it. Everyone else reclined on the floor, which was padded from wall to wall with a thick mat of dried, long-bladed grasses. The mud-brick walls were bare. The only exception was a tattoo of soot, spattered from a kerosene stove, and a brass crucifix with wood inlay that hung over the doorway. Below the crucified figure of Jesus was a miniature skull and crossbones, a design common on German crucifixes of the early twentieth century.

An old man sat against the opposite wall. He was flush-eyed and cradled a long-necked, hollowed-out gourd in his lap. He slurped from a reed straw that was poked into the gourd, which was filled with *rubisi*, the sour-fermented drink made from bananas.

Gosbert spoke quietly, almost fawningly, with the man for several minutes before he introduced us. Gosbert switched to Swahili to explain to me that Silvanus was very old. He was so old, in fact, that no one knew his age, not even him. Practically bald, he bore a toothless grin and had cataracts.

The rheumy, white glazes covering his obsidian irises mixed to yield a bluish hue, and his voice was husky and hoarse as though he'd been shouting all day in the market.

Silvanus recounted how he had been a foot soldier in Kaiser Wilhelm's army when he was just a boy. He told of their drills and physical fitness routines, and at one point he laid down his calabash, hopped up, and marched out into the yard. Standing at attention, he shouldered and presented imaginary arms to a platoon of coffee trees. He also told of a battle against the British near Bukoba that his regiment had won, although they suffered heavy losses. After that he lost his enthusiasm for reminiscing and again became old and feeble and lay back down.

Tanganyika was part of German East Africa from 1885 until 1919 when the Treaty of Versailles was signed at the end of World War I. If Silvanus had fought in the German infantry near Bukoba, he was at least in his early nineties, even if he had been a very young foot soldier. I wondered about the stories this man could tell, and the changes, mostly social, he had seen in his lifetime.

Sofia had disappeared while Silvanus was speaking. She reappeared carrying a freshly cut banana leaf, two aluminum pots, a pitcher of water, and a plastic bowl. She laid the four-foot-long banana leaf in the center of the floor and poured heaps of beans and rice onto it. Gosbert and I took turns washing our hands with a nub of soap over the plastic bowl while Sofia trickled water from the pitcher over them. Washed in the customary way, we sat on the floor around the banana leaf with the soles of our feet respectfully bent back from view. Then we closed our eyes and Silvanus prayed over the meal. After he finished, he crossed himself in the Catholic manner. The rest of us followed suit, even I. Propped up with our "dirty" left hands on the floor, each of us reached forward with our right hand to pull a dab of rice and beans onto our own portion of the leaf. Talk turned slow and ordinary as food became the focus.

After a while I asked our hosts if they would tell me about the cave. They agreed, so I licked the rice and bean sauce off my fingers and rummaged around in my daypack for a journal and pen.

Silvanus and Sofia were poor but respected elders, healers, and shamans. Each month when the moon was made new, elders from nearby villages gathered with them at *Lwemboi-jole*, the Cave of God. The cave, they said, was filled with a pool of clear water, water you could drink, water that went very deep into the earth. "Rain" dripped from the cave's ceiling and kept it filled. The Cave of God was a powerful place where they made special appeals to the ancestors for more rain, or fish, or better health, or other things. The ancestors then spoke on their behalf with Ruhanga, the highest god and primogenitor. As circumstances warranted, the elders brought a sacrifice of coffee beans or boiled milk, or perhaps a chicken or a goat if their requests were dire, and they beat a special drum to summon the spirits. They also called on nature spirits who inhabited certain rocks, trees, and springs.

As Silvanus spoke, I realized I was in the presence of a shamanic tradition that reached back many millennia, deep into the heart of Africa. These sacraments were spiritually reproductive. They atoned for a people's sins by restoring their connections to the natural world and sustaining life. They were systems of belief that were here long before the Germans arrived and introduced Christianity and bolt-action carbines.

The Sahara Desert broadly divides the ethnic groups, languages, and religions that span the African continent. Islam became established in northern Africa and along the east coast of Africa in the seventh and eighth centuries C.E. It did not enter the tropical interior until the seventeenth century. Christianity established itself in Egypt and Ethiopia in the first few centuries after Jesus' life but spread more slowly elsewhere in Africa. Only in the latter half of the nineteenth century did Christian missionaries bring their faith to the interior. Today, Christianity and Islam dominate the continent, and in Nigeria they have fused to produce a syncretistic faith called Chrislam. These religions are interspersed with pockets of Hinduism, Sikhism, Buddhism, and Judaism.

Nevertheless, indigenous beliefs are still widespread. In most cases, African religions have blended with each of the orthodoxies mentioned above. In northern Africa, tribal Muslims indulge in ecstatic spirit possession ceremonies, such as the Zär cult in Sudan. Zulu Jews in South Africa consult their *Mujaji* rain queen, a powerful magician-goddess who has the ability to conjure rain clouds over the semi-arid veldt. Christians in Buhaya in northwestern Tanzania propitiate the spirits of their ancestors with ambrosia as the moon becomes black and spirits run loose upon the earth. And across the continent, witches are consulted for augury and condemned for misfortunes.

The essence of all these beliefs is an overarching spirit world. It is made of people, living and dead, and vibrates with a spiritual reality that includes all created things.

We finished the food and stories and reclined on the grass floor. Broad, green banana leaves flopped and rustled in the late afternoon breeze. I brushed at a mosquito whining past my ear.

Silvanus raised his sagging eyes to Gosbert, who turned

to me and rubbed his thumb and forefinger together. They wanted payment, not for the food and hospitality per se, but for their time and information. I was about to bring my hands up empty when I had an idea: the rope. Maybe they could sell it to fishermen for a good price. I asked Gosbert.

"Hmm. It is good," Gosbert said. His face was focused and cautious. "I will ask."

He also told them I had no money. They understood. I was white, and therefore rich, but I was still young and not too bright. The rope, however, was acceptable.

Silvanus climbed to his feet. The rest of us followed his lead, and with full bellies we toddled outside. Gosbert and the others went on in Kihaya. This was their first language, their mother tongue, as they were fond of saying. For them, Swahili was a utilitarian second, and even I with my limited vocabulary and grammar skills had noticed elderly folks out in the villages mismatching their Swahili noun classes.

I untied the rope. Silvanus felt it between his coarse hands like he was seeing it with them. He mumbled something to Sofia, and she answered quietly. Gosbert translated. "Silvanus and Sofia, they say they like this rope. It is a good one, but it is too much and too strong. You must make a promise to return soon so they can give to you a gift."

I didn't want them to feel obligated. I also knew the matter was not open to debate. So I accepted their offer and asked Gosbert to tell them I promised to return.

I handed the rope to Sofia. She thanked me and said I was welcome to come to a New Moon Ceremony anytime. Also, if Gosbert and I wanted, we could take the path behind their house to see the cave. From there, she said, the path wound up to the road and was not difficult.

Gosbert and I thanked them again and walked our bikes over to the path, which snaked through tall, squeaky grasses.

The forest was looped with vines and creepers and all manner of untamed foliage that thinned out at the foot of a cliff.
Lwemboijole, the Cave of God, gaped like a howling mouth
that leaned out of the earth. The entrance was about twenty
feet from side to side, fifteen feet high, and a near-perfect
arch, but the ceiling sloped down toward the back. A languid
pool filled the floor of the cave with the most pure, transparent water. Who could say how deep or into what subterranean secrets it reached? And as Silvanus had said, it rained
in the cave; drips of water seeped from all over the silica-
encrusted ceiling and plunked into the pool.

The prehistoric-looking grotto reminded me of the Jean
M. Auel novel *The Clan of the Cave Bear*, and I imagined
how it might look on a moonless night by firelight. Countless
generations of frenzied worshippers had congregated here to
throw the bones and read ringlets of smoke and dance and
entreat the spirits. I could not fathom how it had found a
place alongside the Gospel of Christ. My world had always
been this or that, black or white.

I saw my reflection in the pool. An image floated beneath
it, submerged in my subconscious, but I couldn't make it
out. Or, as it says in 1 Corinthians 13:12, "For now we see
through a glass, darkly; but then face to face." Intuitively, I
knew the only way to rescue myself was to dive in and swim
through the belly of the beast. More than descending into
caves, this meant I had to test myself on bigger, steeper, and
more dangerous African mountains where I could exorcise a
demon and call God's bluff: Was He really there?

An ibis squawked, and a flock lifted off from a huge old
gum tree backlit by a retiring red crescent, the color of God.
Gosbert and I stood outside his shop. We thanked each other

for a memorable day, and he reminded me I owed him some cash.

"Yes, *bwana*. Five hundred shillings. I will remember," I said.

"There is no worry, Bill-William, because what is better is a boat, and a motor having the strength of twenty horses. It is called a Mercury. Do you know this kind?"

I was tired from the day, and I nodded. But then it sunk in. "Huh? No, I have no boat, *bwana*, and I am a very poor *mzungu*. Five hundred shillings, yes. Boat and motor, no. I cannot."

We shook hands and extended open invitations to come and visit each other. I hopped on my bike, kicked off to get the unwieldy thing moving, and turned south toward Bukoba. I had been away for three full days, and it would be good to get back, bathe, and fall into a soft bed. But the air was already cool, and I knew I'd be pedaling into the night, maybe until 10:00. I'd be alone, too, because villagers rarely went out after dark, especially when there was no moon. Evening was when people cooked dinner and told stories— this time, perhaps, about a crazy *mzungu*, some toothpaste, and a skeleton.

The road was soon kindled by starlight. I heard the crunch of sand and the ping of red pebbles flinching from under my tires, but no city lights, planes, or cars. The Southern Cross pointed the way and asked a question I couldn't make out. With blind faith, I cruised on and trusted the road ahead.

CHAPTER 13

God Willing

"**PLEASE, MR. BILL!** We are wanting only one picha, please!" Farida and two of her Muslim friends stood at my front door. They were decked out in their Friday best, and they were begging me to take their photos. I was in a hurry, but I gave in.

"Hang on, kiddo. Let me get my camera," I said. The other two girls picked up on the nickname I'd given Farida and exchanged furtive grins.

Eight months had passed since my trip to the caves. I hadn't climbed any mountains as I had promised myself—Meru was the last one—but I had dreamed about it daily. I had written Cynthia and Rolf about Kilimanjaro, and as fate would have it, they planned to take some of their students to climb Kili over the break. They had arranged it so I could join them. I was in seventh heaven. I had done push-ups and chin-ups and gone for a run almost every day. I'd also read my Bible every night and prayed about it, too. Now I felt ready to climb the highest holy mountain in Africa to see if I could find God in a harsh yet heavenly land.

Now it was the end of May, and the end of my second semester at Rugambwa had finally arrived. Rich had come over from Ihungo to help take my things down to the port.

In a few minutes we would have to leave, but there was still time to take a picture of my students.

"Can I give you a hand with your camera?" Rich asked.

"No, thanks. I got it." I knew that as long as the ship was still docked—or the train hadn't left, or the bus was still parked—I would have little trouble boarding by virtue of my skin color alone. At first, I had gone along with this custom without much concern, but then I had started to notice a subtle, self-delusional bigotry in myself whenever I'd taken advantage of it. I increasingly tried to line up like everyone else, even when Tanzanians beseeched me to take my "rightful" place at the front of the line.

"All right. Does this work?" I stepped down off the porch with my camera in hand. "Here? How about here?"

Farida flapped her hand at me. "Yes, yes. There is okay-fine."

"This okay? *Sawa*." *Okay.*

The British volunteer who had lived in this house before me had finished her contract at the end of the previous semester and went home to England. When I returned from traveling over Christmas break, I moved out of Saito's place and into this one. It was located at the end of the row of faculty houses next to the road to town. Be it ever so humble, it was all mine, and I had secured my claim by decorating its walls with the emptied wrappers of Crunch bars, M&Ms, Kit-Kats, Hersheys, even flattened Cheez It boxes. Each one was the remnant of a care package that had made the three-month postal voyage from my mom.

Since moving in, I had strode around in my underwear playing my guitar, singing, and reading authors like Edward Abbey, Robert Pirsig, and Richard Bach—except when the power went out. Thankfully, this hadn't happened as often as it did in the rest of the country. The electricity powering Bukoba was more dependable, as it was supplied by the Owen's Falls Hydroelectric Plant on the Nile in Uganda.

But my new abode was not without its issues. Nearly every night it was bombarded by a virtual squadron of bats that also called the place home. Around dusk they cruised in, full speed, aiming for the half-inch gap between the iron roof drip-edge and the particle-board ceiling tiles. They frequently missed their target and slammed their little bodies into either roof or the outside wall. This was in spite of their touted echolocative sensing apparatus. I also regularly found pea-sized bat turds sprinkled about the mini-fridge, the grain bin, and the veggies. I got used to it, though, and as I was fond of saying, you can eat almost anything if you boil it or fry it long enough.

As for water, the house hadn't received any from the school's elevated tank since the pipes—plumbed on top of the ground—had all been stolen years before. Still, I didn't mind filling a pair of five-gallon buckets at a creek a few hundred yards away. The creek always buzzed with frogs and crickets, and I especially enjoyed the walk when Farida was able to make time in her studies to give me a hand. I would carry my bucket at my side and have to stop to rest every hundred feet or so. Meanwhile, Farida would politely wait with her bucket balanced on her head.

She was helping me fetch water one day the previous October when we stopped to take a break on the way back. "Mr. Bill, you must be very weak."

"That's why I'm a teacher."

Farida wore blue flip-flops and an old *kanga* wrapped around her like a skirt below her white, untucked school shirt. These weren't her nicest clothes, but they did let her natural beauty shine through. I tried not to stare, or at least not be obvious that I was. I was attracted to her. I admitted

that to myself, and I was fascinated with how unradical it felt
to regard a beautiful black woman. Such feelings were quite
new to me. Yet I reminded myself that I was her teacher, and
any expression of my feelings would be completely inappropriate. Besides, I didn't know if any feelings she might have
for me were genuine or if they would be influenced by my
relative position of authority based on my gender, nationality, and race.

"Oh! But this is reminding me. Maybe you can be teaching
me more after school," she said.

I felt a flush of emotion. I picked up my bucket and hobbled
onto the path behind her. I cleared my throat. "You mean like
tutoring you in geography."

"Yes, of course, it is geography. But you know, I am somehow curious about this thing you are telling us in class."

"Which thing?"

"You are calling it religious ecology, yes?"

"You mean how religions affect their environment."

"No, no. What I am meaning is how *environments* are
affecting the *religions*."

"What do you mean?"

"For example, this idea of heaven. I am thinking it must be
a cool place, with streams and many green vegetables growing, and this other place, the bad place, it must be too hot
and dry. Therefore, I think our religions, Islam and Christianity," she said, turning to point at my cross necklace, "they are
deciding what is good and what is bad from their environment."

"Maybe, but you know not every religion has a heaven
and a hell. Like Buddhism," I said, though I really had no
idea about Eastern religions.

"I do not know this Buddhism. But even Buddhism, it
must be having its holy places and gods and devils, all of

them made from what those people, their eyes can be seeing and their hearts are needing. Is it?"

"So you're saying the mind makes whatever it needs out of the physical environment to express itself—"

She stopped and turned to correct me. "To express our *soul*, because God, He is living in all things."

"Sounds like you're saying religions are different because of their physical location. And that, as you know, is environmental determinism."

"It is physical *and* historical *and* spiritual, all together, *mwalimu*." *Teacher.*

I stopped again to rest. "I think you're hedging your bets, kiddo."

"Hm?"

"It's like you're being careful, 'just in case.'"

Farida's smile curled into dimples, and she looked away. "*Ndiyo, mwalimu*," yes, teacher, "I say it 'just in case.'"

The previous November, at the end of my first semester, all government schools in the country closed two weeks early. Tanzania planned to hold its first multi-party elections in late 1995, so it dug under the proverbial sofa cushions for spare change with which to fund it. One of the first cuts was education. Since Rugambwa was a government-funded school, we teachers administered our premature testing, sent in our grades, and prepared for a long Christmas break. Some of Rugambwa's students stayed on campus during the break, though most boarded steamers to cross the lake and spent time at home with family. The break lasted eight weeks.

During that time, I met up with Josh and a few other volunteers. We traveled south to Malawi, where we camped on the beach, swam, partied, and ate "crazy cake" laced with marijuana. My friends continued south to Victoria Falls in Zambia, but I left them in search of wilderness. Along the way, I befriended a member of the so-called Ostrich-foot tribe, each of whom has only three, elongated toes per foot. His name was Houston Texas Banda, and the two of us hitched a ride on a sailboat across Lake Malawi with the intent of hiking into Mozambique's Livingstone Mountains. However, I was intercepted by the Mozambican police for entering their country without a visa and was locked up in jail. Luckily I was released after an hour, when I agreed to board another small sailboat—filled with machetes and hoe heads—headed back to Tanzania. After a rambling adventure on vehicles occupied mostly by livestock, I made it back to Bukoba with only 150 shillings, or about twenty-five cents, in my pocket.

Culturally, the trip was eye-opening. Spiritually, it was unsatisfying. I didn't fulfill the pledge I had made to myself at the Cave of God; namely, I'd failed to lose myself in a mountain wilderness and search for God. I anxiously awaited climbing Kilimanjaro with Rolf and Cynthia after school got out in May. Until then, I decided to let my religious guard down and visit a mosque with a new friend, who happened to be the owner of a bike shop in town.

One early Friday evening in April, Chris, Rich, and I sat perched atop Lookout Rock, a flat-topped boulder just downhill from Rugambwa.

"So Raza invited you to attend mosque with him?" Rich asked, referring to the bike-shop owner.

I nodded. "Can you believe it?"

"Which one is it?" Chris asked.

I pointed down into town. "Right there, the blue one next to the army statue," I said.

"A *blue* mosque? For Muslim Smurfs?"

"I heard they're called 'smurfy' mystics," Rich said, chortling at his own Sufi joke.

The joking was harmless, and none of us knew that blue is often the color of choice used for mosques. In the Islamic tradition, it represents safety and heaven.

"No, but I think it's great that Mr. Raza invited you to go," Chris said.

"Yeah, well, I'm not Muslim or anything," I said. "I just thought it'd be cool to see how they do things in a mosque . . . service."

"So it's tonight?" Rich asked.

"Yeah. In fact, I better get going."

Raza Ramji and I had gotten to know each other after I purchased a bike bell and a carrier. Now whenever I showed up at his shop door, he stopped business to entertain me. He especially liked to talk about the O.J. Simpson trial, the bombing of the Oklahoma Federal Building, or any other CNN news he'd pulled in on his satellite dish.

"Billy, Billy, Billy! Goodness me. Here. Please. Come in." In a flash, Raza would find a chair for me to sit on behind the counter and send a boy off to buy a Pepsi or a Mirinda. He was courteous to a fault, and visits with him promised pleasant conversation and a warm soda pop. At one point he handed me an Islamic religious tract that looked a lot like the Christian cartoon adventures I remembered reading in Sunday school, but even as a kid I had thought they were corny. Nevertheless, I indulged his well-meaning evangelism.

The attention he gave me was nice, though it made me feel uneasy. I wondered why he treated me better than anyone else who walked through his door. I hoped it had nothing to do with my nationality, or lighter skin, or that our faiths shared the same God, more or less.

The British imperialists of the nineteenth and early twentieth centuries had held the view that morality was linked to complexion. To them the brown-skinned South Asians exhibited a slightly higher moral and intellectual caliber than the black-skinned Africans. Colonial administrator Thomas Macaulay presaged these sentiments in 1835 when he declared, "We must do our best to form a class who may be interpreters between us and the millions whom we govern, a class of persons Indian in blood and colour, but English in taste, in opinions, words and intellect."

Under this mandate, traders, shopkeepers, and merchants were later imported from British India in the nineteenth century to serve as indentured laborers and middlemen in British East Africa (Kenya and Uganda). The British overlords maintained a sense of supremacy over the Indians by referring to them as "coolies," a racial slur taken from an Urdu word that meant day laborer.

For nearly a century, Indians complemented the labor of black Africans when they helped to build 906 miles of railroad in British East Africa. For their part, the Germans administered the labor of mostly black Africans when they built 1,003 miles of railway across the semi-arid interior of German East Africa (Tanganyika, Rwanda, and Burundi) by 1912. But when the British took control of the German protectorates after World War I, they again employed Indians to help extend those lines an additional 192 miles and build hundreds of bridges.

Racially favored, the Indians were permitted to serve as secretaries and regents of minor offices, while the Africans were not. Indians soon became part and parcel of an emerging industrial economy. As such, they gained higher proficiency in English and acquired greater wealth than their autochthonous brethren.

Over the decades, this contributed to an undercurrent of resentment from the native, often Christianized, Bantus.

It also created a reciprocal suspicion among the Indians. A black Rugambwa teacher once explained to me (as if I needed clarification) how the hierarchical system of prejudice worked: whites were on top, blacks were at the bottom, and Asians were in the middle. My Rugambwa colleague had been successfully indoctrinated by the same dogmatic conventions as my forebears.

As Raza and I became friends, his proselytizing efforts grew more fervent. "This Jesus—you know Jesus?" he asked. "Yes, so let me be frank with you, Billy, because we are also believing he was great prophet, like Adam and Noah and Abraham. By golly, all of them written in the holy Quran, just like your Bible, I'm telling you now!"

Raza's brother, Mohammed, owned another shop down the street. Mohammed's shop sold cameras, magnifying glasses, calculators, telephones, batteries, watches, lightbulbs, "and all these many necessities." You need it, they had it. The Ramji brothers had medium builds, medium-dark skin, and a spare tire around their middles. I guessed they were both in their fifties.

When the Ramji clan heard I had agreed to accompany Raza to a mosque, opportunities for romantic involvement with their many relatives suddenly became promising, at least in their eyes.

"Billy, you must please come to visit," Mohammed said. He was fond of pistachios. He reached into a bag of them and popped one in his mouth. "You know, we are just there, above my brother Raza's shop, and we can make for you a fine dinner." He said it with the air of a man about to do business, and I knew what was coming. "You know, Billy, I have these three daughters. None are married. So you should come to my home to see for yourself, why don't you?" He popped another pistachio into his mouth, reminiscent of some Godfather film. I did end up having dinner with them, but I made it clear I was not yet (again) in the market for a wife, or wives, as the case may be.

The night I was to accompany Raza to the mosque I wore my good jeans, a new, long-sleeved silk shirt I'd bought in town—blue with white floral embroidery—and my best bandanna to manage my lengthening hair. By the time I walked down the path from Lookout Rock and crossed a stone footbridge into town, it was dark. The expansion gate was locked across the door of Raza's shop. He stood out front wearing a long, light blue *galabiyya* gown, and a white *taqiyah*, or prayer cap. His hands were clasped behind his back in a pedantic way as he kicked pebbles in the glare of a naked, overhead bulb.

"Oh, Billy. Goodness gracious, but you are here and I am so sorry. You see, I talked to our mullah, and he is visiting mullah, not one we are normally knowing, and he said he cannot prepare for you in the English, so you cannot come this time. I am very sorry."

I was confused and a little irritated. "Well, I don't mind if he speaks in Arabic, or Uja—"

"Gujarati. Yes, I see, but he cannot be comfortable, and to be proper for the more beneficial, he is wanting to say for you in the English."

Raza's face was sad and his voice remorseful. I felt bad for both of us. I had really wanted to see what went on at a mosque, just as I had gone to the Catholic service with Patrick in Arusha. Sure, it had been different, but I found the differences interesting. In my youth, Islam hadn't been spoken of, or if it had, it was in hushed tones laced with some nebulous, ill-begotten fear. I recalled when I was married and starting grad school I'd gone to my pastor and asked him to pray for a Muslim friend in one of my classes. I had requested nothing less than divine intervention to help my friend see the light and see that his was, at best, a system of belief that had gone astray. My pastor had taken the request to heart, and one Sunday morning he asked the entire congregation to stand, hold hands, and ask God to help my friend.

"Dear Heavenly Father," he had prayed, "we ask you to please come into this young Arab boy's heart so that he might know you as his personal savior, and that he might know your infinite love, and accept Jesus into his heart and be cleansed by the blood of the lamb. We thank you now, Father, in Jesus' name we pray.

"And everyone said amen."

I was genuinely concerned for my friend. I later witnessed for the Lord when I advised my friend that if he knew what was good for him, he'd convert to Christianity. Muslims were, after all, unsaved and would burn in hell for all eternity.

Held up in limbo outside Raza's shop, I began to view those former, well-meaning intentions as naïve and even foolish. My view of the world had been so small. As the muezzin's call to prayer got underway at the blue mosque down the street, I felt a chill of embarrassment shiver up my spine.

"Maybe another day?" I asked.

"Oh, goodness yes, Billy. Another day, *Inshallah*." *God willing*.

A month later, at the end of May, I felt like a fashion photographer as I turned my plastic point-and-shoot camera this way and that, snapping photos of the girls. They changed their expression with each pose; first smiles, then stern, then demure. I ended the session after a dozen shots.

"All right, you ladies enjoy your school break now, and I'll see you back here in August. *Late* August, *sawa*?" I said.

"*Sawa*, Mr. Bill. Please bring to us our pichas then, okay?" asked one of the girls.

"Yes. I'll bring them all to you then."

"Okay." "Thank you, Mr. Bill." "We will be seeing you then," they said, waving as they walked away, giggling under their breath the way teenage girls sometimes do. Farida turned and smiled at me. I smiled back but quickly looked away. No one else noticed.

"You're a patient man, Mr. Hatcher," Rich said.

"Yeah. No, I'm a pushover, you mean."

The sun had gone down, and the light grew duskier by the minute. Boarding would begin soon, and because I was determined to make my way through the line like everyone else I needed to get moving.

Rich checked his watch. "Hey, we better get you down to the port. You got a mountain to climb."

CHAPTER 14

Rites of Passage

MOUNT MERU GLISTENED in a brilliant armor of gold and silver. The sprinkle of overnight rain at Ilboru secondary school had fallen as snow up there, 10,000 feet higher. Early morning sunshine had already melted most of it off, though it continued to highlight rocky nooks and crannies and other yin places above treeline. It made me wonder what awaited us on the snows and glaciers of Kilimanjaro.

The morning was still damp and cool. I sat on a convenient stone, writing in my journal, when a pair of bush babies stole my attention. The fully grown prosimians were only about seven inches long, not including their tail. The two I watched tossed and shook about in the orange blooms of a silver oak tree on the far side of Cynthia and Rolf's garden. It was funny how a cuddly thing like a bush baby could make such a ruckus.

I re-crossed my legs. I had tucked my khaki, polyester trousers into my laced boots and knee-high gaiters, and they looked more like riding breeches than hiking pants. Some of their effect, however, was lost beneath the oversized purple sweater I wore, which drooped down past my butt. The pattern of the sweater featured hearts and poodles, but I was counting on its practical rather than fashion value on the mountain. I had rounded out my wardrobe with extra wool socks, red mittens, a tan ski balaclava with a built-in hat bill, and a synthetic blue coat that looked better suited for operating an aluminum disk sled on a snowy Christmas Day. Still, I expected it would keep me warm, and it almost fit.

I had pieced together my outfit from the mountains of clothes sold at a bazaar in Arusha. Church groups and other aid organizations distributed shirts, shoes, hats, dresses—every kind of apparel. One morning at the port I saw a big guy wearing a T-shirt that almost covered his bulbous tummy and declared him the WORLD'S FAVORITE GRAND-MOTHER! I also once saw a little kid, naked from the waist down, who had worn a T-shirt airbrushed with GUNNISON, COLORADO!" and a glittering, polymer elk.

While at the bazaar, I had been approached by a man who sold shirts. In English, he had asked, "Why is it? Why do you people give away so many fine things? If you do not need them, you must all be very rich!"

I had answered him with some BS about relative scales of economy, but he had me there. Most Americans, even poverty-stricken folks, had vastly more stuff than the rest of the world. (If each person in the world lived as your average American did in the late twentieth century, *six more planet earths* would have been required to meet everyone's "needs"!) Even I, who had yet to earn more than a few thousand dollars in any given tax year, still had clothes to wear, food to eat, and my education. (As for my car—an '85 Ford Escort—I had sold it before leaving for Africa.) But suddenly, here I was buying *even more* clothes to wear to climb a mountain. No local person in their right mind would dream of undertaking such a pointless activity, unless they were a porter or a guide and were being ridiculously well-paid for it. In a country where the average per capita income hovered near U.S. $250 per year, fashion was foolish. For most people, there were much bigger—or rather, smaller—fish to fry.

"William!" Rolf yelled from his front porch. He and several others from the training group still called me by the name I had used with my host family.

"Yeah?"

"You finished? I'm locking up!"

"Yep, all set!" I slapped my journal shut and zipped it into the top pouch of my JanSport. I hauled it around the house, where students were loading gear onto the open bed of a lorry. Ten young men from Ilboru had signed up to climb Mount Kilimanjaro with us.

Rolf and Cynthia had completed all the legwork for the Kilimanjaro trip. They had rented and scheduled the lorry for drop-off and pickup, dug up all the necessary gear, and purchased some of it with their own funds. They had also supplied six days of food for fifteen people—ten students, two teachers, a guide, a porter, and me. The students had been up late the night before cooking chapatis and sorting rations for the trip. They were excited, and I could tell that Rolf and Cynthia had been pumping them up for weeks.

Rolf handed me a clipboard as he jogged past to talk to the driver. "William, make sure they have everything on the list. Thanks!" Rolf had already climbed Kilimanjaro twice in the previous year. He had quickly become an expert on the rations and gear needed to manage a safe and efficient expedition.

I jumped into the bed of the truck. "All right! *Sikilizeni, tafadhali!*" *Listen up, please!* "Each item on this list should be in your pack. If it is not in your pack right now, raise your hand so we can get it before we leave. *Sawa?*" *Okay?*

"*Sawa, mwalimu,*" *Okay, teacher.*

"Good. Here we go; hat, coat, water bottle—or something to carry water in . . ."

After we finished loading, the lorry began its lumbering descent toward town. Rolf and Cynthia directed from the front seat with the driver, while I rode in back with the students. When we reached the tarmac in Arusha, we stopped for gas at a Total station and then headed east. By mid-morning, clouds started to roll in. By the time we passed the little highway towns of Usa River and Maji ya Chai, the sky had skimmed over in a cool, gray overcast.

I stood into the headwind and scoured the skyline, but I couldn't find Kili. The giant had once again invoked a moody veil of drama. I squinted like a terrier with its snoot stretched out the window, and I pointed upwind into my imagination. "Whoohoo! Kili, baby!"

The students heard me shout and turned to look, but they had all been well aware of Kilimanjaro's location since birth. Like the seasoned travelers they were, they hunkered back down out of the wind to conserve energy.

But every so often, they peeked out with new and uncertain interest. Despite their youth, their faces wore grave lines and their eyes were pensive. They looked like they were revisiting every fact or fable they could remember, whether from books or white-haired elders huddled around crackling campfires. They were becoming men, but traditional rites of passage had been swept away a hundred years earlier during European colonization.

Rites of passage call attention to milestones in life and ease one's transition to a new social status. The event is often effected by removing a person from their everyday, mundane world and pitching him or her into an alien one. Special objects, clothing, words, and the place itself correspond with images hidden in the subconscious mind. These images symbolically dismantle one's former persona and can be called upon to help the initiate make the transition. Anthropologist Roy Rappaport of the University of Michigan wrote of sacred places, "They are often unusual, or even remarkable in several respects. They may be difficult of access, located in high places, for instance, or in the depths of caves. As such, they are separated from the daily world. . . ." As for the preparation of initiates, Rappaport wrote, "The destructuring of identity in certain rites of passage is especially profound . . . [The initiates] in passage may be 'symbolically' destructured to the undifferentiated state of generalized matter . . . thus facilitating its reformation into that which it is to become."

Climbing Kilimanjaro required the use of strange equipment, clothing, and customs that would sustain us through a beguiling and potentially dangerous challenge. Perhaps the climb served as a ritual proxy that would usher these boys toward social maturity—and usher me toward spiritual maturity.

They were all good, Christian young men, and I was sure they prayed about it. I prayed, too. I thanked Jesus for the chance to be there, and I petitioned Him for deliverance into a promised land.

My Peace Corps cohorts and I had traveled this road on our way to Dar nine months earlier, so a lot of things on the drive looked familiar. After we passed through the town of Moshi, however, we turned off the main highway and rounded the southeast side of the mountain. From here, the air grew progressively more damp and flimsy and faintly acrid where fields of tea bushed out in long, manicured rows. Eucalyptus and ironwood trees frothed over the murram road, and clouds sat heavy and close to the ground. The lorry's exhaust pipe snorted black smoke each time the engine ground into a lower gear, which was the only way I could tell we were climbing. Any one of us could have outrun the truck for a short distance.

In a little while we pulled through the park gate into a gravel parking area. Dozens of people off-loaded bags and boxes from Land Rovers and trucks. I sized up the other teams of climbers and gear, and saw ours was a comparatively shabby lot. Our students' water bottles consisted of plastic, half-gallon cooking-oil containers that dangled from strings tied to the outside of their threadbare, aluminum-framed packs. The students also carried plastic market bags that held anything that hadn't fit inside their packs. The bags were the kind with cutout handles and were printed with red and black facsimiles of the Marlboro Man.

Our driver parked the lorry and we started stacking gear into piles of cooking fuel, lanterns, packs, and so on. Meanwhile, Rolf went over to the park office to register our group and meet the guide he had commissioned to hire. Hiring a guide was a legal park requirement on Kilimanjaro. Most groups also hired several porters to help carry loads, though they were not mandatory. We hired one porter to help our guide manage his own gear and food. As for the rest of us, we planned to carry our own belongings and cook our own meals. We felt this was more than reasonable since we had received complimentary park passes as residents who were supervising a local school group.

Many paths led to the summit of Kilimanjaro. They went by such colorful nicknames as the "Lager Route" or the "Whiskey Route," depending on the degree of difficulty involved. Our route, the Marangu Route, also known as the "Coca-Cola Route," started from the Marangu Gate and was used by more than 90 percent of all climbers. It began at

8,000 feet above sea level at the park headquarters and was a virtual highway to the top. In fact, the first few hundred yards of the trail were paved. Designated campgrounds were managed along the way, complete with A-frame bunkhouses, solar-powered lighting, and pit latrines.

Despite its ease of approach, the Marangu Route is not to be taken lightly. Contrary to what some outdoor magazines advertise as an "easy" 19,000-foot mountain, 30 to 50 percent of all climbers fail to reach the summit, depending on the season. Furthermore, a dozen or so people die each year on Kilimanjaro from hypothermia, altitude illnesses, or rockfall.

Beyond the risk, there was the grandeur. The trail began in a lush, tropical rainforest, wrapped in twining vines and ferns. Blue monkeys lounged in webs of branches that arced high above the wide, maintained corridor. They chattered at us as we passed under them.

I strolled near the back of the line. I took it all in—the musky smells, the traffic of other climbers, the massive trees leaning high over the trail like Guardian Ents. I was happy. Mere breathing was delightful.

Rolf walked up next to me. "This is so awesome."

"In-credible," I said.

We continued to walk. The trail petered out from asphalt to gravel and now to dirt. Red thistles and stinging nettles hung into the trail and encouraged us to move in single file. Rolf was in front.

He asked if I had ever taken a NOLS course, which stands for National Outdoor Leadership School. I hadn't, but he had.

"One summer in college," he said, "I spent a month on a NOLS wilderness course in the Wind River Mountains in Wyoming, and it was a—I don't know—a life-changing experience." Rolf's eyes shone with memories behind his wire-framed spectacles, a perfect extension of his wiry physique. His pack looked like it weighed more than he did.

"What do you mean, 'life-changing'?" I asked.

Rolf bobbed his head, and after several seconds I thought he had misunderstood my question. I was about to ask it again when he broke into laughter and glanced back at me. "You know, William, I'm not sure I know how to answer that. Maybe I had questions at that point in my life—you know, I was still a kid. And being up there in those mountains was just—*wow*! I think it helped me see what was important in my life and what wasn't. Does that make sense?"

I nodded even though he was in front of me. "Yeah, I think it does," I said. But it didn't. Not really. Whatever it was, I sensed that Rolf had experienced a kind of turning point or a rite of passage on his NOLS course in the Rockies. I saw that he and his wife had organized this field trip with something similar in mind for their students. Which was great, though it shed a different light on my own situation: I, too, was a student, and I was here only for myself.

We arrived at the first camp, called Mandara, at 5:00 P.M. The mist had started to coagulate into real droplets. After checking in to our assigned A-frames, we set to work cooking up a group dinner of beans and spinach soup with samosas.

A soft patter of rain helped everyone get a good night's sleep, in spite of the raspy sawing noises that came from the trees around the camp. Our guide, James, told us the sounds were made by hyraxes, eastern tree hyraxes to be exact. Hyraxes are furry, nocturnal critters about the size of a groundhog, though distantly related to the elephant.

The rain continued to fall the next morning and throughout the day. Raincoats were donned, tested, and eventually failed. The rain slowed us down, and we eventually split into two hiking groups, one slow, the other slower, and since I had never been mistaken for an aerobic athlete I hiked in the second group. Rolf, Cynthia, Faustini the porter, and two of our students were also in the slow group. The other eight boys went ahead with James.

The vegetation transformed rapidly. Camphor and yellow-wood trees, dripping with goat's-beard mosses, were common at Mandara Camp. As we went higher they were replaced by African redwoods and succulent *Proteas*. Bushy *Ericaceaes*, mum-like Helichrysum flowers, and bursts of pink and red impatiens took advantage of the open spaces close to tree-line. Every so often, a *Kniphofia*, or Red Hot Poker, also made a spicy cameo. I remembered reading a passage about Jesus pointing out beauty in nature: "Consider the lilies of the field, how they grow; they neither toil nor spin, yet I tell you, even Solomon in all his glory was not arrayed as one of these" (Luke 12:27).

We left the forest behind when we ascended onto the heath moorland. The summits can typically be seen from here, but not on that day; we were still immersed in the long rainy season that runs from March to May, and sometimes into June. For better or worse, this was the only timing that worked for these ten Ilboru students who had finished their exams but hadn't yet returned home.

Fog rolled in. My clothes were drenched, and I was glad when Rolf called for a break. I knew if I ate something it would help generate body heat, so I sat down on my pack and dug out a bag of peanuts and raisins. Suddenly I froze. Not fifty feet away, several hulking apparitions materialized out of the gray haze. They pushed short, stumpy arms over their tousled heads, and each one must have stood twenty feet tall. Two became three, then five, with smaller ones beside. A ghostly legion of trolls appeared to be advancing.

I relaxed when it dawned on me what they were. *Senecios* are giant groundsel trees that inhabit the middle-high slopes of Kilimanjaro and a handful of other alpine areas in East Africa. To me they resembled Joshua trees from the American Southwest.

I chuckled at myself. "Cynthia, Rolf, see 'em?" I turned to see Cynthia sprint five yards and barf her *chai* and sweet rice all over a pretty little *Protea* flower. I winced. I looked for the *Senecios*, but they were gone. Rain was closing in again.

Rolf went to help his wife.

"Is she okay?" I asked.

"I think she may have a little altitude sickness," Rolf said as he unzipped her pack for one of her bandannas. "She'll be fine to Horombo Camp, but we'll have to take it slower."

He gave Cynthia the bandanna. She wiped her face with it and gazed into the foggy rain. Her body language said she was disappointed in herself. A strong, go-getter type, Cynthia was the kind of person who knew her own mind and was not afraid to tell you about it. She would take it hard if she couldn't make it to the top, but we weren't even halfway and it bothered me to think she might sidetrack the whole trip.

I stopped in mid-thought. I was embarrassed at myself.

"You okay, Cynthia?" I asked.

"Yeah. Thanks, William. I'll be okay. I feel a lot better already."

Rolf kneeled next to her. "Honey, maybe we should take some weight from your pack and make it easier for you."

But she was already up, shaking her head. "Nope. I'm fine."

Rolf helped her on with her pack, and with a little greater care, we went on.

We arrived at Horombo Camp at 4:00 that afternoon.

Horombo sits at 12,000 feet and is perched like a gull atop the only buoy in the harbor at high tide. The surrounding country is open and wide and broken only by ribs of black and orange rock. From here on, the vegetal-mineral inventory tips in geology's favor.

We were tired, wet, and hungry. Thank God that James and some of the students were busy cooking dinner in the smoke-plumed cook hut when we arrived. Cynthia, however, was not doing well, and right before dinner she threw up again. Her chances to continue looked slim. She might even have to go back down. I felt bad for her, and for Rolf, but I was also assaulted by my own selfish thoughts of how this might affect my chances of reaching the peak. We still had ten miles and 7,000 feet of elevation to gain. At least we had arrived at our scheduled layover camp. The next day would be a day to rest, dry out, and acclimatize before moving higher.

We ate vegetable soup and bread for dinner. Temperatures were colder here, close to freezing, but still wet and slimy. Lights were turned out early that evening.

A cold rain fell the next morning. The outdoor thermometer on the dining hut leveled steady at 33°F. A soggy coldness pruned my fingertips and made me want to pee every fifteen minutes. It was a good day to rest, eat, play gin, and pee some more.

The original plan for our rest day was to take a walk over to the base of Mawenzi, the second-highest peak on the mountain. Standing out in the cold drizzle, Rolf pointed north in the direction of Mawenzi and also northwest toward the main Kibo summit. "If it wasn't raining, we could see both of them from here," he said.

People from other climbing groups milled around, fading

in and out of A-frames and fog. Tourists in the mist. Movement was stiff and depressing. Grim faces hunkered down under dun cloaks and lent a mien of Soviet proletariat to the scene at "Horombo-grad." A wheeled stretcher stashed under a mortared hut foundation added little encouragement.

Rolf and I retreated inside the dining hut. We sat down at a long, wooden table etched with the initials of former climbers who had been held hostage to the rain. Rolf confided in me that one of the reasons he had wanted to hike over to Mawenzi was because he was hunting for a serious alpine challenge, and he wanted to scope it out for a long, multi-pitch technical climb. It was also, he confessed, an ulterior motive for inviting me along to climb Kili. Cynthia wasn't into technical climbing, and I was the only other person in our training group who had shown any interest and know-how.

In Bukoba, Rich had given me book called *Guide Book to Mount Kenya and Kilimanjaro*. I had brought it with me. The Mountain Club of Kenya had published it in 1963, and it was complete with stories, climbing advice, and natural history pertaining to both mountains. I mentioned it to Rolf and sloshed back over to my A-frame to see if the scriptures in an old mountaineer's canon might have anything wise to say.

Mount Kilimanjaro is forty-five miles long on its northwest–southeast axis, thirty miles wide, and stands 19,341 feet high. It is one of the world's largest, free-standing mountains. The earth's crust actually down-warps under its gargantuan mass like the dent that a bowling ball resting on a mattress would make.

Many legends surround the origin of Kilimanjaro's name. Most assume it comes from two root words, *kilima* and *njaro*. *Kilima* is the Swahili word for little mountain, or hill, and may be a term of affection, or comic antonym, as when a big man is nicknamed "Shorty" or "Junior." *Njaro* is more puzzling; it could have come from the local Chagga people's word for caravan. This suggests the mountain was once a landmark for traders moving between the interior and the coast. In any event, Kilimanjaro continues to be regarded as a holy mountain and God's primary home by many of the surrounding culture groups.

My guidebook gave these facts and many more, but it did not tell me if climbing it would serve as my rite of passage to a higher, spiritual plane. I did not know if it would elevate me above my petty, religious concerns, or if God awaited my arrival at the top.

The next day we packed up and started moving to our high camp. Green tufts of *Ericaceae* struggled here and there, but even these soon drew an invisible line of surrender to maximum altitude, minimum precipitation. We had arrived at what geographers call an alpine enclave of the Sahara. Hardcut and lean beyond starvation, this landscape made even the Marlboro Man look effeminate. And in the middle of it all, as if it were necessary, a wooden sign read: THE SADDLE.

Thankfully, the weather had cleared overnight. From behind my Julbo glacier glasses, I gazed upon the summit for the first time and saw Kibo encrusted in snow and shimmering white. Mawenzi, too, stood firm and streaked with snow-packed chutes and toothy gendarmes. Great runnels of cloud retreated below us and gave no hint as to the whereabouts of the rest of the planet. It gave the impression Kilimanjaro had withdrawn its earthly membership and become a satellite. Now it orbited a little ways above the earth and had turned us all into extraterrestrials.

Surprisingly, Cynthia had perked up and seemed to be doing much better. However, the boys were mostly quiet, nearly morose, and not sure what to make of things. One of the boys, named Shile, hiked close to me that morning. Like the rest of us, he wore an outfit that had been cobbled together specifically for this trip. His secondhand cowboy boots were at least three sizes too big, and his double-breasted topcoat made him look like a sea captain. But his hat was what set him apart; a fuzzy tassel of yarn topped his red-and-green-striped balaclava and, to me, looked like something worn by a Who from Whoville.

"So, sir—" he began.

I tongue-shifted the caramel Blow Pop I'd been sucking on. "Bill. Call me Bill. Or William, if you want."

"Yes, sir. So you enjoy this climbing mountains?"

"I love climbing mountains, Shile."

"But, so why then? Why is it?"

I knew why he asked me this question. The weather had been poor, the food was different, the clothes did not fit, and the work was physically hard. For all this effort and suffering, where was the payoff? I could answer him only by saying I enjoyed a challenge, that it built self-esteem and showed me what I was made of, and that it made me self-reliant. But I sensed his question had a deeper motive.

I decided to stall. I pulled my Blow Pop out by the stick. "Well, Shile, why are *you* climbing this mountain? Why Kilimanjaro?"

"It is Mr. Rolf, our teacher. He said to us that it will be very beneficial, and we will see many beautiful things."

"Right. Well, have you? Seen beautiful things?"

Shile looked around. "Yes? I think it is, uh, quite splendid. Yes. Especially this snow," he said, and pointed toward Mawenzi with his lips. "I cannot understand this thing."

"Well tomorrow you can touch the snow when we climb to the top. Maybe even *taste* it!"

As expected, he reacted with wide surprise. "*Sho!*" *Wow!* "Can it be good, to eat?"

"Well it's only water that's frozen, so it has no taste, but it's very cold, and it melts in your mouth."

"*Allah!* I say!"

I noticed his choice of words but let it pass to make sure it felt right. Then I asked, "So, Shile . . ."

"Yes, sir."

"Are you, uh, you know, Muslim?"

"Oh, no, no, no," he answered, mildly amused. "I am Christian. I am saved by the blood of the lamb. We can only be saying this word, 'allah,' to show the excitement. I am believing in God, and Jesus His son. He is our Father in heaven," he said as he pointed toward the sky, this time with an index finger. "Even yours also, sir."

The direction he pointed reminded me of something I'd heard. "I see. Well, you know, some people, even your tribe, I think, they say God lives on top of this mountain. Do you believe that's true?"

We walked and Shile thought. His head bobbed as he stared at the ruddy trail. He probably still had relatives who thought God lived on Kilimanjaro full-time. "Hmm. It could be true. Yes? But that was too long ago. Therefore, I am thinking this thing, it is no longer possible, sir."

"Bill," I said, pointing at myself.

"Yes, sir."

I breathed and let it go. We went on under the creak of our backpacks and the crunch of our boots on the trail. As I had come to expect from the more clever, A-level students, he flipped the question on me. "And you, sir? Are you also Christian?"

His tack briefly reminded me of Farida. In that moment—
before his question sunk in—I also felt the crush of her
absence. I missed her, and it surprised me. I shook off the
daydream. The full import of his question hit me, and I was
flooded with memories of Sunday mornings, youth-group
revivals, and the pre-marriage counseling I had received
from my pastor at Brown Street Baptist Church. "There are
no hidden books in here," my pastor had told me. I had sat
across the desk from him in his study. "I have nothing to
hide from you," he'd said. I didn't argue. "There's nothing
to refute the Gospel of Christ," he had assured me over and
over. I hadn't even brought it up, and I again wondered why
he doth protest so much.

"Yes, Shile, I'm Christian. Yes. Since I was a small boy, I
learned that God is in heaven with, you know, our ancestors,"
I said, motioning to both of us. "But God can be everywhere
at once, right?" I thought he was nodding, though it was
hard to tell, loping along under the weight of his pack. "So
He can be up there, too," I said, pointing at Kibo. "Right?"

The group had stopped to take a pack break. Shile and I
took off our packs.

"This thing you are saying, it may be so," he said. His forehead was stitched in uncertainty.

I was uncertain about the direction of my sermon. I decided
to give both of us some time to think, so I walked away from
the group. I had to pee again, and the only place with any
privacy was a lone, erratic boulder in the middle of the plain.
When I got close to the boulder I noticed miniature flags
flapping close to the ground on the other side. I should have
guessed. Decades of tampons, pink and blue tufts of toilet
paper, and all the rest littered the red, gritty earth. But there
were no flies, not even the stench one might expect, thanks to
the chilled, desiccated air.

Mawenzi loomed pristine above it all. Alternating bands of sunlight and shadow shot through sheets of clouds sliding up from the south. The sacred and the profane created each other. As I peed, I stared up at Mawenzi's fissured ramparts and roiling clouds and wondered about Shile's question. I asked myself, Why was *I* so crazy to climb mountains? I knew it had something to do with my paternalistic, Christian world-view, which had become increasingly cramped and arbitrary. In the past year I had learned so much about the world that I had to go farther and farther out of my ontological way in order to make my original worldview work. And when it did not work, I had to make up excuses and just "trust in Jesus" that everything would be okay.

I zipped my pants. I didn't know what to think anymore, except that my Blow Pop was gone and our group needed to keep moving. The clouds had ramped up against the peaks and bearded God's face from view. Our clothes were finally dry again. It was critical we get everyone across the Saddle and into Kibo Hut—warm, dry, and fed.

As I made my way back over to Shile and the others, I tiptoed around the poop midden, trying very hard not to backslide.

CHAPTER 15

Catechism

THE ROOM WAS dark as pitch, and choked with a morbid brew of body odors. Kibo Hut is a plain block-and-mortar structure situated on the barren wastes of Kilimanjaro at 15,500 feet. All fifteen of us slept in a single room. Rolf and Cynthia were in the bunks next to mine, and many times that night I heard Rolf's breathing become shallower and shallower until no sounds came at all. An eerie silence crept into the corners of our white, plastered room. He had stopped breathing and remained in a state of suspended animation for ten, fifteen, even twenty seconds. The first time it happened I got up to try and do something, but his lungs abruptly heaved into action like a swimmer breaking the surface. Then his breathing relaxed again, returned to normal, and repeated the cycle.

These were symptoms of a normally harmless ailment experienced by mountaineers called Cheyne-Stokes breathing. Simply put, it describes a respiratory system struggling to rebalance the body's arterial gases and blood pH levels under abnormal atmospheric conditions; namely, low oxygen levels. Rolf and several of the others wrestled with it throughout the night.

Me too, only I struggled to breathe and rebalance in a different way, inside my own version of a cold, sealed room.

Relief came at midnight when James and Faustini brought steaming hot cups of *chai* around to resuscitate us and wind us up for the big day.

Only my greed for the summit persuaded me to pull on my stiff, cold boots and my crusty, sweaty clothes. When I stepped out into the glacial air my little plastic thermometer—designed for "the tropics"—quickly bottomed out at 20°F, its lowest gradation.

Shortly after 1:00 A.M., each of us stood swaddled in every stitch of clothing we'd hauled up the mountain. We also wore scaled-down versions of our backpacks that held only water and a little fruit or peanut butter. The tea had been finished, and because a couple of the students had already thrown up, no one cared much for breakfast. Minds were numb. We turned on our torch bulbs and lined up single-file behind James and the Delta Theta Delta logo on his secondhand daypack. Heeding his leaden mantra, "*Polepole, asteaste*," *slowly, carefully,* we trudged off in pursuit of a three-foot circle of light cast onto the next person's boot heels.

Hiking warmed me up. I soon unzipped my blue snow coat to keep from overheating. Important details like this helped to keep the nausea in my gut from oozing its way up my esophagus. I swallowed hard. I was determined not to hurl, but my resolve was challenged by steaming puddles of puke alongside the trail. After an hour, we stopped to rest and sip water. The rocks were too cold to sit down on, so we slumped over and propped ourselves up with our hands on our knees. From there we watched the tiny, bobbing dots of light, which were climbers who crawled above us and below us on the mountainside.

Consciousness penetrated the matte blackness when Cynthia called out from the back of the line. "Rolf! *(breath)* It's Shile! *(breath)* He can't go on! *(breath)* He's stumbling, *(breath)* not making sense! *(breath)*"

Cynthia's headlamp shone up through silhouettes of students and squalls of exhaled moisture. A dark blob sat on the ground next to her. Rolf, James, and I went back to find Shile gibbering to himself about seeing flashes of light. His words were an incoherent mix of English, Swahili, and something else, and we knew he couldn't go on. No longer the simple headache and nausea associated with Acute Mountain Sickness (AMS), Shile exhibited symptoms of the much more serious, even fatal, High Altitude Cerebral Edema (HACE). James gave the order to Faustini to take Shile down to Kibo Hut while he could still walk, or further down if his symptoms did not improve. We helped Shile to his feet.

He leaned close to me, and with eyes wide like a man possessed, he whispered, "*Mungu!*" God! "You find Him! *Find Him!*"

I was shaken, but I nodded. "Okay. Don't worry. I will."

Cynthia interpreted the remark as a sure sign of dementia and turned to Rolf. "He's got to go down. Now."

Rolf stepped into the ring of headlamps. He spoke in Swahili to James. "*Bwana*, I have been to the top before. I can take Shile down so you and Faustini can continue. *Sawa?*" Rolf was firm in his decision, so James agreed and reminded them to drink plenty of water.

Rolf took Shile by the arm and led him down into the darkness. The rest of us stood by, feeling helpless. I watched the light from their headlamps shrink away. It made me sad, but it was too cold and my head hurt too much for the melancholy to linger.

Like any good guide, James got us up and moving again and our half-conscious stupor resumed. We were tired from carrying full packs up to Kibo Hut. We'd also had poor sleep, little food, some vomiting, AMS was setting in, and it was so cold. Each of us was fully occupied with lifting one foot, then the other foot, then breathing. One foot, the other foot, breathe.

The ground beyond the perimeter of my headlamp glided away like deep oil into the heavens. Thankfully, I spotted an old friend to help keep my bearing—the Big Dipper sat on the horizon slightly below my right shoulder. On my left, the Southern Cross was planted among a boneyard of con-stellations that I didn't know. If it hadn't been for the spray of stars, I could have reckoned myself hobbling troll-like in some subterranean chamber. Either that or else the heavens had descended to abut the mute fringe of my headlamp, and now I swam in an intergalactic sea of pagan astrals, all green and blue and white. I counted no less than a dozen meteoric spates diving in by the minute, but the moon was nowhere to be found.

I imagined Silvanus and Sofia singing at the Cave of God. They beat the sacred drums while younger ones danced lithe and erotic. PUDA PUDA PUM! PUDA PUDAPUDA PUM! I stared down. I saw my naked feet, ghost-white and ten-der. They shuffled out of tempo with the drums, and knots of straight, green grass clogged and squeaked between my toes. The night air smelled restive and tangled with sweat and wood smoke. Silvanus puffed on a sacred pipe. Bod-ies pulsed. Naked skin vibrated. Eyes flared with the divine intoxication of *rubisi*, firelight, and the bubbling, red flesh of goat. The ululations of women's voices in high tremolo seduced me. The orgy of life consumed me. I tossed nine cowrie shells into a sacred pool, where they plopped unseen into the rippling black void. Glowing from deep within, they ripened into florescent violet, then indigo, then bright blue, and poured out over the water's edge to bathe my feet and metamorphose into hands that washed over me, caressing, drinking, anointing, blind and wet and free . . .

"Mr. Bill! Mr. Bill! You okay?" a student behind me called out.

My fantasy dissolved. I had wandered off the path and tripped over an oblate stone. I caught myself before I fell.

"Yeah. I'm okay." Confused, I hurried back onto the path. I wasn't sure if I had awoken from a dream or fallen into one, but the brimstone helped; a nearby fumarole coughed up puffs of sulfur dioxide. God appeared to be a smoker, although the fumes reminded me more of rotten eggs than my dad's Half & Half tobacco.

Without warning, the light from our headlamps and flashlights bled away into a buffed glow. Dawn approached. We had marched into the recesses of our collective subconscious for nearly six long hours, but now, one by one, we switched off our headlamps. The rocks were now gray blue and were soft-looking with powdery soils all around.

I glanced uphill but there was no more uphill to see. The angle of the mountain rolled off and stopped a few dozen yards above. We were at the crater rim, Gilman's Point, and it gave us a much-needed boost in morale.

I stopped and turned around. Amber shards of sunrise shot up from behind Mawenzi, but ahead of us the crater dropped open. It was immense and gaping, much broader than I had expected. Concentric ridges within the crater were bracketed by long, white slices of snow that resembled fillets of fish sautéing in a pan. Snow lay daubed in patches between rocks. Most impressive, however, were the austere, white glaciers that buttressed the rim on the north and south sides.

Rolf and Cynthia's students had never seen snow. They were busy at the next break touching, tasting, and wringing it from their bare fingers.

"It is so cold!" one student said. He marveled at the crystalline water that stuck to his magenta palms. I thought about starting a snowball fight but reconsidered. No one, including me, had that kind of energy to spare.

"*Sawa, rafiki zangu,*" *Okay, my friends,* James announced to the group, "drink more water. Very important. Then we keep going. The top, it is one and one-half hours, but not difficult." He leaned in so only Cynthia and I could hear. "Besides, God, He is waiting for us."

I smiled, and an exquisite bead of blood cracked the center of both my lips. Tears filled my eyes. When I blinked, a tear was immediately absorbed by the polyester weave of my hat, now pulled down into its face-mask mode.

Piercing, almost unbearable beauty surrounded me. My head split with oxygen deprivation and I had trouble forming sentences, but my heart pumped like mad with an excitement that expressed everything my mind could not. *I made it!*

Mount Meru poked through a lower deck of clouds, eighty miles to the west. When Josh and I climbed it almost a year earlier it had seemed so immense and mysterious, but now I could reach out and cup it in the palm of my hand. Scrolls of warm, seasonal moisture unraveled to the north, where a wreckage of cumulus rumpled against an obstacle, maybe two hundred miles away, as the crow flies. I wondered if that could be Mount Kenya. And to the east, platinum-looking and on time, the sun gathered speed above Mawenzi and reduced the last of dawn's pastels to ashes. All of Africa—indeed, over 99 percent of the earth's surface—lay below my feet. I pivoted 360 degrees, and my naked eyes took in 100,000 square miles and more. All this, yet it was as quiet as the squeaky stillness in a chapel at midnight.

I remembered a verse from the Book of Amos. I had quoted it each time I summited a mountain in the United States: "He who forms the mountains, creates the wind, and reveals His thoughts to man, He who turns dawn to darkness, and treads the high places of the earth—the Lord God Almighty is His name." I had always liked that one.

In the New International Version of the Bible, the words "mountain" and "hill" occur 541 times. High points served as divine portals of God's revelation to humans, as well as His abode. These ethereal places could be gentle but also severe, benevolent yet judgmental. They symbolized both a fatherly God and a godly father.

"William! You going to sign?" Cynthia held up the summit registry.

"Yep. Coming." I waddled over to the students. They passed around a tablet and a pencil that was kept in the registry box for signing in. After we finished this rite, a punch of euphoria hit us like a joke. We burst into numb, dazed laughter. Limp high-fives were thrown. Cynthia rounded everyone up for a big group hug and a series of photos that recorded shriveled smiles and waxy, bloodshot eyes.

In a moment, James introduced us to a traditional Chagga song he liked to sing when guiding a group to the summit. The lyrics were bouncy and repetitive and described how Kilimanjaro resembled a colossal serpent that had split through its old skin and now sidled across the dry savanna, bestowing water and life as it went. When he finished, we clapped our gloved hands and gathered up our things to head down. But I couldn't get the words of his song out of my head and what they meant to me—"transformation is life."

James reminded everyone to drink water and take it slowly on the way down. With any luck, we'd meet up with Rolf and Shile at Kibo Hut later that day and hike across the Saddle to

Horombo Camp before nightfall. The next day, we planned to reenter the land of green and living things. We looked forward to warm baths and fat calzones in Arusha.

I looked around and everyone was happy, but I felt a mixture of elation, nausea, and disappointment. Sure, it was an extraordinary moment full of magnificent views. I had completed a daunting, physical test—as far as the summit, anyway. But I was also on top of a patriarchal pyre in my psyche. The only thing left to do to transform myself into a new creature was to light the fire, except I had no matches, no spark. The first half of a passage from Psalms now seemed more appropriate: "I lift up my eyes to the hills; where does my help come from?"

I scanned the horizon for God, or someone, anyone, who could help. I was troubled that my personal relationship with Christ could falter so easily. Was I that shallow, I asked myself, or were we Christians merely masters of self-deception who shared a mutually affirmed pie in the sky? Ignorance of the full menu was bliss.

The answers were implied in my questions.

I was confused. I looked down, and a sparkle on the ground caught my eye. A small stone glistened with rhomboid crystals. I picked it up and rolled it around in my gloved fingers the way a penitent turns the beads of a necklace. It reminded me of the serpentine I had swiped from the top of Mount Meru. I wished I had it with me now to bolster a little honest repentance and stave off fleeting madness.

Or maybe not. The porphyry in my hand was a different species than the one I'd gotten at Meru: less iron, more crystalline. Less repentance, more redemption. I admired how it caught tiny pieces of sunrise in its web like a promise. I tucked it into a pocket and hustled to catch up with my group.

Five other climbers staggered to the top as we were leaving. I glanced into their pink faces and their thin blue lips. Like me, their bloodshot eyes were dazzled and fixed on a shining goal that lay just ahead.

Just ahead.

CHAPTER 16

The Prophet

FIVE O'CLOCK A.M. Most mornings I put a pillow over my head and went back to sleep. However, when the wind came in off the lake, the muezzin's ghostly call to prayer floated up from the blue mosque and spilled in through the screens on my bedroom windows. In that case, I got up and made a cup of coffee.

Seven o'clock A.M. I chomped down a bowl of Weetabix drowned in creamy, fresh-squeezed whole milk, and brushed my teeth. Then I ran up to the school in the nick of time to join my fellow teachers on the portico of the administration block. From there we appraised the 650 young women ranked and filed on the main lawn as they feathered their voices into harmonies elegant and unconcerned.

The semester was off and running—my third—and as happened each morning, the students sang the national anthem as the Tanzanian national flag was raised. After the anthem, they sang the school song. Formalities were often interrupted by the deep blast of an air horn down at the lake. They announced that one of the ships had survived its passage and was steaming into port. The interruption, however, was only audible. The singing went on, undeterred. "*Shule Rugambwa, nakupenda sana . . . ,*" *Rugambwa School, I love you very much.* Classes were back in full swing. The school grounds swarmed with uniformed young ladies shuttling notebooks and chairs and buckets of water on their heads. The regular faculty directed and admonished between sips of black *chai*. This meant the kitchen was also back in operation. Great volumes of steaming, white rice and doughy *ugali* were cooked in hundred-gallon vats and stirred with wooden paddles you could row a boat with. We volunteer teachers were back, too. We were primed for students and classes, and we swapped tales of travel concerning the previous twelve weeks.

I had now gone through one full year of course topics, so I recycled my material from previous terms. I discarded stale parts and replaced them with newer bits to help spice things up. This tactic allowed me to feel more confident in front a fresh crop of Form Five students. My old Form Fives were now Form Sixes. As for my old Form Sixes, they had graduated at the end of the previous semester and scattered to the four winds. I heard they had done about average on their national exams in May, though a few of them expected to be invited to the University of Dar es Salaam. I was happy for them, but I missed their faces and their laughter around campus.

The person I would have missed the most, however, was still there. She kept me on my toes and kept classes interesting. "Mr. Bill. I do not understand this thing you are saying," Farida said. She flexed her new, Form Six muscles and let no inconsistency escape her comment. One of the first classes of the semester involved an old favorite of ours—the religious ecology of North America. "You are saying people from the United States, they go to worship these spirits in the deserts and the mountainous areas. But Mr. Bill," she said, leaning forward on her desk and shooting an open hand at me, "as you have said, United States, this is Christian nation, with some Muslims and Jewish ones in cities. So how can this be?" She plopped back into her chair and folded her arms.

As a Muslim, Farida had been instructed from an early age that the Abrahamic Religions—Islam in particular—were superior to the superstitions of the common, uneducated, rural folk. For her, the prophet, the Koran, and Islam were *the way, the truth, and the life.* All others were infidels— Islam's version of "everyone else."

"Yes. That's true," I said. "Eighty-one percent of people in the United States are *mo-no-the-is-tic.*" I pronounced each syllable as I chalked it out on the board. "Monotheists are people who believe in one God; for example, Christians, Muslims, and Jews. It's interesting to note that only 53% of the *world's* population is monotheistic. The rest have other faiths, and some don't believe in a god at all. And remember, one of the functions of *any* religion is to balance the relationship people have with their physical environment."

"But Mr. Bill." Another student, a Catholic nun named Zawadi, spoke up. "Has God not given to us this earth to consume until Christ returns?" Her question sounded more like a challenge. It was embedded in theological self-righteousness and shared the same foundation as Protestantism, which for me had recently become riddled with doubt.

I nodded at Sister Zawadi and mustered my courage. I told the class that geography can study the effects religions have on the landscape, but only religions can say *why* they believe what they do. I knew it was a copout. Sister Zawadi hunched down in her chair with a pouty frown on her face. A girl next to her whispered something. Sister Zawadi nodded and whispered back to the girl.

I returned to Farida. "So, like we were saying, rivers, mountains, trees, even caves—in fact, any natural feature could be an example of a *sacred place*." I chalked out the words on the blackboard. "Even in major world religions. We've already talked about the River Ganges in Hinduism. Mountains are also considered sacred, like the Mount of Olives in Christianity and Mount Fuji in Japanese Shintoism."

"For Mr. Saito," Farida said.

"Yes. I think so. In the United States, places like Mount Shasta are pilgrimage sites and worship centers for many cult religions."

"They do not believe in God?" Sister Zawadi asked.

"They are not Christians—or Muslims," I said, glancing at Farida. "But they believe that a god *in some form* lives in these natural places."

"And Kilimanjaro," said another girl.

"Yes, exactly. Like the Chagga people near Kilimanjaro," I said. "Other groups near Mount Shasta believe that there are *many* gods or goddesses or spirits inhabiting natural objects in that area. And others believe there is one, great everywhere spirit in all of us and all of nature, like Native Americans."

The classroom erupted in chuckles. In previous classes, I had finally convinced my students that, yes, even though the U.S. government did give some money to some people, most people in America actually did have to work. Furthermore, I had explained that, no, machines did not do all the work for us, as they had heard rumored, with things like clothes washers, dishwashers, and farming machinery. But now I professed there were people in the U.S. who worshipped rocks and trees. What's more, there were "native" peoples who lived there, too. Well, this was just too much.

"I say! Mr. Bill! You are wrong!" said a girl from the back of the classroom. She tipped her chair over on the concrete floor as she leaped to her feet. "United States, it is greatest country of all! You have cities with sufficient streets and so many automobiles. Therefore, it must be a nonsense to have these forests or mountains, I think, not since long ago."

"Because they are Christians! Witnessing for the Lord," Sister Zawadi said, and the classroom spontaneously combusted. With frowns intent on rebuttal, Farida and her Muslim allies swung into a huddled knot and prepared to engage the Catholic sisters. In the center of the ring, Farida wheeled around and shook her fist at Sister Zawadi. "Then they shall straightaway be going to hell!"

I clapped my hands twice, then twice again as I had seen Tanzanian teachers do. I also conjured my most authoritative voice. "Ladies! Ladies! Sit down! *Sit! Down!*" Some students began to shush the others.

Suddenly the classroom door pitched open and Mr. Rwelengera poked his round head in. The classroom fell silent. "Mmm, is there a problem, Mr. Bill?"

"No, sir. We're just having a geographical debate." Giggles squeezed out from the back row.

"I *assume* you are aware of the school's policy for loud and distracting behaviors?"

"Yes, sir. I'm sorry. We'll keep it down."

"Mmm. Very well, then. I am next door in Miss Chris' room if you need me." His eyes looked skeptical as he closed the creaky door.

I leaned onto the chalk-dusted, wooden teacher's desk and puffed a sigh of relief. I surveyed the class. No one spoke. We listened to Mr. Rwelengera's footsteps echo down the concrete corridor. We heard him open Chris' biology room door and close it behind him.

Farida broke the silence. "To *assume* will make an 'ass' out of 'u' and 'me,'" she said. Several girls broke into laughter, but Farida's snort laugh stood out. Sister Zawadi looked confused and conferred with her companions. I smiled and shook my head.

"*Sawa*. Tomorrow, ladies," I shouted, holding my hands out to calm the levity. "Tomorrow I will bring photographs that prove there are forests and mountains in the U.S.A. I may even have one of Mount Shasta."

"Are you also worshiping gods in the rocks?" Farida asked in her impertinent way.

"Ah, no. No, I do not. But to help everyone get a clearer understanding of religious ecology, I want you all to answer these questions for tomorrow."

Papers shuffled and conversation dwindled as I chalked out the assignment on the board. After I finished, I went to the back of the room and sat on a lab table next to one of the tall, glassless windows. While the students copied the questions, I looked out north over the rolling, forested hills in the direction of Kashozi and the Cave of God.

No one made a peep for the remainder of class.

Evenings were full of possibility. The brassy, fuzzy light of sunsets poured down over glens of blue gum, papaya, and banana trees. Frisky bugs flitted about, golden and shiny, and made easy pickings for hornbills, bee-eaters, and flycatchers.

I loved going for runs at dusk. Running worked something like a miracle on my body and soul, especially when I was pursued by a brigade of smiling kids who shouted things like "Rambo" and "American Ninja." When I exercised I got away with wearing shorts like their professional, soccer-playing folk heroes. Any other time it had to be trousers. (Not to be confused with "pants," which is what Tanzanians understood to mean underwear—yet another nonessential for pampered foreigners.)

Exercise, everyone knew, was a senseless activity, and anyone involved in it must be cultivating superhuman powers. This was another lucky side effect for me, since I had started to exhibit paranoid tendencies. I kept all doors in the house locked, interior and exterior, night and day, and I kept a three-foot section of two-by-four next to my bed, just in case.

Chris told me that a young man who was mentally ill but harmless had stumbled onto her front porch a week earlier. He had seen her clothes hanging out to dry, so he disrobed and slipped into a pair of her jeans and a shirt. The moment she saw him, she had screamed bloody murder. Mr. Rwelengera and another neighbor had raced to the scene and threatened him with a beating. They had persuaded him to surrender Chris's clothes and never come back, but before leaving he had peed on a pair of her socks.

I am certain episodes like this played into my feeling of unease, but they only reflected a deeper dilemma. Since the last school break, I had behaved more tentatively around friends, more reservedly with students, more carefully with regard to everything. I was like someone with a fever who just wants to be left alone. I even considered getting a dog, more for protection than for affection.

I was on my way back from one of my runs when I stopped in at the school store. The store was tacked on like an afterthought to the end of the administration block, and mainly served as an after-hours social venue for students and teachers. Every afternoon at 5:00, Mr. Rwelengera brought out his handheld radio. He turned it on and navigated the dial through the high-pitched whirs and whistles to locate a martial band lining up for a familiar British accent that announced, "This is the BBC News, Radio Free Africa."

The store traded only in the most basic utilitarian goods:

notebooks, pencils, sugar, bar soap, Vick's lozenges, Blue Band margarine, and Double Cola. Modest piles of bell peppers, onions, and tomatoes from teachers' gardens were also sold. One of the more specialized products was bundles of soft-hued toilet paper stocked mostly for the foreign volunteer faculty like me.

The most important item, however, arrived every two or three days after a teacher made the round-trip hike to the school's post office box in town. I checked my mail every week. Now and then I got a letter from a friend back home or a care package from my mom, but on that day I received only one slim envelope. Mailed from within the country, it was return-addressed to Rolf.

Habari gani William!
Cynthia and I hope that you are doing well. We are fine. Our students are still talking about the Kilimanjaro trip. (Shile is fine with no lasting effects.)

I have been corresponding with the Mountain Club of Kilimanjaro and Mount Kenya. They call Mawenzi a "death trap" with loads of crumbly, unstable rock near the peak. They suggested Mount Kenya instead. It's supposed to be good climbing with several technical routes. The summit is 17,057 feet and the Normal Route looks like the best option for us. It's only rated at 5.6, but it covers 21 pitches. The best opportunity for climbing it would be over Christmas break.

One last thing: I talked to Brad and he wants to join us. He has not done much technical climbing, but I think the three of us would make a good team. Write soon with your opinion. I'll be making plans.

Salaam,
Rolf and Cynthia

Rolf included a photocopied route description and an old article on Mount Kenya from a climbing magazine. I skimmed over it. My insides tingled with butterflies. I rushed home, studied the map, and re-read his letter. Then I studied the map again. I dug out the old guidebook Rich had given me and spent the rest of that evening dreaming about Mount Kenya. A technical climb covering twenty-one pitches would far exceed anything I had ever attempted. I estimated it would take us three days to hike in, two on the climb itself, and then hike out again—over a week. An expedition to Mount Kenya promised true adventure.

Right after I had climbed Kilimanjaro with Rolf and Cynthia, two of my old friends from the States came to visit me. The three of us had gone on a camping safari in the Serengeti, Ngorongoro Crater, and Olduvai Gorge—the so-called tourist circuit. They had also talked me into climbing Kili again, though it really hadn't taken much convincing.

After Kili, we had headed for Zanzibar, the original Spice Island. Zanzibar is girdled with sandy beaches, palm trees, and a population that exudes a rich mixture of Bantu-Indian-Arabian heritage, especially the women. I'd been caught off guard by my attraction to their dark, mysterious beauty. Mostly I was surprised by how much they reminded me of Farida and that an interracial relationship for me might be possible after all.

I had delighted in every part of our trip, but one event stood out. On our second day in the Serengeti, our safari guide had squeezed in time for us to visit Olduvai Gorge. Unfortunately, we arrived too late. The last tour group of the day had already left to view the discovery sites of *Zinjanthropus* and his ilk. The docents were about to close the visitor center. Disappointed, we ambled over to the museum to have a quick look around. The museum was small and tidy yet comprehensive. Fossils of wild animals and copies of hominid artifacts all related the tale of evolution. Olduvai Gorge is the famed excavation site first explored by Dr. Louis Leakey and his family in the 1950s and 60s. Discoveries made here pushed human evolution back two and three million years. Since then, other discoveries made in the Rift Valley have filled in the gaps, completed the links, and unearthed grist for new quandaries and debates.

Such thinking had been anathema to my religious upbringing. Olduvai Gorge itself was blacklisted in the unwritten, evangelical Christian code as a vortex of evil. It was hard to believe Dr. Leakey could be a proponent of evolution when his own parents had been Christian missionaries in Kenya. Yet he had the gall to say, "Nothing I've ever found has contradicted the Bible. It's people with their finite minds who misread the Bible."

Impossible. He was no biblical scholar. But then, neither was I.

The Baptist Church had only recently declared that dinosaur remains were legitimate. Young Earth Creationists now shoehorned them into their worldview by whatever gymnastic means necessary. Dinosaurs, they concluded, had walked the earth alongside Adam and Eve, though any form of evolution—especially its human stripe—was still considered blasphemy. These "human bones," I had been told, were the products of bad science, competitive and sensitive egos, and outright contempt for the church. In short, they were lies. One only need look at hoaxes like Piltdown Man.

The Institute of Creation Research, of which I was an ardent member, continued to send monthly pamphlets to me in Tanzania that confirmed its scientific *and* biblical veracity.

From the flood of Noah to a literal six days of creation, all were produced by the all-powerful, all-knowing, Christian God. That's how it happened. End of story.

I was sure scientists made mistakes, both innocent and guilty. They were only human. One of my emerging problems with the Creationist position was how scientists the world over could have been so hopelessly and consistently wrong for such a long time. After all, their methods were based on the same science used to make airplanes, telephones, breakfast cereals, and a thousand other things that worked just fine.

A human skull was mounted on the museum wall at Olduvai, and I bent down to take a closer look. Its forehead rose up higher and wider than an ape's behind thickly set orbits, and its jawbone was more gracile. I thought it looked more like a gorilla than a chimp, but not exactly. I flashed back to Dr. Goodall's talk in Dar. She and others in her field were convinced that humans had co-evolved from the same pre-ape, pre-monkey, proto-hominid around 6 million years ago. Present-day humans, she had said, were 98.7 percent genetically identical to bonobos and common chimpanzees.

I asked myself, Why was it so hard to believe we were "merely" animals or, by extension, that animals were "merely" people? Turning the phrase like this meant all life was related— genetically, integrally, spiritually. I'd wondered if approaching the problem this way might instill in us an ethic to renounce our self-mandated hubris of domination, overuse, and waste. As a species on the brink, could we stop what we were doing long enough to see that we were not what it was all about? Or was the human ego just too damn big?

I laughed, put my hands in my pockets, and looked down at the museum skull. I was unsure about a lot of things, but at least I had the assurance of salvation, "because the Bible tells me so." Nevertheless, while I'd been embarrassed about doubting my faith—in the caves, on Kili, here—I had not asked God for forgiveness. Maybe I was ashamed of what I'd been thinking, but I was not ashamed *of thinking—and feeling.* Of being human and milking the sacred cow for an unpasteurized sip of awareness.

On the same day that his letter arrived, I wrote back to Rolf to tell him he could definitely count me in. The route he suggested looked serious and risky, much more so than Kili, but doable for three young studs in our prime.

After the sun went down, I grabbed a Coke from the fridge and went out on my front porch. Fireflies blinked green and yellow. I imagined they danced to the music drifting up from the Lake Hotel in town. "The Lake," as we called it, was a colonial-era hostel that claimed Humphrey Bogart had once stayed there while shooting *The African Queen* with Katharine Hepburn. Apart from that and the occasional hippo lumbering ashore out back, the place was unremarkable. The choices were Pepsi, Coke, or Mirinda Fruity.

Every week or two, several of us in the expatriate pool met up at the Lake. Among our membership were Americans, British, Japanese, French, and Norwegians. With silly talk and laughter, we diluted classroom pressures with lagers, hacky sack, and Sportsman cigarettes. Less successful were our attempts to ignore the television in the adjacent bar. It perpetually played an old VHS tape of Michael Jackson, yelping and groping his crotch, and I cringed at the thought of Tanzanians concluding he epitomized the typical American.

From my porch I saw orange strings of fire on the hillsides around Bukoba. Farmers cleared their fields this way by slashing and burning them. I couldn't help but wonder what would happen if they lost control of their fire. What would they do if they lost control and were consumed from the inside out?

A muffled warmth hisses from each step in the soft sand. The lake moves endless and wise like a living thing. Behind me, I hear her. "Mr. Bill?" I turn to Farida. She stands barefoot in a long, red dress. She isn't wearing her shawl, and her hair falls in long, wavy curls around her face and neck.

A thunder clap chases a flash of light across the sky, and a delicious rain begins to fall. She smiles and reaches up to touch my face. I press her hand into my cheek, but she backs away into the rain, smiling. She stops and waves good-bye.

More rain and a peal of thunder, as if the sky is tearing apart, ripping . . .

. . . like a knife through a wire screen. I gasped once and sat bolt upright in bed. My head brushed against the mosquito net. My heart jumped. Light rain tapped on the iron roof and made it hard to hear, but I heard it again. Someone was breaking into the house.

I threw the net behind me and grabbed the two-by-four next to my bed. I slipped into my tennis shoes. I crept toward my bedroom door and turned the skeleton key in the keyhole. The ripping continued and sounded like it was coming from the living room. I tiptoed onto the concrete floor in the hallway. The hallway door was also locked from the inside, with its key left in the hole. I turned it and it clanked into place. I cracked the door open. In the dim light, I saw an arm hinged around the pane of the screened-in window. Its hand groped for the dead bolts on the front door.

I flipped on the front porch light. The arm retreated, but

the curtained image of a man remained. My heart pounded. With a jolt of adrenaline, I ran to the door and threw it open. I sprang onto the porch and raised the club over my head. I hoped there was only one intruder.

Instantly, my gaze fell. My would-be thief was five feet tall. He wore a smudged, pink winter coat at least three sizes too small, and his shorts hung in torn, limp vines around his thighs. I squinched my eyes and recognized him. He was the fellow Saito and I had seen in town lounging on a heap of slop over a year earlier. His confused expression made me realize he was also the mentally ill man who had tried on some of Chris' clothes; retarded or blighted with Schistosoma parasites that ate away at his brain.

My resolve was about to falter. I only wanted to scare him away, so I shook the club over my head, but he didn't flinch. All at once his eyes flew open and he screamed. His scream caused me to scream. Maybe I looked like a Neanderthal standing over him in my underwear, wielding a club, but he leaped off the porch and raced down the path. I chased him out onto the road. We both shouted and leaped as we ran. I shook my two-by-four high in the air, following him in hot pursuit—but not too closely.

As I ran I tripped on an untied shoelace and ground to a stop, facedown, in the muddy road. I looked up and saw his silhouette in the glow of light coming from the port. He jumped and bellowed like crazy as he ran toward the light.

I was spent. I rested my forehead on my two-by-four and closed my eyes. I felt the warm sting of blood ooze from the abrasions on my knees and elbows. Deeper than that was a hard knot of fear metastasizing in my gut. I was so afraid, locked up inside. I was afraid to be imprisoned, yet petrified to break out.

Maybe the little man in the pink coat wasn't so much

a thief in the night as he was a prophet in the wilderness? Maybe he only wanted to summon me from the tomb I was locked up in and point me toward Mount Kenya?

I felt sick. My insides squirmed. I turned my head as acid filled my mouth and nose and spewed onto the road. I coughed out the last chunks. I balled up on my side in the rain in the middle of the red, muddy road. Shamelessly, like a baby, I wept.

CHAPTER 17

Journey to the Center of the Earth

A SPEED TAXI in Tanzania is a Toyota or Peugeot wagon able to seat up to seven passengers plus a driver. Silk tassels fringe the windshield and dashboard, and most taxis carry a photo of the president, or Arnold Schwarzenegger as *The Terminator*, or some other heroic figure. One last thing: the word "speed" not only refers to a taxi's relative velocity (and higher fare) but also the higher rate of thrills a passenger can expect to experience. Circular red-and-white signs posted along the roadside advertising some two-digit number aren't even suggestions to the speed taxi driver. If anything, signs are used in timing and bluffing strategies with other drivers who squeeze their vehicles around trucks and cars; and between pedestrians, bicycles, livestock, and even the occasional zebra. NASCAR, Formula 500, and adventure video games have nothing on your run-of-the-mill speed taxi driver.

Brad, Rolf, and I left Rolf's house before daylight. By 8:00 A.M. we had hired a speed taxi in Arusha and were racing across the termite-mounded savanna toward the Kenya border. Along the way, the driver entertained us and our African co-passengers with a cassette tape of *Legend* by Bob Marley and the Wailers. At the border town of Namanga we switched to a Kenyan speed taxi. The Kenyan driver preferred the 70s rock superstar ABBA and played hits like "Take a Chance on Me" and "Dancing Queen."

"Shazam!" Brad said, recognizing some old faves. Months earlier, Brad said he had once played a bit part in an MTV music video, though I had never seen it and was skeptical. I changed my mind, though, when he persuaded the Africans in the taxi to sing along with him and groove the "butter churn."

Brad and I were similar in build and height, though he was a much stronger runner. He was also a proverbial class clown and an unconventional thinker, which helped him connect with his teenage math students. Another talent was his ability to remain calm and levelheaded under pressure; a possible life saver on a steep mountain.

We arrived in Nairobi early that afternoon. Downtown Nairobi is essentially a modern city and is known as "Nairobbery" by many of its residents. With this in mind, we kept an eye on one another's backpacks as we hiked to the nearest bank to change our Tanzanian shillings into Kenyan shillings. Unfortunately the tellers would not exchange them for notes that held approximately one-tenth the value of their own nation's currency. Time was running out. Our bus to Mount Kenya was about to leave, so we asked around and were soon led down a filthy backstreet alley to an upstairs "dealer." His henchmen corralled us into a smoky room and guarded the door. Flakes of blue paint had peeled off the cinder-block walls and the only furniture was a heavy, steel desk. The fat cat himself sat behind the desk and smiled as he eagerly changed all our cash into Kenyan shillings at, shall we say, his advantage. He knew he had us. We were in a pinch and on his turf, but since we left the place unharmed, with all our gear and enough cash to make do, I still thought we got a bargain.

By late afternoon we were on a minibus crammed with twenty-some souls bound for Chogoria. Traffic was slow as we drove north. Several police roadblocks made it go even slower. Most vehicles were stopped and inspected for registration, adequate tire pressure, matching headlight power, or anything else the police could invent to collect bribes. But not our minibus. The police waved us through each one. When I asked the driver why, he told me Kenya receives so much foreign aid and tourism dollars from *wazungu*, white people, that a vehicle with a white face on board is never stopped. This explained why he had insisted my two friends and I sit at the front of the bus.

We pulled into town not long after dark. Chogoria is a mountain town that is in direct antithesis to a chic, upscale resort like Aspen or Val d'Isère. It hunkers down rosy-cheeked and evergreen at 5,000 feet on the eastern slopes of Mount Kenya, and misty nights are cool, temperatures in the fifties. Residents wear knitted caps, scarves, layers of secondhand coats, and woolen trousers tucked into knee-high rubber boots.

Tired and hungry from traveling all day, we hauled our gear into a seedy guesthouse bar that reminded me of the cantina in the original *Star Wars* movie. The place was lit only by two guttering kerosene lanterns and the air was thick with the smoke of Sportsman cigarettes, which made it even more difficult to see. Chogoria had no electricity.

The only entrées available were steak—cow or goat—and meat soup, or meat shish kebab, and the only beverage was beer. Forced to break my self-sworn affidavit for avoiding meat, I ordered the soup, à la carte. I preferred to drink my nutrition instead of rending it from rubbery gristle. A few globs of the jelly-like ketchup Peptang squeezed into my soup improved its flavor dramatically. I also settled into my very first Tusker lager. I found the flavor slightly hoppy, but the carbonated smile it put on my face more than made up for it. *Sweet and fruity, the pride of Kenya.*

Local observances mandated a small portion of every fermented drink be poured onto the dirt floor in courtesy to the ancestors, a custom that made the floor sticky. I respectfully poured out a few drops of my beer. It seemed wherever I turned, there were these little reminders of everyone's impending mortality. At first I had found it depressing, but now I began to see how the ever-present uncertainties of life—especially in a place like Africa—were hereby equalized.

The mood was cheerful. Throaty laughter came from porters and guides padded up in wool and acrylic blends. People had that hard, weather-beaten look and the accessories to prove it—tired gaiters, re-stitched hiking boots, ice axes. One fellow even carried an AK-47 assault rifle—in a bar! Since guides were optional on Mount Kenya, patrons had already looked us over and dismissed us as being self-sufficient, doing our own thing, and therefore not in need of their services.

After dinner we pre-arranged a ride in a park service truck that was headed up to the entrance the next morning. Then we checked into a room. Our unheated, cement-block room was chilly and dank, so we unpacked our sleeping bags. We unrolled them onto the complimentary, open-cell foam mattresses and turned in. The town was quiet by 8:00 or 9:00. All I heard was a random muffled voice, a door close, a pail of water being thrown out. Right before I drifted off, I also heard a sawing, rasping sound in the trees outside our room. I was back in the land of the hyrax, the mountain's gatekeeper. I heard in his peculiar language both a greeting and a warning.

* * *

Each of us nursed a cup of hot, black *chai*. The steam that swirled around my face smelled like green, moist earth and relaxed me like a masseuse's towel. I cupped a hand over the warm vapor. Rolf's glasses had fogged up from taking sips, so he dipped his chin to see over the circular rims when he reached for another scone, deep-fried in lard and still sizzling.

The early morning air was chilly, but the sunshine was fresh and bright. Townspeople busied about as if they were already halfway through their day, but the three of us woke up more slowly. We huddled around an old, Beckwith pot-belly stove, all cozy and crackling, and dunked our scones in our tea the way locals did. I peered out a frosty window and saw a little church up the street. Since it was Sunday, it had already attracted a congregation. I couldn't tell its denomination by the architecture of the building, though it certainly looked too plain to be Catholic.

I hadn't been to church since I had gone with Patrick in Arusha, eighteen months earlier. I thought I would feel guilty about it, but I didn't. Worse was how I'd begun to feel for inheriting a worldview that had been used to divide and exploit people, and sponsor imperialism and warfare.

A book I had purchased in Bukoba entitled *A Short History of Africa* explained how it happened. The Age of Imperialism in Africa ran from the mid-nineteenth century to the early twentieth century, though precursors of it reach back to the Portuguese slavers of the fifteenth century and aftereffects continue to the present day.

Victorian England famously misused the principles of Darwinian evolution when it applied them to politics and sociology. The result was a high-sounding notion called scientific racism, or social Darwinism. Pseudo-sciences such as phrenology (measuring the skull) and physiognomy (determining personality from appearance, especially the face) were invented in an effort to legitimize Eurocentrism and sanction imperial expansion across the globe.

Lord Frederick Lugard was an explorer for the Imperial British East Africa Company in 1889. He was also the military administrator of Uganda from 1890 to 1892. In his opinion, "[The African mind] is far nearer to the animal world than that of the European or the Asiatic, and exhibits something of the animals' placidity . . . Through the ages, the African appears to have evolved no organised religious creed, and though some tribes appear to believe in a deity, the religious sense seldom rises above pantheistic animalism . . . In brief, the virtues and defects of this race-type are those of attractive children . . ."

Nineteenth-century German philosopher Georg W.F. Hegel was a notable contributor to scientific racism. "It is characteristic of the blacks," he wrote, "that their consciousness has not yet even arrived at the intuition of any objectivity, as for example, of God or the law . . . [The black person] is a human being in the rough." Hegel went on to prescribe a religious antidote for Africans' "inferior" condition: "The destiny of the Germanic peoples is that of serving as the bearer of the Christian principle."

Of course, the British and the Germans were not the only Imperial racists who took aim at Africa. In 1904, the American missionary Samuel Phillips Verner purchased the Congolese Pygmy Ota Benga from Belgian slavers and took him to St. Louis, Missouri, where he was featured in an anthropology exhibit. Commenting on the exhibit, American scientist William John McGee said the exhibit showed how culture had evolved from "the darkest blacks to the dominant whites." Ota Benga was later shipped to New York and displayed in a cage at the Bronx Zoo and touted as the "missing link" between humans and orangutans. He committed suicide in 1916.

Cultural hubris was only able to achieve such lofty heights under the aegis of its missionary efforts. The church strove to convert the "heathen," a mandate eased by the Africans' high regard for the spirit world and their openness to alternative spiritual practices. The takeover and subsequent underdevelopment of Africa were made simpler after African worldviews had been shifted onto Western foundations.

Bishop Desmond Tutu acknowledged these abuses when he quoted a popular African proverb: "When the missionaries came to Africa, they had the Bible and we had the land. They said 'Let us pray.' We closed our eyes. When we opened them, we had the Bible and they had the land."

Brad, Rolf, and I finished breakfast and went out to the truck. I continued to glace at the ramshackle church and its misguided flock, and I wondered if they had any idea. Did they realize the main reason they worshipped a Christian god was due to the imperialist fantasies of men in far-flung, ivory towers? I was ashamed.

We loaded the bed of the truck and hopped in. As the truck bounced over the rutted road past all the people waiting for the church doors to open, they started to sing. Sonorous basses, tenors, and altos, with tremolos on top, sang "*Hallelujah, hallelujah, hallelujah* to the Lord. . . ." The music was simple yet rich and multi-layered. My flesh prickled with goose bumps. People around town stopped to look and listen, too, and some joined in. The moment was beautiful, as if the mountain itself made a joyful noise unto the Lord.

I felt so sorry for them.

* * *

The road climbed a fairly straight line through the forest and meandered only to avoid a ravine or an outcropping of rock. Before long we reached the forest boundary. We went to the park gate and bought three eight-day passes into Mount Kenya National Park that cost U.S. $20 per day, or 160 bucks apiece. We thought the amount was outrageous, since we had climbed Kilimanjaro and Meru for free. However, we might have been less irritated about it had we known that in only a few short years a guided climb like ours would cost up to $5,000 per person.

Once through the gate we shouldered our packs and hiked up the four-wheel-drive road. The road gradually withered into a single-track trail entombed in a canopy of eucalyptus and camphor trees. The towering trees obscured our view of everything around us, including the mountain itself.

Late that afternoon we reached the heath moorland and set up camp. The trees were gnarled and crowded into stream beds, and for the first time, the country opened up and refreshed our sweat-soaked skin with mountain breezes. Fragments of sunlight shattered across an unforeseen high country and spilled long, cold shadows into distant vales and cirques. Temperatures stiffened into the thirties that night.

After a breakfast of oatmeal and cocoa heated on our mini kerosene stove, we set off toward a designated camping area at 12,000 feet. The day was gorgeous, sunny, and blue. We hiked through meadows of flowering *Proteas*, *Ericaceas*, everlastings, lobelias, Red Hot Pokers, and many others— alpine gardens of Eden. We also saw giant groundsels, or *Senecio* trees, similar to those on Kilimanjaro. We had heard reports of elephants and hyenas. However, our only encounter with wildlife came when we were awakened one night by a herd of Cape buffalo. Several of these half-ton animals snorted hot blasts of air and nuzzled us through our paper-thin tent. Fortunately, they decided we were not a threat and wandered off into the moonlit night, but we were reminded of them each time we stepped over splatters of poop they had left behind on the trail.

I was fascinated with how rapidly the landscape transformed around us. Greens were replaced with yellows and then shades of hard gray and frozen brown. The trail wound onto a ridge broken on both sides by immense, U-shaped valleys carved by ancient glaciers, and craggy arêtes towered above us. Cumulus clouds bubbled up behind the central peaks.

I swallowed hard. A knot of anxiety tightened in the pit of my stomach as my day of reckoning drew near.

The drone of a single-engine plane had bored holes in the sky most of the day. The plane was a yellow Piper Cub, and I wondered if a hiker had been hurt or was lost. Or maybe poachers had been spotted and the pilot was working with an anti-poaching patrol on the ground.

The plane continued to come and go when we arrived at Minto's Hut, our camp for the night. As we looked for a level spot to put our tent, we noticed several other tents already up. Each tent was embossed with a pert, blue-and-yellow cross pattern, and a dozen people, all white, jumped and danced and ran around between them. The people frequently broke into laughter. It reminded me of 4-H camp when I was a kid, and I recognized some of the group games they played—trust walk, amoeba, Tom & Jerry.

Solitary men were posted at intervals at their camp's periphery. They were not pleasant-looking fellows. When they saw us, they alerted a man in the main group, who came over and introduced himself as Ian Howell, a British-Kenyan mountaineer and the author of several climbing guides to East African mountains. We shook his hand.

"I'm afraid I have to apologize," he said, his accent round and authoritative. "The king of Sweden and the royal family are camping here tonight." He motioned to the people near the blue-and-yellow tents. They stood in a circle, laughing. Ian leaned in close and brought a hand to the side of his mouth. "All a bit daft, if you ask me." We chuckled with him. "Anyway, rotten luck, but I'm afraid you'll have to move your camp a little farther off."

Ian looked to be in his fifties. He was friendly and talkative but made it clear that a royal perimeter of one hundred meters had been established around the Swedes. They were there on vacation, he said, to climb Point Lenana, a nontechnical mountain and the third-highest peak on the massif. As Ian spoke, the Piper Cub buzzed overhead not 200 feet off the ground. The wings waved in quick jerks. Ian looked up and waved back.

"Is he with them?" I asked.

Ian nodded. "He's an aerial guard that the royal family commissioned. Makes them feel safer, I suppose." We watched the plane bank left over the valley and return to make another pass, but Ian's attention had turned to the helmets tied to our packs. "Ah! I see you're climbing the peaks. Which one?"

"The Normal Route, Batian," Brad answered.

"Yes, very good. One of my true favorites. Actually helped build the sleeper hut on Nelion, several years ago now." He chuckled lightly. "There are, of course, several tricky spots, especially the Gate of Mists." He stopped talking and surveyed our packs. "You have your ice gear?"

Brad, Rolf, and I glanced at one another but no one answered.

Ian cleared his throat and rubbed his nose. "Right, well whichever one of you leads the pitch into the gate and up the other side will need a stout pair of crampons and an ice ax. No getting around that, really."

We turned to face the peaks. The plane buzzed overhead, but we scarcely noticed.

"Now because there are three of you," he went on, "the going could be slower than you expect. Teams of three are always slower than teams of two."

We stood in silence for a moment, trying to comprehend what we had let ourselves in for.

Ian spoke again. "One more thing; there's an old, metal bivvy box. It used to be called Bailey's Bivvy, and you could sleep in if you had to. Anyway, it's anchored to the main wall perhaps eight or nine pitches up. From Top Hut you can see the sun reflecting off it in the morning. Keep that under your hat in case you need it. Not at all pleasant—quite grim, really— but there it is."

The next morning, we packed early and left for Top Hut. Austrian Hut and Top Hut sit adjacent to each other on a glacially scoured backbone of rock at 15,500 feet. But since we had a tent, we moved off a couple hundred yards and set up camp next to the Lewis Glacier. Later we walked up to the huts and talked to a Kenyan guide. For 500 Kenyan shillings, about ten dollars, we rented an ice ax and a pair of crampons.

We made plans over dinner. Steam and bubbles chugged out of the pot of rice as Rolf pulled the lid off and gave them a quick stir.

"Beans are in that pink bag," I said, pointing at the food bag with the blade of my Swiss Army knife. Brad grabbed a can of cooked beans from the larder. I breathed on my bare fingers to warm them up and went back to dicing an onion. In between cuts, I stole steep glances up at Nelion. "Damn, she's big!"

Brad didn't miss a beat. "Hey, the bigger the better, the tighter the sweater."

I tried to finish it. "We must, we must—"

"—we must scale the earth's crust!" Brad polished it off. We cracked up like junior high school boys.

Rolf gazed up at the mountain, too. His mouth was slightly open and his forehead was wrinkled. "This could be interesting," he said, mostly to himself.

I didn't hear him over the blowtorch noise from the stove. "What?"

He shook his head. "Gonna be a hell of a climb!" He sounded concerned.

"Exactly!" I said, adding naïve confidence. "We sleep in tomorrow, get some rest, and in two days we'll be rockin' up that baby!"

"Amen, brother," Brad toasted and raised his Nalgene to his lips.

Rolf had no comment. He went back to his rice. "Yep— hey, does anyone care if I add the beans to the rice and mix them in?"

The mountain archetype is primordial and powerful. Ritual details may vary, but mountain symbolism is expressed in cosmologies the world over.

Buddhism, Taoism, Hinduism, Confucianism, and Shintoism each worship aspects of mountains, as well as the mountains themselves. In Chinese Taoism, for instance, mountains are considered to be the body of God, its rivers are God's blood, the rocks are bones, vegetation is hair, and clouds are God's breath. Many Native American cultures link their origin myths with mountains as well. The Navajo identify a sacred mountain as the axis mundi—world axis or the center of the earth. Tibetan Buddhists also recognize a mountainous axis mundi, though theirs is mythical; Mount Meru (not the mountain Josh and I climbed) is 80,000 miles high and stretches to the corners of the earth. The cosmic tree of life grows from its summit with branches that reach to heaven.

Romanian historian of religion Mircea Eliade argued that mountains represent the struggle to achieve deeper insight and higher enlightenment. Mountains, he said, symbolize a link between heaven and earth, the sacred and the profane; religions imitate them with temples, minarets, steeples, and pyramids. Freud claimed mountains were also symbols of masculinity with their flame-shaped, barren steeps standing erect over fertile, feminine valleys.

Much like the world I had grown up in, Mount Kenya was masculine, monolithic, and absolute. I considered it even more imposing than Kilimanjaro, both in metaphor and structure.

In geologic terms, Mount Kenya's viscous magma broke the floor of the Rift Valley one million years ago. Over the next few hundred thousand years, its volcanic base grew to sixty miles and its summit to 23,000 feet. The highest peaks on Mount Kenya today are the skeletal remains of magma that cooled and crystallized inside the volcanic necks of their cones. Eventually, the outer, less-consolidated cones eroded away to expose the more resistant plugs. Similar to granite, these plugs are made of porphyritic trachyte-diorite, interposed with feldspars, olivines, and nepheline syenite. In English, this means the rock quality for technical climbing is considered fair to good and offers reasonable protection placement.

The name "Kenya" itself is a corruption of the Kikuyu people's name for the mountain. Originally pronounced "Kirinyaga," or Mountain of Whiteness, it is the traditional home of their great god, Ngai, and the location of their axis mundi. Many of the highest peaks on the massif are named in honor of holy men and women of the nearby plains people, the Maasai. These include Batian, who served as a Maasai holy man in the late nineteenth century; Nelion, his brother; and Lenana, successor to Batian.

That evening I studied Mount Kenya's profile in the moonlight. The summit vanished into the clouds, and I imagined there being no top at all, like the Tibetans' world mountain. Perhaps, I thought, it reached to infinity and penetrated Paradise. If I could just get there, maybe I could climb out of a subconscious dungeon. To fail would be to risk losing myself to that old-time, habitual complacency and the half-truths I had taken on blind faith . . . or worse.

It was a risk I willing to take.

CHAPTER 18

The Marble Room

PAPER BEATS ROCK, which meant I lost and Rolf led the first pitch. But first, we stashed the tent and nonessentials behind a boulder and scrambled up to the base of the main wall. Even though it was twilight and the sun hadn't come up yet, we found the starting point for the Normal Route without much trouble. Temperatures were in the teens, so we quickly racked the gear, flaked the ropes, and started climbing.

The first few pitches served as good warm-ups. None of it was difficult, though on average it took us about an hour-and-a-half to complete one pitch. (A pitch can be as long as one rope length, or 165 feet, though it is often shorter. Also, we climbed with two ropes—one from the leader to the second person, and a second rope running from the second person to the third person.) We spent most of that time tied in to an anchor point, stationary, so the climber was the only person who stayed warm. The trade-off was that the climber's hands and fingers went gloveless to improve grip, turning them into numb stubs of flesh by the time he had made it to the next anchor point.

We soon found a rhythm—climb, belay, drink rationed sips of water—but twelve hours was a long stretch for anyone. Clouds had packed in tighter throughout the day, and by late afternoon it started to snow.

Toward evening, Rolf was leading a pitch while Brad belayed. I sat huddled in some rocks out of the wind. Suddenly I started to shiver. I tensed my muscles and the shivering stopped, but it started again when I relaxed. Hypothermia had set in. I knew I should generate body heat, so I stood and hopped in place while I swung my arms up and down. Swathed in harness, rope, and various jingling paraphernalia, I reminded myself of the ghost of Marley.

I hopped like this for a minute and it helped a little, but I thought I should let Rolf know, so I tottered over to the rock face. He was only thirty feet up, squinting through the snowflakes as he tried to find the best way ahead. Rolf had stayed positive all day, but he was also a clear and reasoned thinker who was not about to over-optimize a situation. He knew we still had nine pitches to go before topping out on Nelion, and at our current pace it would take twelve more hours.

"Rolf!" I yelled through chattering teeth.

"Yeah!"

"What's it look like?"

"Not sure. I know it goes right, but I see a piton up left."

"Six of one, half dozen of another," Brad said, trying to keep things moving.

Unexpectedly, Rolf stopped and beamed down. "Hey!" Brad and I squinted into the flurries. "Remember Ian? Bailey's Bivvy?"

Brad perked up. "Shit, yeah! I am down with that, bro!"

In a few minutes, Rolf had downclimbed to the belay anchor and all three of us scrambled to the edge of the cliff behind us.

We leaned out over the wall. Brad pointed through the snow. "There. Is that it?"

A dull, metallic object roosted on the wall about twenty yards below. We anchored a rappel line and I went first. In a minute, I arrived at a box made of aluminum sheet metal that was eight feet long, four feet deep, and four feet high. It resembled an oversized coffin. The "door" was an open-framed hole about two feet square that faced away from the cliff. The entire structure sat perched on a ledge of questionable merit, hardly bigger than its boxy girth.

"This is it!" I yelled back up.

"Does it look safe?" Rolf asked.

"Yeah . . . I think so." I stuck my head inside. A trickle of water had dribbled into the back corner on warmer days. It had frozen into the shape of a ramp that came down to coat the entire floor in a floe of ice. I pulled my head out and yelled up, "Bring the ice ax!"

After Brad rappelled down, we took turns using the ax to chip out the hump of ice. I wondered if we were undermining our own foundation. Rolf brought the rest of the gear down. To insulate us against the ground, we laid out a foil emergency blanket and uncoiled the second climbing rope over it. For safety, whoever sat in front of the doorless doorway stayed tied in to the fixed line we had rappelled down on. Likewise, whoever needed to pee or poop did so out the door while remaining tied in. It was a bit like I had imagined space travel—spartan dining, cramped quarters, no privacy, and lots of room outside.

After unrolling our sleeping bags, we broke out the stove and rewarded ourselves with a chopped bell pepper boiled up tender in a bouillon-cube soup. We garnished our dinner with chapati fry breads.

"I think we have enough food to continue for one more full day," Rolf said, taking inventory, "which means at our present speed we'll be doing well to make the summit of Nelion tomorrow. We would have to rappel down in the dark." Rolf didn't mean to sound pessimistic. He only wanted to lay out the facts. But the odds were stacked against us, and I could sense the conclusion he was heading for: we should bail out the next day.

"Right. So what's the climbing like tomorrow?" I asked, probing his observation for weak points. I had to get to the summit.

Rolf reached under his hat and kneaded his unruly scalp. "According to what I've read, it's slab-climbing, some easy gullies—certainly nothing more difficult than today, with nine pitches to the top."

"Of Nelion."

"Of Nelion. Yes," Rolf said.

"And after that we're basically there, right?"

Rolf studied me as he chewed on his chapati. "After Nelion," he said, "we'd have to cross the Gate of Mists."

"*And then* we must fight the invisible swordsman!" Brad said. Hot soup dribbled through his stubble as he swash-buckled his titanium spork into the low ceiling.

Rolf chuckled. "I hope not."

I remembered a passage from my little guidebook. "The Diamond Couloir?" I asked.

"Yep. That's the top of it. Like Ian said, most climbers anchor a fixed line on Nelion and rappel into the couloir wearing crampons. Then they climb three short pitches on the other side to the summit."

"Three pitches," I said, usurping his narrative. "So we could get to the top of Nelion tomorrow, scoot over to Batian the next morning, then back to Nelion and down the same day. We'd have to go down the day after tomorrow anyway, right?" Again, I was greedy for the top.

Rolf nodded thoughtfully. "Yep. Yep, that could work if we cut way back on food and water."

"And fuel," Brad added.

"And fuel, starting now," Rolf said.

Brad wrapped the remaining portion of his cold chapati in a plastic bag and handed it to me. "Here you go, brother. Put this in the bank for me."

I tucked it into the food bag. I was tired, but I lobbied hard. "So I say we go for it. I mean, when's the next time we'll be back here again?"

"I'm with you, bro. Let's do it," Brad said. He reached across with his fist and knuckle-bumped me. "Wonder-twin powers, activate!"

Rolf nodded with a downward-puckered mouth.

Like Meru and Kili, I wanted this mountain bad, and come hell or high water I was willing to put our lives at risk to see it come to pass. Subconsciously I needed it to cleanse me of my sins and of the person I used to be.

"Sure. I'm in," Rolf said.

Brad and I presented him with fists of fellowship.

The subject changed, and we agreed the accommodations at Bailey's earned absolutely zero stars, and we would never recommend the place to anyone. Nevertheless, not being ones to look a gift horse in the mouth, we raised our water bottles and gave a toast to Mr. Howell and Mr. Bailey.

Whirling spin drifts of hail-like graupel flogged our aluminum box throughout the night. We slept fitfully, if at all. It didn't help matters that we had to line ourselves up—one, two, three—and sit with our backs against the rock while our feet stuck straight out against the sheet- metal wall. I was next to the door, so I stayed tied in to the rope on which we had rappelled down. It snaked in through the door hole, into the face hole of my bag, and down to my midsection like an umbilical cord.

I had not been asleep for long when I awoke to the dawn silhouette of Point Lenana. Deep purple and fuzzy on its shadowed side, Lenana was about one horizontal mile due east. The Lewis Glacier bridged the gap 600 feet directly below our toes. However, I made this estimate using only monocular vision, since the vapor from my breaths had iced the lashes of one of my eyes shut. I squirmed my hands free to pry it open.

The three of us extracted ourselves from our sleeping bags like pupae butterflies in cocoons. Daylight came late over Point Lenana, so Rolf hung his headlamp—our only one, to save weight—on a bent, sheet-metal screw in the ceiling. Half asleep, we stuffed our feet into our frozen boots and ate Snickers bars and Gatorade for breakfast.

Brad mimicked Mr. Rogers: "It's a beautiful day in the neighborhood, a beautiful day for a neighbor, would you be mine, could you be mine? . . . And this is how we put on our gaiters, yup, do ya see that?" At least he sounded refreshed.

We moved in better sync that day, though the weather closed in again and slowed us down to about the same speed as the day before. Brad stepped up to the plate and carried out his first lead climb on the last pitch of the day. After that, we coiled the ropes, racked the gear, and clambered over a jumble of boulders for the last bit. Visibility had fallen to less than fifty yards, but an oddly symmetrical structure stood out.

In comparison with the previous night's lodging, Howell Hut was a veritable Hilton, not the least of which was due to its situation on highly prized, level ground. True, it was another aluminum box, scarcely bigger than the last one at six by eight by four feet high. This one, however, was furnished with plush, yellow foam mattresses. Foam insulation had been installed in the walls and ceiling, too.

We stumbled over to find its exterior walls and door plastered with graffiti and bumper stickers—everything from beer mottos and condom slogans to a quote from Bishop Desmond Tutu: "God is not a Jew or a Christian or a Muslim; God is beyond those definitions."

I leaned a gloved hand against the hut as I read the bishop's proverb, not sure what it was doing here. Not sure what I was doing here.

Brad was less impressed. "Put it in your pipe and smoke it later, *bwana*," he said. He shuffled past me and yanked the door open.

We were greeted by two British climbers. "Hello!" said one.

"Bugger! Let's keep the white stuff outside!" said the other, as he brushed kernels of snow from his sleeping bag.

We ducked in and introduced ourselves to Paul and Oliver from Sheffield, England. They had started climbing the previous morning at 6:00 A.M. on a classic ice route known as the Diamond. They had arrived at Howell Hut the same day. Summiting Nelion in one day meant they were exceptionally fast climbers. However, they admitted to getting a late start that morning. They had crossed over to Batian, tagged the summit, and re-crossed to Nelion only an hour earlier. In their words, they were now "a trifle knackered."

Nice chaps, but food topped our list of priorities. We found a spot shielded from the wind behind some boulders and cooked our dinner. The menu that evening included soup with rice and the other halves of our chapatis.

We had a potentially brutal day ahead of us, so I set my watch alarm for 5:30 and prayed for sun. Wind howled throughout the night. Volleys of snow and windblown grit flailed against the little shelter and made it sound as though the walls might collapse. The storm kept me awake for hours, and when sleep finally came, I dreamed.

I am in a room with high walls made of white marble. Cracks in the floor are inlaid with green serpentine. The cracks are widening before my eyes, growing into the walls. Across the room are two tall double doors. They are also made of stone, and they are closed. I panic and walk toward the doors to get out.

Just then a small figurine of white marble spins through the air and strikes the floor at my feet. On impact, one of the statuette's arms breaks off and releases a tiny ball of light. The light curls off into the room. I continue toward the doors. A second statuette glides past. It, too, strikes the floor, breaks another arm, and releases another ball of light.

I reach the doors, but they are locked. I pull on the handles and pound on the doors. A third figurine crashes into the threshold at my feet. This one shatters. A hundred balls of blue white light fly out and converge at my wrists and ankles.

The lights pick me up into the air. They turn me to face the opposite wall, which is one enormous mirror. In the mirror I see my arms stretched out and my legs pinned with fiery stigmata. I see the reflection of my own crucifixion.

I watch myself in the mirror being turned to face the high ceiling. The ceiling is filled with a blindingly pure white light. I am lifted closer and closer, until I merge and fuse with it. I have become the light!

I awoke with a jerk and sat up. My heart thumped so hard it caused my nylon sleeping bag to rustle. I remembered where I was and looked around for the others, but it was too dark. I felt for my wristwatch and pressed the Indiglo button: 5:20 A.M. I laid back down and tried to relax, but I was too disturbed by my nightmare. Like a missive sent from my subconscious, it warned that my identity was about to implode and cave in. Yet escape by the usual means—physical or mental—was impossible.

My watch alarm went off. No one stirred. I was now completely awake. I looked past the toes of my sleeping bag and saw a thin, red glow from the east bleed through the Plexiglas window. I savored the last moments of warmth in my nylon womb and pretended the glow on the Plexiglas meant heat. But there was no pretending about my dream. The collapse had begun.

Brad, Rolf, and I hunted around in the rocks but found no registry box or notebook sealed in a jar. The summit area on Mount Kenya was less than thirty feet on a side, so we decided against celebrating with a game of hacky sack. At least the overcast and undercast had thinned out. We caught glimpses of lower mountains and forests and even the Aberdare Range to the west.

Our situation was paradoxical. We had achieved the summit but had exhausted our rations. We ate the last of our peanut butter. We drank the last of our water. The rest of our supplies were stashed at the foot of the main wall, with nothing between here and there but a mountain of vertical rock and ice. We may as well have been on the moon. I stumbled over to the edge to pee. A dark stream of liquid dotted off into space, a sure sign I was dehydrating like always.

For me the hardships were more than physical. I had pushed my limits and crawled to the top of this godforsaken precipice, but I asked myself: Where was the joy, the enlightenment? The summit was sublime and ethereal, but where was the peace? I instead felt numb and empty like I had received no return on my investment. I was a nil Bill, a cipher.

My mind grew quiet. Piss dribbled on my boots.

It then occurred to me that no mountain by itself would ever be high enough or steep enough or even beautiful enough to consummate enlightenment. Suddenly the soft, empty clouds below seemed an attractive alternative. I wondered if I could get back down the mountain, or if it even mattered anymore.

The sun was down. A moment of strawberry-copper alpenglow burnished the mountainside before it dimmed and faded and was gone. However, the blackness of night did not follow. Folded buttresses and spiny gendarmes waxed pallid beneath a brilliant full moonrise.

We had rappelled for several hours and were on the west side of an arête—an alcove above Bailey's Bivvy. It was a simple catwalk, one we had scurried across the day before without roping up, trying to save time. Now we were back, doing it in reverse, and once again we were unroped. I wore the gear pack.

The area was eclipsed in moon shadow and as dark as the center of the earth. The pupils of my eyes were fully dilated, but I saw nothing, only Rolf's headlamp bobbing up ahead, scouting the way. Brad was about fifty feet in front of me, feeling his way along. I could hear him, but I couldn't see him, couldn't see anything. I remembered that the slickrock to my right immediately sloped off. After that, there was nothing but air all the way to the Lewis Glacier, a half mile below. I couldn't help but lean into the wall on my left, even though doing so stole traction from underfoot.

I felt for the ground with my feet. I hoped it would be there. Sweat prickled my face and I heard my breaths come quick and shallow. Moisture condensed on my face and reminded me of my last supper—cold peanut butter.

Another blind step, and another. Then one more.

Then it wasn't there.

I turned on tiny stone, round like a ball bearing. My arms flew out. "Whoa! *Fuuuck!*"

I wheeled around in the dark, unattached. I was faceup. A powder of stars sprayed across the heavens. I felt weightless, floating, and a warm tranquility filled me and relaxed me. I forgot what had happened, when it started, or if it should end. I no longer existed. I was confused, yet it was peaceful and quiet and I didn't care.

"William!" Brad shouted, and I slammed onto my back-pack, faceup.

I bounced slightly, slid a few inches, and stopped. Neither Brad nor I knew the other's position, but I heard his voice move closer.

"Holy shit, brother! You need a hand?"

"No! I got it."

But I didn't. I was a few inches from the point of no return, and I flopped and slapped around like a turtle on its back. I groped for anything at all. I held my breath and heard a flash of intuition or an inner voice: *Reach left and roll!*

My pack began to grind over the slickrock. In a second or two I wouldn't be able to stop my slide. I stretched out to my left, found something solid, and pulled as hard as I could. I rolled onto my stomach and locked off.

Rolf's headlamp beamed out from the moonlit side of the arête. "Hey guys! It's over here!" he shouted.

I saw Brad's backlighted silhouette. "William! Here!" Blindly, I reached out. He found my hand and dragged me up as I kicked against dead air. He said something, but I didn't hear him. I was too shaky and full of adrenaline. Carefully, he led me to the moonlit side of the arête.

We caught up with Rolf, but I didn't say anything about the incident and neither did Brad. After we crossed the traverse, we began a series of long, exposed rappels on the main wall. I felt weak in the knees and unsure of myself, so I followed Rolf's lead for the rest of the night. He thought I was just tired. We touched down at the base of the main wall at midnight, January 6th—Epiphany.

Along the way, I tried to make sense out of what had happened—the dream, the summit, the fall. My identity and my grasp on reality were crashing down around me, and in the midst of it all I floated in an existential purgatory. I knew there was a way out, but it wasn't one I could walk through. To know life I would have to finish knowing death.

CHAPTER 19

Books of Revelation

TEN DAYS AFTER my last shower, I peeled off my Polypro long underwear, brushed out my matted hair, and baptized myself in a bath of hot, soapy water. Washing my hair required two liberal doses of Pert Plus. I had lost ten pounds that I really could not afford to lose. Brad and Rolf were about the same. We did our best to put some of it back on at the Naro Moru River Lodge. The lodge was a relatively posh resort on the western piedmont of Mount Kenya that had a restaurant and bar complete with a billiards table and a dart board. It also had several racquetball courts we decided not to use. On the following day we took a speed taxi back to Tanzania.

While recuperating at Rolf and Cynthia's house, we inspected all our gear, checked the cams, and felt the ropes for worn spots. We also hand-washed our noxious clothing with extra-strength, all-purpose Vim in their outdoor sinks. That evening we cooked homemade pizzas to the tunes of Eric Clapton's *Unplugged*, grooving from a GE cassette player in the living room. Now we only needed for the electricity to stay on.

Over dinner we told Cynthia about the climb. Rolf described the views and the Cape buffalo. Brad told her about the long, exposed rappels. My nerves had settled down, so I mentioned the moon shadow and how I had tripped.

Cynthia gasped. Rolf's mouth fell open. "Tripped? When?" he asked.

Everyone at the table watched and waited. It was like I was on the witness stand. "Right," I said, and put my pizza down on my plate. I went on to give the bare facts but avoided the moment of singularity and the voice in my head.

Rolf had stopped chewing. "Whoa."

He looked at Brad for confirmation, but Brad waved his hands. "Hey, all I know is I heard him fall, and—he chuckled and redirected his comment to me—"use certain expletives I ain't *never* heard you say before!"

I forced a smile and nodded. My cheeks felt red. "Yeah, well, it brings out your best when you think you're taking the big ride home."

"You mean the pearly gates?" Brad joked, aware of my Christian roots. God and heaven, however, had not crossed my mind; not when I stumbled, not even when I was hanging over the valley of the shadow of death.

I scrambled. "Yeah, except they were more misty than pearly."

The three of them laughed and the subject changed, but not for me. I knew I needed time to think and find out where I had landed. In the meantime, we finished dinner and Cynthia dealt out a deck of cards for a few rounds of euchre.

The next morning new plans commenced. Brad was heading back to his school, and Cynthia and Rolf were taking a short trip out to Zanzibar. I had a plane ticket to Mwanza, but my flight wasn't scheduled for another week. Cynthia and Rolf said I could stay at their place until then.

I was brushing my teeth in the bathroom when Rolf came in holding a book. "William. If you have time, I thought you might enjoy reading this."

I spit the Colgate foam into the sink, wiped my mouth, and read the title. "*The Gospel According to Jesus.* Is this like the Dead Sea Scrolls or something?"

"No, actually it's the author's interpretation of the New Testament, published pretty recently, I think. Anyway, it made a lot of sense to me when I read it, and since I know you're into stuff like this . . ."

I took it from him, not sure how I felt about it. "Thanks. I'll give it a read."

"Great, and help yourself to any of the books you see in the living room."

I followed Rolf out the back door and wished him and Cynthia bon voyage. Brad was leaving at the same time, so we all said our good-byes. We had two group hugs before they put on their backpacks. I stood outside the house and watched the three of them walk down the shaded, dirt road. I waved again as they disappeared around a bend. A blue clapboard kiosk sat vacant at the corner, its Pepsi sign reminding passersby, *Chaguo Ni Lako. The Choice Is Yours.*

I walked back inside and made a cup of hot *chai.* I took the tea into the living room and sank into a comfortable reading chair in the corner. The sweet concoction was warm and satisfying and encouraged me to gaze out the window at Mount Meru.

Below the scene in the window sat a bookshelf decorated with African knickknacks and a copy of the paperback Rolf had showed me. I reached over and took it off the shelf. I read the title again: *The Gospel According to Jesus* by Stephen Mitchell. The small print at the bottom of the cover read, "By the translator of Tao Te Ching and the Book of Job."

The muscles in the pit of my stomach and low back stiffened as if they were guarding against a threat. But I didn't care anymore. I was ready. I opened the book and began to read.

What is the gospel according to Jesus? Simply this: that the love we all long for in our innermost heart is already present, beyond longing.

I was drawn in. My insides stretched thin and tight, yet I did not resist. My defenses had finally collapsed on Mount Kenya, so I let go and embraced it. I soon waxed appalled, mollified, ecstatic.

Like all the spiritual Masters, Jesus taught one thing only: Presence. Ultimate reality, the luminous compassionate intelligence of the universe, is not somewhere else, in some heaven light-years away . . . It is always right here, right now.

The author revealed the nature of the Kingdom of God, and I leaped onto its message, soaking it up like a man in the desert who stumbles upon a pool of clear water. I read all day, all night, and on through the next day. I stopped only to wave flies away from the now two-day-old pizza I had left out on the table. I snacked on it and then dived back into the book. I repeated sections I had earmarked to make sure they were still there and that I hadn't simply imagined them.

No good scholar, for example, would call the Christmas stories anything but legends, or the accounts of Jesus' trial anything but polemical fiction.

Polemical fiction? I didn't know what polemical meant. But fiction? Were these so-called theologians and scholars implying that the manger and everything after was a one-size-fits-all illusion? I laughed and shook my head. It was total heresy! Blasphemy! Sacrilege! And I loved it! I was thrilled and relieved to *finally* read it, to see the truth of it, and realize I would not be eternally damned for thinking it.

> [T]here is not a trace of difference between the teaching of Jesus and the teaching of Buddha . . . And Jesus, like the Buddha, was a man who had awakened from all dreams.

Jesus may have been a great spiritual teacher, but he was no more (or less) divine than anyone else. His peers branded him a bastard child, an issue he grappled with for the rest of his brief life. Nevertheless, he had something to say, something that people who labored under the tyranny of the Roman Empire—and tyrannies of every age—longed to hear: You are loved, you are legitimate, and help is on the way. (Perhaps he himself longed to hear these precepts.)

Jesus was one of many christs and mystics who wandered the hills of Judea. He happened to be in the wrong place at the wrong time. Martyrdom clinched the deal. After he was crucified, his grief-stricken friends latched onto his allegories, elevated him to divine status, and began spreading the gospel. As time went on, the legend of Jesus grew larger than life—certainly larger than his. It did not take long before human egos found currency in his message and used it to justify their earthly desires and manipulate the masses.

> Once the sectarian passages are left out, we can recognize that Jesus speaks in harmony with the supreme teachings of all the great religions: the Upanishads, the Tao Te Ching, the Buddhist sutras, the Zen and Sufi and Hasidic Masters.

The Hindu master Ramana Maharshi said, "The ultimate is so simple. . . ." He continued:

This is all that needs to be said. All religions have come into existence because people want something elaborate and attractive and puzzling. . . . Only mature minds can grasp the simple truth in all its nakedness.

And the Sufi Mystic, Hafiz, said:

I have learned so much from God that I can no longer call myself a Christian, a Hindu, a Muslim, a Buddhist, a Jew.

My mind reeled with excitement. I ravaged the shelves and found a copy of the Tao Te Ching. A slim volume of romantic mysticism, it was written by China's Lao Tzu in the sixth century B.C.E. and pointed to an ineffable way, or natural process, of all things.

The Tao that can be spoken is not the eternal Tao;
The name that can be named is not the eternal name.
The nameless is the beginning of heaven and earth.
The named is the mother of the ten thousand things.
Ever desireless, one can see the mystery.
Ever desiring, one can see the manifestations.
These two spring from the same source, but differ in name;
  this appears as darkness.
Darkness within darkness, the gate to all mystery.

The gate of misty mystery moves in godlike ways. In accord with the universal Tao, the road to reconciliation with myself, my true self, promised nothing less than authentic peace. I was intrigued. Still, I couldn't pretend to understand every allegory woven into the text, and God was pretty much left out, unless the Tao, or way, *was* God.

There is a being, wonderful, perfect; It existed before heaven and earth. How quiet it is! How spiritual it is! . . . All life comes from it.

I easily connected with how Taoism regarded nature. Taoism's landscape art often depicted a tiny human form trudging beneath a burden or poling a boat. The individual ego was minimalized on its journey, immersed in sublime nature.

I scanned the shelves and moved on to a commentary on Buddhism. Siddhartha Gautama was born around 563 B.C.E. and experienced many trials on his journey to enlightenment. He hinted that nirvana was an eternal state of godhead bliss attainable by any human spirit. I was most captured by one of the Buddha's greatest dictums:

Betake yourselves to no external refuge. Work out your own salvation with diligence.

What the fuck? My own salvation?

My laughter echoed off the walls in the living room. I felt dazed and dumb, like I was high, like my old religion lay in ruins around me. It was insane! I began to view my formative beliefs—maybe all beliefs—as a big joke! *The biggest ever!*

I scoured the shelves for more books. After I had exhausted the religious literature, I moved on to pseudo-spiritual texts with titles like *Hero with a Thousand Faces* and *The Tao of Pooh*. It was preposterous fun. My mind leaped into virgin territories by the hour, by the minute, and lit up like floodlights flipped on at a stadium, panel by panel. My body quivered with excitement and exhaustion. Until finally, after forcing consciousness for nearly three days, I felt a chill and stopped.

In a matter of minutes I began to shiver. Cold seeped into

my marrow and froze like spears of blue, glacial ice. It was nearly midnight and the air was cool anyway, so I covered up with a thick wool blanket, and then another. I put my down sleeping bag on top of that, but I couldn't get warm.

In a flash my goose bumps vanished. Now I sweated profusely. The only way to find relief was to sit on the cool cement floor in the kitchen and pour cupfuls of water from the rain barrel over my head and arms and legs. Afterward, I went to lie down in bed, where I shuddered and was seized with nausea. Shortly, I made a run for the bathroom to vomit and then squat. I limped back to the kitchen to repeat the cycle, and spilled more cool water over skin so fiery it crackled with heat.

The misery was unbearable. In my agony I wondered if this was God's puerile idea of I'll-show-you retribution. If that's how it was, I thought, then *screw him*!

I was exhausted and dehydrated—a condition with which I had become an old hand. Late in the night my fever broke. I fell asleep and lay there, still and dreamless, for more than twenty-four hours.

Five days after Brad, Cynthia, and Rolf had left, I awoke to the shrill whistle of a pair of bush babies playing in the trees outside. I moved to get up, but my head whirled in rushing Technicolor. I eased back down. For the moment I was content to watch the morning light gradually warm the room.

In a few minutes, a bird twittered past the window, sending its shadow across the wall and floor. It cheered and encouraged me, so I rolled onto my side and hoisted up on an elbow. I rested there for a minute. Then I kicked my legs off the bed and used them like a counterweight to help me duck under the mosquito net and sit up. I put my feet on the cold cement floor, palmed off the wall for balance, and came to my feet.

Hobbling like a ninety-year-old man, I worked my way

into the living room. I smiled when I saw it filled with beams of sunlight fresh from Mecca and a fastness of color that seemed to say, "Let's get cracking! Much to do!" But I had barely eaten in a week. As my mom would have instructed, I heated a kettle of water for tea and made some toast. I spread the toast with honey and took it and my tea to the living room table and sat down.

At least a dozen books lay in a heap on the table—trade paperbacks, an old Webster's dictionary, and my journal. All seemed to buzz microscopically, ready at my command to start the next round.

The dictionary caught my attention first and I remembered a word—"deism." I had read it somewhere in the stack, but I wasn't clear on what it meant. I paged through the Webster's. "Deist: One who believes in the existence of a God or Supreme Being but denies revealed religion, basing his belief on the light of nature and reason"

Nature and reason. Was I a deist? After evacuating my guts for the past two days, I knew one thing beyond any shadow of a doubt: I was definitely no longer (I breathed deeply) a Krishtean.

I stopped. The word, which had once been so familiar and inseparable from my identity, was now strange. The taste of it in my mouth was like the sweetly puffed PEEPS candy (made in Bethlehem, Pennsylvania) that I'd gobbled up on Easter mornings as a boy—full of nothing substantial.

I took another bite of toast and honey. A timid smile edged across my face. It was a little scary, like driving my first car, but felt liberating at the same time. I had given myself permission to feel and think and become who I already was. "I am not a Christian anymore." There, I'd said it. This was *way* past falling by the wayside. I was siding with the way-fallen, and I reveled in it.

I remembered something I had read in a book on the table. I found the book and opened it to a page I had earmarked.

> *This is the most important single moment in Oriental mythology, a counterpart of the Crucifixion in the West. The Buddha beneath the Tree of Enlightenment (the Bo Tree) and Christ on the Holy Rood (the Tree of Redemption) are analogous figures, incorporating an archetypal World Savior, World Tree motif, which is of immemorial antiquity . . .*

The passage came from *The Hero with a Thousand Faces* by renowned mythologist Joseph Campbell. He described a fundamental structure common to almost every story ever written, from the biblical account of Christ to more recent epics like *Star Wars*. Such stories portray the transformation of a hero through three basic stages—a call to adventure, a trial in the wilderness where a goal is achieved, and a return to the ordinary world with new knowledge.

I scanned down to a paragraph I had bracketed in pencil.

> *A hero ventures forth from the world of common day into a region of supernatural wonder: fabulous forces are there encountered and a decisive victory is won: the hero comes back from this mysterious adventure with the power to bestow boons on his fellow man.*

Mr. Campbell's lesson was this: Each of us is our own hero. We have all the gear and provisions needed to map the soul's wilderness. Becoming conscious of this insight is the first step in the journey.

I could certainly understand the atheist perspective. Atheism, however, was not an option for me because I'd been so deeply initiated in the mystery of nature and felt a kinship with its inherent wisdom. Pantheism seemed more in tune with my truth. In pantheism, all existence was a manifestation of the universal, immanent deity. Everything was divine, which turned earth into Earth. But I had to ask myself if that was where the question came full circle and the snake bit itself on the ass? That is, monotheism, one god?

On this subject, thus spoke Lao Tzu:

Do you have the patience to wait till your mud settles and the water is clear? Can you remain unmoving till the right action arises by itself?

My mind spun into the mud. I was stuck, and I did not have enough information to go on— not yet, anyway.

After I finished my toast and tea, I went to brush my teeth in the bathroom sink. I was glad to finally get the pukey taste out of my mouth. As I spit, rinsed, and wiped my face, something caught my attention in the mirror. Hanging brightly around my neck was the gold chain and cross my ex-wife had given me five years earlier. I had worn it ever since, and it had often comforted me in uncertain times. I had worn it for such a long time I'd forgotten about it. Now it felt ugly and fake.

Cautiously, like petting a dog you don't know, I unclasped it and studied it in the palm of my hand. The tiny, delicate-looking nodules were arranged in cruciform, and I admired how they caught the light and glittered. I flipped it over and my tentative regard eased into a sour grin. Finely printed engraving on the back of the cross read "EP GOLD," which stood for electroplated gold—shiny on the outside, junk metal on the inside.

I wrapped it in a wad of powder blue toilet paper and tossed it into the bathroom trash. When I heard it thud in the bottom of the can, a pang of guilt shivered through me. Bound up in that little golden lie was an intricate web of guilt spun from an inheritance of racism, sexism, religious jingoism, resource exploitation, and my own failed marriage.

I shook it off. I had only one more day in Arusha before heading back to Bukoba, and I needed to get out and walk and heal and work out the kinks. After I got dressed, I packed some food and water and went for a hike in the lower forests on Mount Meru one last time. Maybe I'd get lucky and find a philosopher's stone made of serpentine, or maybe a butterfly would lead me to a tree where I could meditate. Or maybe, just maybe, I'd run across an old man wearing a blue hat and ask him a question.

Where do I go from here?

BOOK THREE

Resurrection

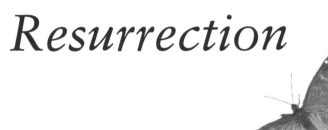

CHAPTER 20

Amulets and Spells

A LIGHT BREEZE had kicked up, and waxy, green leaves as big as umbrellas flopped and flashed about in the pellucid air. Gleaming puffs of white scooted out across the wild blue yonder. The rainy season had been a soggy one, but the farmers were happy, which included almost everyone.

The hard-packed dirt yard was still damp from all the rain, and an olive-drab nursery of moss suckled at the base of a mud-wattle house on the other side. Sofia stepped through the doorway. She walked over to her husband, Silvanus, and handed him something small I couldn't make out. He bowed his head to his wife, took the object, and turned to gaze into the *shamba*. I looked, too, but saw nothing out of the ordinary, only more banana and coffee trees.

He surprised me when he shouted into the *shamba* and shook whatever it was Sofia had given him. I got the impression he was incanting a spirit from beyond the grave. In a few moments he stopped shouting and extended his thin, wasting arms to the invisible interloper. When he opened his hands, five tinkling shafts of white dropped to the end of a string. They looked like small bones.

Silvanus turned to Gosbert. He spoke in a softer tone, though he still emphasized certain words by shaking the talisman in his hands. Gosbert translated the story to me in Swahili. "Silvanus, he says these are claws of the spirit-leopard. They are very old. Before Silvanus was born, when his father was a young boy, a leopard came to the Cave of God. It was night, and the people were dancing and speaking with the Chwezi ancestors. He says no one moved, no one spoke. His father, he was just a boy, and so afraid.

"But Silvanus's grandfather, he was also there. He was a holy man. He greeted the leopard and spoke to it in a strange language, and the leopard lay down and died, just there, at the Cave of God."

Silvanus shook the string of claws and spouted something that sounded important. Gosbert stopped to listen. "Mhmm. *Sawa, mzee*," *Okay, my elder,* he said, and turned to me. "Silvanus, he says his grandfather has just now spoken to him, there, from the *shamba*. They are wanting you to take these things because they will protect you as you travel, and help you to know life. But first, you must know death."

"Huh? You mean what happened on Mount Kenya?"

Gosbert smiled patiently. "Not here," he said, grabbing my upper arm, "and not here." He tapped my forehead. "But here," he said, and tapped my chest. "It is most strong, and it is time."

"But—"

A wind whipped up through the trees. Dust and twigs blew around in the air and the four of us squeezed our eyes shut and waited.

When it passed, Silvanus took my hands. He placed the amulets in my open palms and sandwiched them between his own gnarled and knotted hands. He closed his eyes and mumbled in Kihaya. When he opened his eyes, he stared into my face. In spite of his massive cataracts his gaze was intense, and almost telepathically I understood the claws were both a blessing and a responsibility. They were at least 150 years old. Europeans had not yet arrived here and the rhythms of tribal life had still been intact when Silvanus's grandfather had received them from the spirit-leopard. In a way, all of Africa since the beginning was smelted into these five ingots of bone.

Twenty months earlier I had given Sofia and Silvanus a rope in payment for information about the Cave of God. However, the rope had been more than enough. The amulets were meant to re-balance the books. They were also, I think, a gesture of approval. Silvanus was pleased I had tried to make it to another New Moon Ceremony, even though I had missed this one, too.

But the claws were so precious I did not think I deserved them. "*Bwana* Silvanus, *babu,*" grandfather, I said, "these things are very good, but they are yours. I cannot take them."

Silvanus' comprehension of Swahili was poor, but he read the tone of my voice. In answering, he patted his chest and gummed a mixture of Swahili and German. "*Mimi kaput! Kaput!*" and something else in Kihaya.

Gosbert translated. "He says he is finished and old, but these claws, they are not his, and they are not yours. We can only borrow them from the spirit-leopard."

Silvanus released my hands and crossed himself. Gosbert and Sofia did the same. Reluctantly, I crossed myself with the hand holding the claws. I then thanked the shamans with the smidgen of Kihaya I had picked up. "Thank you. Good very. Good keep." I wished I could say more and tell them how honored I was, but I think they understood.

Silvanus returned a grandfatherly smile, and this time he replied in German-American: "*Welkomen,* Bill-William. Okey dokey."

Gosbert and I thanked them again for their hospitality

during our unexpected visit. Having no telephone and a sporadic mail service, they were used to guests dropping in unan-
nounced. They thanked us for coming and extended open
invitations to return anytime. It was a powerful moment. I
felt like I had found my first ally and a whole continent of
allies, living and otherwise. Yet in the midst of all the pleasant sacraments, it was sad knowing I would likely never see
them or this magical place again.

Gosbert and I walked our bicycles to the path at the
edge of the yard. I stopped to wave. Sofia held up both
her hands, waving in the customary way, but Silvanus just
stood there, stock still. His outer eyesight had left him,
though his inner sight was keen and bright and would
accompany me always.

"*Bwana* Bill, you must return and visit—you, and Miss Chris,
and Mr. Rich, and the others," Gosbert said as he shook my
hand. "We will be missing all of you very much." He and I
stood outside his little shop, the only real building along the
road in Kashozi.

"Yes, my friend. You have helped so much. I will try to
visit. Someday." We paused. Each of us picked our nose. The
silence was awkward, and Gosbert reached over his shop
counter to turn on his favorite album, *Happy Nation* by Ace
of Base.

I looked out over the fields behind his shop in the direction
of the Cave That Ate the Bride. "Oh! *Bwana*, I am forget-
ting." I reached into my pocket for the paperclip I used as a
money clip. I pulled off a blue 500 shilling note and handed
it to him. "For the rope."

His eyes shot open. He had forgotten all about it, or at
least he hadn't brought it up. His surprise turned into laugh-

ter, and he slapped his thigh and held his chest, feigning heart failure. I couldn't help but join in.

When the laughter eased, we smiled at the ground for a long time. He sighed and extended his hand. "*Bwana* Bill, travel well, my friend." We shook hands, and I straddled my bike and kicked at the pebbled road.

I eased down into the seat, and from behind me I heard Gosbert's voice call out. "And *Bwana* Bill! Remember, it is a boat! With a Mercury motor! I will wait here!"

Sam arrived with the newest group of Peace Corps volunteers in January. Since he needed a place to stay, and my departure was fast approaching, I offered my house.

"Oh, it is very favorable that Mr. Samuel is here with you, Mr. Bill," Mr. Rwelengera said.

"Yes?"

"Oh, yes! Like you, he is coming from Illinoiz, so he is from your tribe."

In any event, Sam was a Stanford alum—not my tribe—sharp as a tack, and taught physics at Rugambwa. He was also a rock climber, so he and I spent off-hours putting up new top-rope climbs near campus. Perhaps his greatest talent, however, was his fiddle playing. He was classically trained and had a good ear, too, so our jam sessions included him on violin, Rich on sax or flute, me on guitar, and everyone else filling in with percussion on spoons, buckets, or whatever was handy.

Several other new volunteers had recently arrived, but Chris and Saito were both long gone, and time for me and Rich was ticking down fast. After my Peace Corps contract ended in June, I planned to climb in the Swiss Alps, eat French croissants, and drink German beer. When I got back to the States, I wanted to enroll in a NOLS instructor course in wilderness education. Sure, grad school was comfy, and researching the sacred caves in Tanzania would have taken me a long way toward a PhD, but for me that direction would have been more about ego and less about my freshly molted soul.

Rugambwa buzzed with so much excitement, though, it was hard to think about going home. My Form Six girls were busy cramming for their National Exams. This exam would determine whether they would go on to university to realize all their dreams or return to the *shamba* to dig root crops, haul water, have lots of babies, and wash lots of clothes—for the rest of their lives. The next two weeks were the turning point. I was busy, too, helping them find answers to questions from former exams. Under such stress, even Farida's normally self-assured composure began to buckle.

"It is especially this one!" she said. "*No one* can answer this question!" She and I sat on the top step of my front porch, going over old test questions.

"Yeah, it's a tough one, for sure," I said. "But there must be an answer, right?"

She looked pouty, like the little girl she used to be and to whom she occasionally reverted, not the young woman of nineteen whose smile reminded me of the glow on the lake at sunset. Or whose slender hands looked as if they could cast happy spells with a single touch.

A vervet monkey galloped across my roof with its tail arced high like a furry question mark. Vervets were little bigger than a house cat and were a common sight, so I refocused on the exam question. However, Farida had a different sort of question in mind, and I wondered if this had been the real reason for her visit.

"Mr. Bill, may I ask a question?"

"Sure."

"Do you . . ." She sighed and reached into the grass and plucked a few blades.

"Go on."

"Do you . . . believe in God?"

My teeth clenched. For a moment the world stopped spinning, second hands paused. I went blank. I didn't know how to tell her I was a born-again pantheist, washed in the "blood" of Mother Nature. True, it was more or less in line with our usual topics of conversation, but the way I looked at the world now was so completely different than a year earlier, I didn't know how she'd handle it, or if I could even express it. I still flinched every time I remembered I was no longer a Christian.

"Yes, Farida. I do believe in God, but"—her eyes blinked concern—"but not the same way you do."

"Oh, then I know this thing." She sounded relieved and pointed to my missing cross necklace. "It is okay-fine because you are Christian. Me myself, I am Muslim. Both children of Ibrahim."

"No. That's . . ." I sighed. "Farida, I am not a Christian—anymore."

Her face went stone cold.

"See, I do believe that God is in all things. *Is*, in fact, all things. Even people. Even you and me, I think."

Her full lips, the darker one above and lighter one below, parted slightly as her expression morphed into one of disbelief. "Mr. Bill!" She sat up straight and leaned away. "You mean like these poor people living in the rural areas? Like the native people?"

"Well, no. Not exactly. But I do respect their religions because they're so, you know, close to the Earth. You said yourself everybody worships God in their own way depending on where they live and what their physical landscape looks like."

"Yes, because, *Mungu*, He is everywhere, in all things."

"Like I said."

"But Mr. Bill, it is different."

"How is it different?"

"It is Allah—praise to Him—He is *in us*, but we are not *in Him*."

"That's your opinion."

"Hmph. But what must it be happening then, when these people who are refusing to believe, when they die? When you, yourself, will die?"

"You know what, I don't know, and I don't think anyone *can* know. Not for sure, anyway."

"But in the holy Quran, it is telling us we will go to heaven."

"Well, yeah, maybe, but no one *really knows*. I mean, you can *believe* and have *faith* in whatever you want, and that's comforting, I guess. But just look at all the science that shows us where we came from and how things work. And history, too, how each one of the holy books has changed and been rearranged and rewritten until it's completely different. See what I mean?"

How could she? Maybe she was too young to understand? Or too old?

Then she surprised me. "I am not sure, Mr. Bill, but I am thinking you may somehow be correct."

"Really?"

"But not completely. You see, what I am saying is this; we have Allah, and the Christian God, and this Jewish Yahweh, yes? Even these pagan ones."

I nodded.

"I think we are agreeing they are names for this one God, who cannot be named."

I waited.

"Therefore, each religion can be correct, but it is because *people* are selfish, mistaking things for themselves that is making each religion incorrect. *Sawa mwalimu?*"

I stared into the yard.

She could see I was having trouble following her, so she simplified it for me. "Perhaps it is like this examination." She pointed to the test paper in my hand. "To be correct is not the same as to be true. Therefore, I think we must not be taking ourselves—or God—too serious."

Pure silence surrounded us.

She abruptly smiled, buried her face in her hands, and snorted a laugh. I was speechless. I was mesmerized by her simple profundity—and by who she was.

"Anyway, I find *my* kind of God in nature," I said, tapping my chest. I hoped to convey my belief in the interchangeable locations of heart, Earth, and divinity.

"*Sho!*" She looked up from her hands. "In these terrible places where you are conquering mountains?"

I leaned closer. "Listen, kiddo, just between you and me, no one can *conquer* a mountain. You can only conquer what's in here," I said, pointing to my head.

"You know, Mr. Bill, these things we are saying, I think I must first pray and ask *Mungu*."

I cleared my throat. "Good. You do that. But for now—"

"And *you*, Mr. Bill, you should also be to pray and listen to God," she said, and pointed to my chest, "in your heart!" On reflex, I grabbed her hand. We stopped, and our fingers curled around each other. Tensions evaporated. We could no longer ignore our attraction to each other and the feeling that we were connected in a special, spiritual sort of way. As we sat hand in hand on my front porch step, Farida put her head on my shoulder and we allowed ourselves a moment of simple closeness. Because we knew it would all soon be coming to an end.

Across the road, three kids shouted and threw stones at a monkey stealing corn from someone's garden. Shadows from eucalyptus trees played about on the grass, and out on the lake another dark and twisting swatch of lake flies wound higher into the sky, shifting at random like a water spout. The world started spinning again, and the lake was calm and wide and blue as always.

And as always, something unimaginable was about to happen.

CHAPTER 21

Limbo

CLASS RAN LATE. The last bell had rung, teatime had come and gone, and the O-level students had started their afternoon chores. In the geography room, my Form Six students had spent the entire afternoon debating every possible exam question and had arrived at either moot, philosophical conclusions or personal opinions. Conversation dwindled until no one spoke.

"Okay. I think we're done," I said. I was tired but satisfied with what we had accomplished, so I closed the reference books on the teacher's desk. "I think you're ready for your exams, and I wish you all *bahati njema*." *Good luck*. The students were silent. As I gathered my things I began to feel as if I were the only person in the room.

Finally, someone in the back row broke the silence. "Thank you, Mr. Bill."

A swarm of others followed. "Yes! Thank you, very much!" "We are thanking you, Mr. Bill."

The moment was melancholy. My students and I had shared in one another's lives for the past two years, and I would miss them all. I would especially miss my "kiddo," even though I hadn't been able to look at her all day. She had avoided me, too. Thinking about it flushed my cheeks as I opened the battered, knobless old door for the last time and made my way home. I was about to leave a land that had fundamentally changed me. What had formerly been unknown was now safe, and what had formerly been safe was unknown. I would again be entering a state of in-betweens.

As I approached the back door of the house, I noticed an army of ants. They were huge and black, and they boiled over an invisible corridor that led to their latest entrée. I stooped down to see what they were dismantling and spied a crisp, translucent film splayed out on the red earth. It was a snakeskin. I had recently seen skins like this almost every day and suspected molting was common after the long rains.

I stepped over it and walked in the back door. I tossed my book bag on the table. Sam sat on the couch reading a newspaper.

"Hey, Sam."

"Bill. How was class?" He shuffled to the next page without looking up.

"Good. Hey, you going to town later?"

"No. I just got back." He let the newspaper go slack between his hands. "I did run into Rich, though, and he asked me to spread the word that he's hosting a big party over at his place Monday night. I just told Dan." Dan was a British volunteer who'd been teaching mathematics at Rugambwa.

I stuck my face inside our dorm-sized fridge, hunting for leftovers. "So a party," I said.

"Yeah. Monday night. His place."

"Cool. What do we bring?"

A lag in his response made me look around the corner.

"It appears that we are in charge of *senene*."

I stood up and took a bite from a plate of last night's spaghetti dinner. "Grasshoppers!"

Sam chortled and shook his head.

"You know, I actually had some last year," I said, "and they're not bad. I think we fried them up with salt and cumin—they're like popcorn, with eyes."

Sam winced.

"Anyway, count me in." I slurped a few more strands of spaghetti and returned the rest to the fridge. "I think I'll take a nap. Class wiped me out. But I'm on for dinner, right?"

"Sure."

I went to my ten-foot-by-ten-foot cement-block room and closed the door. I lifted the corner of the mosquito net and crawled in. As I lay there, I reviewed the day: the muezzin's call to prayer on the mosque's loudspeakers in town; the girls assembling in the main yard at 7:00 to sing the school song and raise the flag; me writing on the chalk board "Vernacular culture regions are neither intellectual creations or formal regions based on specific criteria."

"Mr. Bill?" Farida had said.

"Yes, Farida."

"Neither is complemented by nor, is it not?"

I had grumbled something and chalked in an N.

As I lay in bed, a heavy, downward-whirling sensation filled my bones. I was on the verge of sleep, but a scritch-scratching sound kept me awake. Every day dozens, maybe hundreds of geckos scampered around the house, suctioning their wee toes onto floors, walls, and ceilings. Other than leaving their teeny turds strewn about, they weren't much of a bother, unless I was trying to fall asleep.

One of them had once climbed onto the inside of the mosquito net over my bed. At the exact moment I woke up and yawned, it lost its footing. Luckily, I had turned my head just as it slapped onto my face and stuck to my cheek. Nevertheless, I much preferred geckos to the rat I'd caught nibbling on my hair one night on a train ride to the coast.

I was thinking too much, and there it was again, a scratching noise right behind my head. I sighed, opened my eyes, and turned my head to look. Instantly, I froze. Wrapped around my bedpost was a black mamba—one of the deadliest snakes in Africa.

My brain kicked in to overdrive. The Peace Corps had told us that after being bitten by a mamba, a victim might live for another twenty minutes, writhing in pain.

I didn't breathe. We locked eyes. Its scales were ashen-drab and its forked tongue zipped in and out of its namesake inky mouth. If I moved too fast it might attack, too slow and it would catch me for sure. I swallowed hard and opted for slow. I moved a hand and then a foot out from under the netting. I watched the serpent. It never moved, just its tongue.

"Sam!"

"Yeah!"

"Bring the machete!"

Sam read the alarm in my voice and entered the room a moment later. He had a machete and a garden hoe.

"Jesus Christ!" he shouted. "Kill it there? Where it can't strike?"

"No time. Hit the bedframe with the hoe. Scare it to the floor." I took the machete. "Wait! Close the door."

Sam shut the door and the mamba flexed its cobra-like neck flaps. Sam hit the bed with the hoe. In a flash the snake disappeared under the bed. Then it shot out at the bottom of the far wall. When it reached the corner, it climbed up to try and escape. It climbed six or seven feet and fell back to the floor. Then it tried again.

"Pin it with the hoe!" I yelled. Sam crammed the butt-end of the hoe into the corner. He pinned the snake. It squirmed and writhed.

"Hurry!" Sam shouted.

I jabbed the machete over the top of the handle until it made hard contact with the wall. I twisted the blade and ground it into the cement. The snake's head flopped over and fell to the floor.

We stood in shocked silence for a moment. Sam finally broke the spell. "Holy shit! How the hell did it get in here?"

I panted hard. I couldn't answer.

Like the professor at the end of *War of the Worlds*, we crept toward the reptilian invader. The mamba's round black eyes continued to blink. Its mouth opened and closed around its fangs as if trying to say something. Carefully I picked up the longer portion of the snake, now limp and completely lifeless on the cement floor. Surprisingly little blood had oozed out.

I was fascinated and I looked closer. Only a minute before it had been a living, breathing creature. A spasm of guilt coiled up inside me even though I knew the mamba could have killed me if it had wanted to. Regardless, I empathized and identified with this serpent, and now I had killed it.

I recalled one of Rolf and Cynthia's books, *The Hero with a Thousand Faces*. Joseph Campbell said many cultures considered the snake to be a symbol of energy and transformative power. Campbell described a moment near the climax of the mythic journey when the protagonist kills the dragon and assimilates its power. This power allows the hero to transcend her former level of consciousness.

I carried the mamba's body out the back door and flung it past a grazing cow. The ants would probably eat it. I saw a twig on the ground and it gave me an idea, so I picked it up and went back inside. Sam was already trying to scoop up the snake's head with the blade of the hoe.

"Hang on," I said. I knelt down and put the twig in its mouth. The head was still conscious and clamped down on it. In this way I carried the mamba's head outside. After about five minutes, its eyes glazed over and its jaw stopped moving.

Sam and I went back inside and promptly set about rummaging through all the pillows, sheets, and couch, also checking under the fridge—everywhere. "Must have come in when the door was open," I said. In recent months I had started to leave the doors unlocked or even standing wide open when I was away, and it was not just because Sam had moved in. I'd been doing it since I had returned from Mount Kenya.

"Or under a closed door. See that space over the threshold?" Sam said. He squatted and pointed to an inch gap between the bottom edge of the back door and the cement floor. "We'll have to cover that or fill it with something, for sure."

I got down on all fours to look. I was reminded of all the old snake skins I had seen lately—telltale signs of growth and change. "Yeah," I said. "Definitely."

A legal-sized parchment was pinned to the bulletin board outside the headmistress' office. It bore a notice in heavy black letters.

FORM VI GRADUATION, SATURDAY, 18TH MAY, 1996, NINE O'CLOCK IN THE MORNING. A CONGRATULATION TO FORM VI.

I knew how Rugambwa's ceremonies worked. If I showed up at 9:00 in the morning on graduation day as the poster advertised, I'd be admiring the pretty landscape all by myself. People started to trickle in around 11:00, and if all went well, commencement might begin at noon. Sharp.

On the morning of the big day, Sam and I walked up to Dan's house, played cards, and kept watch from his back door. Noon came and went. Several people had started to congregate around the doors to the dining hall, the site of the ceremony, but the guest speaker—a bigwig from the Ministry of Education—was late. He was red-eyed and punchy when he finally showed up at 1:00. On that cue, I tied my hair back, cinched up my skinny black tie—the only one I owned—and the three of us walked over to the school.

Graduation was always a combination of liturgical protocol and boisterous fun. Teams of girls put on skits that always had a moral message to the story. For this occasion the Form Five girls role-played a Tanzanian family whose eldest daughter was enrolled in secondary school (very apropos). The family's youngest daughter happened to be in the throes of romantic love (which was, I could only guess, also very apropos). The recipient of her affections was played by a Rugambwa girl. As fate would have it, the younger daughter wished to marry immediately; alas, custom required the older one to wed first. The studious, older girl, however, had no interest whatsoever in such trivial, unintellectual affairs as love and marriage. She instead preferred to partake of the more cultured, Western things in life. The younger girl then enlisted eligible bachelors (also played by Rugambwa girls) in a desperate attempt to interest her sister in love and liberate herself from her lovesick purgatory.

All lines were spoken in unamplified English, which was a stretch for the younger students to comprehend. Still, everyone understood the trajectory of the plot and delighted in the performance. All 600-plus students were present, including teachers—Mr. Rwelengera officiated—so it was a full house of celebration. Even the churlish headmistress, Ms. Coelestine, caught herself chuckling. The play was followed with song, drum, and dance performances.

Speeches came next. The visiting Minister of Education had sobered up, and rambled on about how the country needed qualified secretaries and assistants to help serve their male superiors. My girls shot sidelong glances at one another. Farida rolled her eyes.

The Form Six students finally received their diplomas right before dinner. Everyone went outside for photos, laughter, and hugs—between students, that is. Farida and I glanced at each other across the yard. She smiled at me briefly and looked back to her friends. She seemed jubilant, independent, and grown-up, and I was happy for her, but sad, too. Part of me wanted to say something, to start something I'd been dreaming about, but my dreams that afternoon fluttered away as carefree as a butterfly. I let them go and walked home.

Two days passed. I hopped over the open sewer ditch on my way to the market to shop for *senene*. To me they looked like grasshoppers, but they were actually katydids. After the rainy season, people carried burlap bags into the grassy *rweya* fields above town, hunting for fresh crops of the bugs.

As I'd told Sam, I had eaten them on one or two occasions a year earlier. After helping Mr. Rwelengera catch some, we'd gone back to his house and sat on his front porch with the writhing sacks next to us. We extracted the goods one at a time and pulled the legs and wings off. Then we deposited the head, thorax, and abdomen—the edible parts—from each one into a bowl. It was something I might have enjoyed as a kid, but as an adult it took some getting used to. Besides, I had practically converted to vegetarianism by that time.

Locals caught other kinds of tasty bugs, too. At night, people often stood underneath streetlamps and whirled burlap bags around in the light. Finer-meshed nets were used to catch lake flies. Great tornadoes of the insects some-times moved in off the lake, and if you owned any sort of

cloth material it could be wetted and waved through the air.
Hundreds of the flimsy creatures would stick to the mesh.
The flies were later scooped out and meted into patties and
fried in a skillet like burgers.

As I shopped for *senene* that day at the market, I had a
flashback of the Cave That Ate the Bride. It was the cave that
Gosbert and I had descended into, and he had told me the legend of how a young woman had been chasing *senene* when
she'd fallen to her death in the cave. The memory made me feel
strange, but it quickly passed. I bought a quarter kilo of *senene*,
which filled a bag the size of a soccer ball, and went back out to
the street where I'd chained my bike to an awning post.

"Mr. Bill!" "Hello, Mr. Bill!"

My former students smiled and waved as they walked over.
Sister Zawadi, Miriamu, Bertha, and Farida were dressed in
their town best. Farida and Miriamu wore ivory-colored silk
shawls, fringed with teardrop-shaped beads. Sister Zawadi
wore her habit. She and Farida had reconciled their differences months earlier and were friends again.

"Aren't you ladies catching a boat tonight?"

They squealed with excitement and spoke over one another.
"Yes!" "It is true!" "We are going home!" "It is a long time
now, Mr. Bill."

"Well, congratulations. I'm very proud of you, and I had a
lot of fun being your teacher."

Sister Zawadi answered first. "Yes. And you, too, Mr. Bill.
We very much enjoyed your classes."

"And the Geography Club," Farida said. "I especially
enjoyed the rock climbing and the waterfall."

"Yes. It was great. But what are you all doing here at the
market?"

"As you know, Mr. Bill," Sister Zawadi said, "we are shopping for these certain foods that can be eaten on the ship."

"We have only these third-class tickets," Miriamu explained, "so no rooms and no food. We can be sleeping in the bottom of the ship."

"Well, then it sounds like a good idea," I said.

"Okay, Mr. Bill," said Farida. "We must shop! Time, it is rushing!"

I tried to think of something to say to her, but there was really nothing left. Infatuated hopes and dreams had melted into memory. I smiled, got on my bike, and waved. "*Safari njema, wanawake!*" *Travel well, ladies!*

"*Asante, Mr. Bill!*" "*Safari njema.*" "*Kwaheri!*" *Good-bye,* they said, glowing in their sterling, new achievement.

I rode into the crowded, dirt street, but a voice stopped me. "I say! Mr. Bill! I say!" I stopped and looked back to see Farida running across the street in her black patent leather shoes. A frailty came over me and my defenses dissolved. Even though I no longer considered "interracial comingling" perverse or radical, I convinced myself I wasn't ready—probably—for *any* kind of relationship.

Farida sprinted up and almost ran into me. I caught hold of her waist. Her face glided up to within inches of mine, and for a moment nothing else existed. As I had on Mount Kenya, I was falling, and life was peaceful and clear. Farida and I floated in limbo between this place and the next, and into it she held up a small slip of paper. "Take this, Mr. Bill," she said, softly but with a flare in her eyes. "It is for you. For a remembering."

I was numb. I had the urge to kiss her in the middle of the street, but I only managed to nod my dumb head and take the paper from her long, slender fingers.

She smiled and darted back across the street to her friends, who closed in around her with surprised and curious expressions. I unfolded the slip of paper. Farida's name and mailing address were penciled in with a note below that read, *Just in case.*

Farida turned and waved from the entrance to the market. "*Kwaheri mwalimu!*" *Good-bye, teacher*, she shouted. I didn't answer. I only waved with the hand that held the note. I could see she was heartsick, and I felt a similar clot of emotion rising in my throat, too. I pocketed the note, turned, and rode on. I didn't look back.

Mpira wa miguu. Soccer. Football. In Tanzania, all refer to same thing—the sport where the expats get beaten, badly and repeatedly, by the locals. We twenty- and thirty-something volunteers stood no chance against the lanky teens who had been playing since they were very young. Mercifully, they suggested we reshuffle players to include some of us and some of them on each team. I suspected they were looking for more challenge.

The game withered as evening approached. I was hungry, so I walked over to Rich's house, a few hundred yards away. More than a dozen friends had shown up. We popped open Tuskers and Fantas, dealt out cards, and loaded the cassette player with everything from Counting Crows to John Denver. A box of Slim Panatela cigars—made in Holland, though Arabic was printed on the cases—made the rounds, but Rich insisted we take the stinky smokes outside. A female Japanese volunteer teaching at Ihungo braided my hair. At one point somebody grabbed a rope and started up a round of limbo. I performed poorly at the game. I wore a purple and red, wraparound *kikoi* from Zanzibar that looked a lot like a dress, and I was certain it limited my normally flexible physique—a likely excuse.

The leopard claws were in my daypack. I wasn't sure why I had brought them along. Maybe I wanted to show them to everybody and tell them what had happened, but I changed my mind. The timing was off. The mood wasn't right. Something wasn't right.

By midnight, folks had crashed on couches or in nests of pillows on the floor. Rich had a couple of guest rooms for those of us still standing. Content with food, friendship, and warm thoughts of home, I dreamed.

Gray mist surrounds a group of Tanzanians. They are young women wearing school uniforms, but they are faceless and I cannot recognize them. Four climb into a small boat. They float onto a lake, not large, more like a pond. A dark murk of forest haunts the far bank.

In the middle of the lake, the boat starts to sink. The young women scream. I want to help, but I am not really there and they cannot see me. The boat sinks and they thrash and flail and try to swim, but only one reaches shore. The others all drown.

I awoke with a shot. Lightning had smacked hard and close. It made the single-paned windows rattle in their rectangular metal frames. Tree limbs clawed at the glass. Rain pounded like steel balls against the bedroom windows, and I thought they would surely break. The sky crackled and rumbled.

I burrowed deeper into my warm, dry woolen blankets. The lapse between lightning flashes and thunder claps soon widened, and the rain eased, its energy spent. I fell into a dreamless sleep.

"Yo, Rich!" I yelled.

"Yeah!"

"Where do you put your bottles?"

Rich stuck his head into the kitchen. He held a broom. "There should be a crate under the sink." He pointed to the floor behind me, and I unloaded the empties I had gathered from the previous night's party. It was late morning, and everyone was more or less conscious, sweeping and picking up. Dan scrambled a few dozen eggs to accompany the toast and jam Rich had set out. By noon guests were at the front door thanking Rich for his hospitality.

"Guess I'll see you Friday at the Lake?" I said as I clipped my helmet on over my new braids.

"Yep. I'll be there," Rich said. "Students are gone, so this week's pretty casual. I'm helping some local kids get started in the new computer lab. And packing up." The grin on his face said it all.

"Me too," I said. "Time to go home." I walked my bike onto the path in front of his house. Fallen tree branches and trash littered the yard. "Hell of a storm last night!"

"Yeah! Guess I have some work to do."

I waved and pedaled off down the well-shaded lane that wound into town. Conditions routinely made it preferable for vehicles to drive around this road rather than on it, but today it was even more rutted than usual. Little rivulets of water snaked their way down. My bike had no fenders, and I felt the red mud spattering up over the back of my shirt. But I didn't care. Nothing could touch me now.

But when I rode into town it was as if I had descended into an alien atmosphere. Streets usually clogged with bicycles and people were almost empty. Tight crowds gathered around certain shops, the ones the Indians owned that had televisions. I heard a peculiar, solemn chatter, too, and mutterings about "Mwanza," and "the storm," and "so many people." Women in the centers of the crowds wept, and everyone wore drawn, cloudy expressions.

I was confused and uneasy, but I decided not to stop. I rode past Raza's bicycle shop, past the blue mosque and the market, the Rose Café, and the Lake Hotel. Sam had left Rich's place earlier that morning and had talked about rock climbing on the cliffs overlooking the port. The day was sunny and cool, great weather for it, and I had told him I'd meet him back at the house.

But the day was getting on, so I geared my bike low and cranked hard up the hill. It felt good to push my body like that. A rhythmic *thump-thump* surged through my temples and filled my muscles with taut yet supple life. I zipped up past the whitewashed Catholic church, where a troop of monkeys had once bombed me with handfuls of half-eaten cashews. Next I passed the place where several men had chased a huge snake, probably a mamba, into a ditch. They had beaten it to death with big sticks.

Finally I turned onto Rugambwa Lane and took the side path up to my house. I breathed hard when I pulled up to the front door. I pressed a button on my sweaty wristwatch. Eleven minutes, thirty-seven seconds from the bottom of the hill. Not bad, I thought. I dismounted and pushed my bike into the house. The front door stood open.

"Yo, Sam!" I parked my bike against the living room wall and turned around as Sam came in from his room. His face was pursed, especially around the eyes. "Sam?" He opened his mouth but was unable to speak. He shook his head.

Abruptly, a man's voice, high-pitched and breaking, shouted from outside. I went to the front step. It was Mr. Rwelengera. He looked shocked and afraid. He raised his trembling hands and held the sides of his head as if protecting himself. "Oh! Mr. Bill! Mr. Samuel! It is so terrible! This ship, the *Bukoba*! It has gone down sinking! And so many, they have all died!"

CHAPTER 22

Metamorphosis

FEATURES AFRICA NETWORK
NEWS BULLETIN, MAY 25, 1996.
LAKE DISASTER TOLL MAY BE 1,000

According to the latest reports from Mwanza, divers who entered the sunken ferry Bukoba *and removed bodies on Friday say they think there are more than 1,000 bodies on board. Tanzanian officials said more than 500 were killed but the exact toll was unclear as they had differing figures for the number aboard when the vessel capsized and sank on Tuesday. The ferry has a legal capacity of 430. Twenty-eight bodies were recovered before Friday. A total of 114 survivors have been officially listed but the ship's owners say more may have survived but not notified the authorities. By Friday rescuers had recovered 158 bodies but stopped the operation at dusk.*

I didn't move. I watched a creature go from one flower to another and then another. Each time it moved or changed direction, it emitted a flatulent sound that made me smile. At first I thought it was a bumblebee, but when I looked closer I saw it was an African sunbird. Sunbirds are related to hummingbirds and are one of the smallest birds on Earth. Darting in and out of a quilt of wildflowers so sprightly and with such precision, it held my complete attention and for a moment I forgot everything else. The flowers, yellow orchids, were pretty, too.

Rubare Forest was a glen of eastern red pine two miles from school. I liked to follow animal trails deep inside its labyrinth, where I could sit and listen and watch. No one ever went through the forest, so for a little while I had the rare luxury of being outside my house and alone at the same time. The forest floor was padded with pine duff. A sparse understory gave it an easy, open feel that inspired deep breathing and thinking and healing. Nature, even planned nature, has a special talent for administering this therapy. Unfortunately, while the Latin word for nature, *natura*, means "to be born," this place rested squarely on its death bed. Loggers had been whittling away at it for over a year. I predicted the entire forest would be clear-cut within a month or two.

I took off my daypack and sat down on the crunchy, red duff and propped my back against a low outcrop of quartzite. Turquoise-colored lichens and mosses shingled the rock. I rested my head on it and closed my eyes. I thought about my climbing friends, Josh, Brad, and Cynthia and Rolf; and folks around school like Sam, Chris, Saito, and Rich; and all my African friends, including Gosbert, Silvanus and Sofia, the Ramji brothers, Mr. Rwelengera, and the Mollel family.

I also thought about Rugambwa, and all the young women who had just graduated and were so happy and bursting with life. They had been so excited to go home and get on with their lives. Many had been my students. One had become my teacher, a special friend, and might have become much more. Now I would never know.

A week had passed since Mr. Rwelengera delivered the horrible news. As soon as he had said it, I felt like I'd been hit in the stomach with a ball bat. My legs had buckled and I collapsed onto the floor. I had almost passed out.

Now, memories and regrets caught up with me and streamed back onto the rock. Farida was gone, never to return. I cried so hard I thought my heart would break in two.

Later I wiped my warm, wet face with my hands as a breeze whispered through the pine branches. I lay there for a while, breathing, and watching the sky. When I noticed my daypack, I reached into it for the leopard claws. Maybe I wanted to affirm my sadness as well as my grasp of what Silvanus had told me, but I held them up to the sky. They tinkled together in the breeze.

Instantly, the side of my neck erupted into fiery pain. Tiny mandibles had pierced my skin, and I violently slapped and plucked a carnivorous *siafu* ant from behind my ear. I crushed it between my fingers. When I opened my hand, I realized that the endless cycle of growth, decay, death, and rebirth are not only *parts* of life, they *are* life, the meaning of which is to live. I looked at the ant in my hand and I finally saw God—dead, buried, and resurrected, every day. Everywhere.

A Form Four student whom I had seen around campus but didn't know was on board the ship that night. She had happened to be above deck when the ship capsized and was later picked up by fishermen. Her name was Heavenlight. She later described how overloaded the ship had been, with trucks and bananas and bags of·grain and all the people—1,200 people on a ship designed to carry 430.

Hundreds of people had bribed port officials to board an already overloaded ship. Raza told me this when I saw him in town a few days after it happened. He told me about one of his friends, a shopkeeper, who had owned a car. The man had missed the ship's departure in Bukoba, so he drove like mad to Kemondo Bay, a short stopover point along the coast. He had bribed his way on board from there.

Many stories like this circulated as death tolls ranged from 500 to over 1,000. Final figures settled down somewhere in between, but the upshot was the same: a massive loss of life. The catastrophe came to be known as the "Tanzanian Titanic."

Heavenlight said she had seen water lapping over the first-floor deck that night. Later, when the storm rolled in, she described how the boat had started to pitch and roll, and many people in the hull came out on deck. Hundreds had huddled together against the wind and rain on one side of the ship, which tipped it sideways. When the ship had started to take on water on one side, those above deck ran to the opposite side, en masse. This created the same situation, only with increased inertia. Back and forth it went, until the ship completely capsized a few miles offshore from Mwanza.

Many of those on board had been newly graduated young people. An entire girls' choir was lost. Rich said dozens of students and teachers from Ihungo had died in transit, and their headmaster alone lost twenty-three relatives. Since Rich was still on campus when it happened, his school's administration had asked him to go to Mwanza and identify Ihungo's dead. Rich was reluctant but finally agreed and traveled third class on the *Serengeti*. He said it was a grisly task. Hundreds of bodies had been recovered by a South African scuba team and laid out in a soccer stadium for identification. Overwhelmed with memories, as well as the sheer number of casualties, Rich said he had reached a point where he felt unable to go on. Only after Josh met him at the stadium to lend emotional support had he been able to finish the job.

Rich also described initial rescue efforts. After the *Bukoba* capsized, the stern portion of the hull had bobbed in the air. A small boat carrying rescuers had gone out to try and help. They heard people inside the ship, swimming, banging on the metal hull, screaming in the absolute darkness. Desperate to do something, the well-meaning rescuers had used a blow-torch to cut an escape hole. After the heavy metal flap had dropped into the hull, a child was passed into the arms of rescuers at the precise moment all remaining buoyancy was lost. The ship glided swiftly to the bottom.

Days into the rescue, divers had found a dead man sitting upright in an air pocket in his first-class cabin. Writing by flashlight, he'd kept a journal for two days until he exhausted his supply of oxygen. Later it was discovered that the man's name was Abu al-Banshiri, the second-in-command of a lit-tle-known organization called Al Qaeda.

Unlike this freak discovery, most of the bodies found by the scuba team were so tightly crammed into underwater pockets they had to be cut out. After the second week of such gruesome recovery efforts, the number of crocodiles and other aquatic scavengers made it too dangerous for the team to continue its work, and diving was called off.

Following the M.V. *Bukoba* tragedy, I heard the cries of Muslims, Hindus, Christians, and others. They prayed to a god or gods, spirits or ancestors, or some divine combination. Whatever an individual's version of the absolute, the timbre of their prayers was hauntingly consistent. "Oh! It is terrible! Unspeakable! We miss them so, but they are with us, and they are with God always."

Across Tanzania and across the continent, millions of prayers lifted from the lips of those at mosques, temples, synagogues, churches, sacred caves, and mountain shrines. In that moment all worlds came together at the mystical bottom line, which cannot be named. It was the root of religion, beyond religion. In my recent experience, it was the door, the way out, but it was not a mere stone to be rolled away from the entrance, because it did not exist in the realm of the rational mind at all.

To me, spiritual liberation intimated that we were *part of* something immeasurably small, empty, and void, yet which held and created all things. We were not separate from it, as religion would have us believe. Death, in each of its transformational masks, is the key to opening that door, and the key to rebirth.

Perhaps to see it we needed only practice what Farida advised and take ourselves and God a little less seriously.

A chainsaw ripped into my daydream. Loggers were working on the far side of what was left of Rubare Forest, and their gas-powered racket startled the sunbird. It buzzed away and left a lemon-colored orchid bobbing in its wake. High above the pine tops, clouds spooled out into cottony curls of ocher and aubergine. They also suggested I should go. I checked my watch; it was 5:30.

I snugged down my floppy safari hat and went to get up. But just as I did, a butterfly alighted on one of my bent knees. I didn't want to spook it, so I settled back to admire its delicate indigo wings, fanning up and down, cooling itself. As I watched, I was overcome with a sudden flush of tears. I closed my eyes. An unstoppable lump dropped into my throat and I reached out to everything I was a part of, into all creation, and with love—for my parents, my world, and even myself—I completed the last step of my transformation. I forgave.

Mr. Bill. What do you call this one?
That is a but-ter-fly, Farida.
But-ter-fly.
Yes. Good. How do you say it in Kiswahili?
It is called kipepeo.
Ki-pe-pe-o.
Yes! Very good, Mr. Bill!

I looked again and the butterfly was gone.

CHAPTER 23

Ascension

THE FLIGHT ATTENDANT smiled and nodded as I handed her my guitar case. She turned and stored it in the coat closet. As I walked back to my assigned seat, I saw an African woman, four East Asian businessmen, and a young couple who looked and sounded as if they were German backpackers. We were all headed in the same direction.

Our plane was a Gulf Air Boeing 767 Widebody. The economy seating area spanned eight seats across and was separated by two aisles—two seats, an aisle, four seats, an aisle, two seats. Mounted on each of the section partitions was a large, flat-screened monitor with digitized maps that showed the plane's speed, direction, altitude, and outside air temperature. It was more high-tech equipment than I'd seen in a long time, and I looked forward to seeing it work.

I peeked out my window at the drab, block buildings of Kilimanjaro International Airport. The forested slopes of Mount Kilimanjaro loomed dark behind them, and a thick layer of stratus obscured the upper peaks and the blue sky. Rolf and Cynthia were climbing Kilimanjaro again. This was their fourth excursion, and this time they were climbing via the Western Breach Wall on the Machame Route, or the Whiskey Route, often considered the most difficult approach to the summit. I wondered if they had made it above that cloud layer by now.

Rolf and Cynthia had left me the keys to their house so I could stay for a night, but I almost hadn't gotten there—or to the airport—on time. Two weeks after the disaster on Lake Victoria, nearly all ship traffic had stopped due to a national, three-day period of mourning declared by the new president, Benjamin Mkapa. I had tried to buy a ticket on the only twin-engine prop plane that flew out of Bukoba once each week, but it was down for repairs. And with the rainy season having just ended, overland travel around the lake was out of the question.

I was stuck. I had airline tickets to Paris in hand but no way to get out of Bukoba. I'd started to get nervous when Rich gave me a tip on buying a ticket for the M.V. *Serengeti*, the mainly cargo shipping vessel. I had been relieved to find a way out of town, but it was sad standing at the ship's rail, listening to the hull plow through the water as the lights of Bukoba drifted farther and farther behind.

That night I had slept in an overhead luggage rack in the lounge. The next morning, the ship had chugged into the frowning bay of Mwanza and given a courteous berth to the salvage vessels encircling the site of the M.V. *Bukoba*. Everyone on board the *Serengeti* had stood at the rail in solemn attention.

I had felt an urge to reach down and touch the water. I'd wanted to see if I could sense all those people, grasp their panic, grasp Farida. But the waterline lapped too low. Instead, I released the note she'd given me over the bow of the ship. When I looked up, I'd seen her radiance in the sunlight, her energy in the clouds, her spontaneity in a butterfly dancing with its reflection on the water.

The moment had been meditative, and I began to wonder

what I was going home to. I was a completely different person, and I wasn't sure how to tell my family and friends in a way they'd understand. It would be exhausting if I tried to pretend to be the person I used to be when I was around them just to keep the peace, and I worried it would crush them and they might ostracize me if they knew the truth.

The truth was that in Africa I had liberated myself from an identity and an outlook on life I found to be misleading at best. My parents never knew it, but their divorce had cracked that worldview. Ironically, this crisis had planted in me an impulse to search for answers. My own divorce widened these fractures along religious and ethnocentric lines of weakness, and after I followed a serpentine path into my subconscious, I discovered a new level of faith where the ultimate answers were the ultimate questions.

Ready for takeoff, I relaxed into my coach-class recliner. I popped a Bob Marley cassette into my Walkman, and in a few seconds "One Love" streamed in through my earphones. As I sang along, I couldn't help but smile as I imagined Bob being called a messiah a thousand years from now . . . if not already.

One love, one heart,
Let's get together and feel all right.

And everyone said, Amen.

Acknowledgments

I WAS THE fortunate child of parents who loved me and wanted only the very best for me. One of the ways they showed their love was to take me outdoors and introduce me to the magic of nature from the time I was in diapers. They fostered in me a connection with the Earth I have found invaluable, and I am deeply grateful to both of them.

My father often took me hunting when I was a boy. He also instilled in me the value of finishing projects that I begin. When I was five years old, my pony, Gypsy, bucked me off the first time I tried to ride her. Immediately my father snatched me up off of the ground—and out of the horse manure—and put me back into the saddle. This training to persevere has served me well on many occasions, not the least of which was successfully completing this book.

Nature was also intrinsically valuable to my mother, who liked to take me and my sister on hikes, picking wild blackberries in our pasture. Beginning with the natural food craze of the 1970s, she taught me to eat healthy foods and get regular exercise, practices I've carried into my adulthood. She also taught me to rise above whatever life throws at you, and to emerge stronger and with a smile on your face. Without the strength of character she instilled in me, much of the material for this book would have never materialized.

My family has given me so much love, yet I use the same

candid portrayal of them in this book as I do for myself, which is often less than flattering. Each scene, whether in Africa or growing up in the Midwest, has been selected to illustrate my transformational journey, and I describe those events to the best of my recollection. This story is my truth.

Figuring large in the shape of my experiences in Tanzania are, of course, the other Peace Corps Volunteers who shared my many adventures, alpine and otherwise. I thank all of the volunteers in my group, plus those I knew in groups immediately before and after mine, as well as the Peace Corps Tanzania staff. In my opinion, never has there been a more earnest endeavor attracting a more quality group of individuals than the United States Peace Corps.

I also wish to deeply thank all those Tanzanians whose names appear in my book as well as those who do not, who watched out for me when I never even knew, and who were part and parcel of Tanzania long before I arrived and long after I left. *Asanteni sana!*

Other friends and family who gave their advice, made editorial comments, or otherwise went to bat for me include Pip and Aaron Conrad, Dave and Avi Beaulieu, Patty Lataille and Jack Sciacca, Yvette Meftah, Lucy Probert, Rick and Bridget Marcus, Carolyn Smoyer, Vykie Whipple, Steve and Cea Tait, Rick Barandes and Leslie Griffith, Pam and Tom Parker, Corrinne and Gordon Schieman, Diane Stover, Debbie Westra, Bridget Hardy and Tom Casteel, Kelsey Hauck, Jean Colgan Gould (author of *Forty Years Since My Last Confession: A Memoir of a Catholic Journey Home*), Janet Goss (author of *Perfect on Paper*), and Polly Letofsky (author of *3MPH: The Adventure of One Woman's Walk Around the World*).

Others who helped to spread the word include Kizzen Laki, editor of *The Crestone Eagle Newspaper* in Crestone, Colorado; Friends of the Saguache Public Library in Saguache, Colorado; Lisa Marvel, owner/manager of The Book Haven, an independent bookstore in Salida, Colorado; and the Creede Arts Council, publishers of *Willow Creek Journal* in Creede, Colorado.

Thanks also to Jim Schneider, who helped in critical ways before I even left for Africa. Jim is formerly a co-director of the Life Adventures program at the YMCA in Belleville, Illinois, and taught me about rock climbing and caving. But more than any outdoor skill, he and his experiential program created a space in which I could incubate a new direction in life.

I especially wish to thank my publisher, Lantern Books; Kara Davis, managing director, for being interested to begin with; Martin Rowe, publisher at large, for giving me a second chance; and Wendy Lee, publishing director, whose patience and guidance eased my fears and helped coax the manuscript to completion.

Special thanks to Michael Henry, executive director and co-founder of Lighthouse Writer's Workshop in Denver, Colorado. As an earlier editor, Michael entered the picture at a crucial point and helped bring my manuscript to a level that got it noticed. He may not realize it, but he gave me the encouragement I needed to keep going when he said, "Bill, I think you have a knack for writing."

Thanks also go to Francelia Sevin and her private business, Education Editor. As my first editor on the road to publication, Francelia offered keen insights for molding my story into a form that would eventually make it coherent and meaningful.

Finally and most of all, I am forever grateful to my beautiful wife, Kim Smoyer, who endured all of my lectures, tirades, and ill-timed requests over the course of six years and twenty-two drafts. In return she gave her endless support, advice, and lots and lots of love. You are my hero.

Glossary of Swahili Words and Phrases

Abey (ah-BAY): What? Used by women, as opposed to the form used by men, which is **Naam?**

Alaa (ah-LAH): Oh! Is that so? Transliterally, Allah, as in God.

Arusha (ah-ROO-shah): The largest city in northern Tanzania.

Asante (ah-SAHN-tay): Thank you, often followed with **Sana**, or "very much." It occurs in the plural form as **Asanteni** (ah-sahn-TAY-nee).

Asteaste (AH-stay-AH-stay): Slowly, carefully.

Babu (BAH-boo): Grandfather.

Bahati Njema (bah-HA-tee n-JAY-mah): Bidding someone good luck (literally, "luck good!").

Barabara (BAH-rah-BAH-rah): A road.

Bukoba (boo-KOH-bah): Largest city in northwestern Tanzania and capital of the Kagera Region.

Bwana (BWAH-nah): Roughly equivalent to mister, or sir. Used alone as a conversational formality when addressing a man whose name is not known, or together with one's name in less formal, familiar situations, as in, **Bwana** Bill.

Chaguo Ni Lako (chah-GOO-oh nee LAH-koh): (The) choice is yours.

Chai (CHA-ee): Most often translated as tea; but also used as slang for a bribe.

Chapati (chah-PAH-tee): An oily, unleavened fry bread, usually round, about the size of a tortilla.

Chakula (chah-KOO-lah): Food.

Dagaa (dah-GAH): Small whitefish, baitfish.

Dar es Salaam (dar ay sah-LAHM): Former capital and largest city in Tanzania. It is centrally located on the coast and most often translated from the Arabic as "Harbor of Peace."

Farida (fah-REE-dah): My student and friend at Rugambwa from whom I learned so much.

Habari (ha-BAH-ree): Always stated as a question, literally, "News?" Though often translated as "How is it?" Or "What's up?"

Habari gani (ha-BAH-ree GAH-nee): Stated as a question, literally, News which/what? Often translated as "What's the news?"

Habari za asabuhi (ha-BAH-ree zah ah-soo-BOO-hee): Always stated as a question, literally, "News of the morning?" Though often translated simply as "Good morning!"

Hapa (HAH-pah): Here. Hereabouts.

Hapana (ha-PAH-nah): Literally "There is not any." Though most often translated simply as "No."

Hodi (HOH-dee): May I come in/approach? Often repeated: **Hodi hodi?**

Hujambo (hoo-DYAHM-bo): Hello. How are you?

Inshallah (een-shah-LAH): God willing, from the Arabic. Also expressed in the Bantu as **Mungu akipenda,** If God wishes.

Jambo (DYAHM-bo): Hello.

Kanga (KAHNG-gah): Rectangular piece of cotton cloth printed with lively patterns and nature motifs. Used as a skirt-type wrap for women.

Karibu (kah-REE-boo): Most often means welcome; but also used as "near to."

Kashozi (kah-SHO-zee): A small village near several caves in northwestern Tanzania.

Kibo (KEE-bow): At 19,340 feet, the highest peak on the Kilimanjaro massif. Also known as **Uhuru** (oo-HOO-roo), or freedom, peak.

Kikoi (kee-KOY): A colorful, rectangular-shaped cloth, usually corded with tassels at the edges. Worn as a wrap-around skirt-type sarong by men—usually Muslim men at the coast.

Kipepeo (kee-pay-PAY-oh): A butterfly.

Kirinyaga (keer-een-YAH-gah): Traditional Kikuyu name for Mount Kenya, which translates as "Mountain of Whiteness," and is the derivation for the county's name, Kenya. At 17,057 feet, it is the second-highest mountain in Africa.

Kiswahili (kee-swah-HEE-lee): The form of the word indicating the language as it appears in that language, as opposed to Swahili, the way it appears in the West by dropping the noun class agreement.

Kitenge (kee-TANG-gay): A colorful wrap worn by women. Similar to a **kanga,** though larger and able to be worn as a full-body garment.

Konyagi (kohn-YAH-gee): Rum-type liquor made from sugarcane (molasses).

Kwaheri (kwah-HAIR-ree): Good-bye. Literally, with happiness, or with luck.

Maandazi (ma-an-DAH-zi): Deep-fried cakes (plural), similar to donuts without holes.

Maji (MAH-jee): Water.

Mama (MAH-mah): Literally, one's mother. Also affectionately used to address any woman.

Marahaba (mah-rah-HA-bah): Literally "As it should be." The customary reply given by an elder to the greeting **Shikamoo.**

Mawenzi (mah-WEN-zee): At 16,893 feet, the second-highest peak on the Kilimanjaro massif.

Mikate (mee-KAH-tay): Breads (plural). (**Mkate** is the singular.)

Mimi (MEE-mee): Me.

Miwili (mee-WEE-lee): Two of something (in the m/mi noun class).

Mount Meru (MAY-roo): Dormant volcanic mountain in northern Tanzania and fifth-highest mountain in Africa at 14,977 feet.

Mpira wa miguu (m-PEE-rah wah mee-GOO): Soccer, or literally, ball of feet.

Mungu (MOONG-goo): God, supreme being.

Mungu akipenda (MOONG-goo ah-kee-PEN-dah): Literally, God (he) if wishes, or, If God wishes. Similar to the Arabic form also commonly used, Inshallah, God willing.

Mwalimu (m-wah-LEE-moo): Teacher.

Mwarobaini (mwah-ro-bah-EE-nee): Tree native to Bukoba and the entire Kagera region, famous as a medicinal tree, with over forty illness applications.

Mwanza (m-WAHN-zah): Primary city on the southern Tanzanian shore of Lake Victoria.

Mzee (m-ZAY): An elder, or any person more than a few years older than you.

Mzungu (m-ZOONG-goo): Any white person, of either sex, singular. Or, most accurately, a European. The plural form is **wazungu**.

Nakupenda (nah-koo-PEN-dah): Literal contraction of the words "I am you loving"; usually translated as "I love you."

Naam (NAH-m): Form used only by men to ask "What?" As opposed to the form used by women, **Abey?**

Ndiyo (n-DEE-yo): Literally translated as "correct." More commonly used to mean yes.

Nzuri (n-ZOO-ree): Generic noun class spelling for "good."

Pesa (PAY-sah): From the old Portuguese, it is the most common word for money.

Picha (PEE-chah): A picture. Also a photograph or portrait.

Pikipiki (PEE-kee-PEE-kee): Motorcycle. The word is an onomatopoeic invention.

Pilau (pee-LAH-oo): Rice pilaf, an originally South Asian rice dish prepared with vegetables and meat.

Pole (POH-lay): Sorry, as in, I'm sorry for you, though when repeated in the same word, as in **Polepole**, it means "slowly," or "Go slowly."

Rafiki (rah-FEE-kee): A friend.

Rubisi (roo-BEE-see): A Kihaya word for banana beer.

Rugambwa (roo-GAHM-bwah): A secondary school for young women located outside of Bukoba, Tanzania.

Rwelengera (reh-len-GEH-rah): Mr. Rwelengera was a chemistry teacher and the second-master at Rugambwa Secondary School.

Safari (sah-FAH-ree): Travel. A trip. Often followed with **Njema** (n-JAY-mah), the adjective or adverb form of "good," as in a wish for good tidings, good travels.

Salaam (sah-LAHM): Peace. Also spelled **Salama** (sah-LAH-mah).

Samosa (sah-MOH-sah): A fried, triangular pastry shell, usually savory, prepared with potato, cabbage, coriander, cottage cheese, onion, tamarind, and sometimes ground meat. Originally from South Asia. Sometimes called **Sambusa** (sahm-BOO-sah).

Sana (SAH-nah): Very much.

Sawa (SAH-wah): Equivalent of okay, often repeated as, **Sawa sawa.**

Senene (say-NAY-nay): Katydid.

Shamba (SHAHM-bah): A farm. Typically a family's plot of land, planted in a variety of tree and root crops around the home.

Shikamoo (shee-kah-MOH): Literally "I hold your feet." Term of respect given to greet an elder, or anyone more than a few years older than you. Often followed with **Mzee** (m-ZAY), or elder. **Shikamooni** (shee-kah-moh-OH-nee) is the plural.

Sho (SHOH): An expression of surprise: Wow! No!

Shukuru (shoo-KOO-roo): Word meaning great thanks, more than **asante.** From the Arabic.

Shule (SHOO-lay): School.

Tafadhali (tah-fah-THAH-lee): Please.

Ugali (oo-GAH-lee): A food item normally made from mixing flour and water into a moldable paste. Eaten like bread to complement other foods.

Wanafunzi (wah-nah-FOON-zee): Students.

Wanawake (wah-nah-WAH-kay): Women, ladies.

Watoto (wah-TOH-toh): Children.

Wazungu (wah-ZOO-ngoo): Plural, two or more white people, either sex. Or, most precisely, Europeans. Singular is **mzungu**.

Wewe (WAY-way): You. Both as the pronoun, and as in the emphatic "Hey, you!"

Zangu (ZAHNG-goo): Mine, as first-person possessive in the u/zi noun class.

Zawadi (zah-WAH-dee): A gift, present, or boon.

Bibliography

Awde, Nicholas. "Swahili–English English–Swahili Dictionary." *Hippocrene Practical Dictionary*. New York: Hippocrene Books, 2002.

Boddy, Janice. *Wombs and Alien Spirits: Women, Men, and the Zār Cult in Northern Sudan*. Madison: The University of Wisconsin Press, 1989.

Bradford, Phillips Verner, and Harvey Blume. *Ota Benga: The Pygmy in the Zoo*. New York: St. Martin's Press, 1st ed., 1992.

Bunker, Susan M. *World Studies for Christian Schools, Teacher's Edition*. Greenville, SC: Bob Jones University Press, 1993.

Campbell, Joseph. *The Hero with a Thousand Faces*. New York: World Publishing, 2nd ed., 1971.

Carleson, Robert G. "Hierarchy of the Haya Divine Kingship." *American Ethnologist* 20, no.2, (1993):312–335.

Clark, Audrey N. "Dictionary of Geography." *Human & Physical Geography Terms Explained*. Essex, United Kingdom: Longman House, 1987.

Cory, Hans, and M.M. Hartnoll. *Customary Law of the Haya Tribe, Tanganyika Territory*. Westport, CT: Greenwood Press, 1970.

Danner, Blythe. *Six Billion and Beyond*. DVD. Directed by Linda Harrar. Linda Harrar Productions, 1999.

"East Africa, German." *The Encyclopedia Americana: A Library of Universal Knowledge*. New York: The Encyclopedia Americana Corporation. Vol. 9. 1918.

"East Africa Protectorate." *The Encyclopedia Americana: A Library of Universal Knowledge*. New York: The Encyclopedia Americana Corporation. Vol. 9. 1918.

"East African Mountains." *Encyclopædia Britannica*. 2009. Encyclopædia Britannica Online. 28 Oct. 2009.

Eliade, Mircea. *Patterns in Comparative Religion*. New York: Sheed & Ward, 1958.

Features Africa Network. "Lake Disaster Toll May Be 1000," *Africa Online, Inc*. May 25, 1996.

Hanby, Jeanette. *Kilimanjaro National Park*. Edited by Deborah Snelson, Illustrated by David Bygott. Tanzania National Parks in cooperation with the African Wildlife Foundation, 1987.

Harris, Marvin. *Our Kind: Who We Are, Where We Came From & Where We Are Going: The Evolution of Human Life & Culture*. New York: Harper & Row, 1989.

Hedges, Chris. *American Fascists: The Christian Right and the War on America*. New York: Simon & Schuster, 2006.

Herbert, Eugenia W. *Iron, Gender, and Power: Rural Transformations in African Societies*. Bloomington and Indianapolis: Indiana University Press, 1993.

Hicks, David. *Ritual and Belief: Readings in the Anthropology of Religion*. 2nd ed. New York: McGraw-Hill, 2002.

Hoff, Benjamin. *The Tao of Pooh*. Boston: Dutton, 1982.

Huxley, Elspeth. *The Flame Trees of Thika: Memories of an African Childhood*. London: Chatto & Windus, 1959.

Jordan, Terry G., Mona Domosh, and Lester Rowntree. *The Human Mosaic: A Thematic Introduction to Cultural Geography*. 6th ed. New York.: HarperCollins College Div., 1994.

——. *The Human Mosaic: A Thematic Introduction to Cultural Geography*. 7th ed. Glenview, IL: Addison-Wesley, 1997.

Jung, C. G. *The Archetypes and the Collective Unconscious*. Translated by R. F. C. Hull. New York: Bollingen Foundation, 1959.

Krishnamurti, J. *As One Is: To Free the Mind from All Conditioning*. Prescott, AZ: Hohm Press, 2007.

——. *On Living and Dying*. Sandpoint, ID: Morning Light Press, 2005.

Lan, David. *Guns & Rain: Guerrillas & Spirit Mediums in Zimbabwe*. Berkeley and Los Angeles: University of California Press, 1985.

Lane, Belden, C. *Landscapes of the Sacred: Geography and Narrative in American Spirituality*. Expanded edition. Baltimore and London: The Johns Hopkins University Press, 2001.

Lwamgira, F. X. *Amakuru ga Kiziba: The History of Kiziba and Its Kings*. 2nd ed. Translated by E. R. Kamuangire. Kampala, Uganda: Makerere Department of History, Makerere University College, 1969.

MacFarlane, Robert. *Mountains of the Mind: Adventures in Reaching the Summit*. New York: Random House, 2003.

McKnight, Tom L. *Physical Geography: A Landscape Appreciation*. Englewood Cliffs, NJ: Simon & Schuster, 1993.

Mitchell, Stephen. *The Gospel According to Jesus: A New Translation and Guide to His Essential Teachings for Believers and Unbelievers*. New York: HarperCollins, 1991.

Nash, Roderick. *Wilderness and the American Mind*. 3rd ed. New Haven and London: Yale University Press, 1967.

Noss, John B. *Man's Religions*. 5th ed. New York: Macmillan, 1974.

Old World History and Geography, Teacher Edition. Pensacola, FL: A Beka Press, 1991.

Oliver, Roland, and J. D. Fage. *A Short History of Africa*. 6th ed. New York: Penguin, 1990.

Parfitt, Tudor. *Journey to the Vanished City: The Search for a Lost Tribe of Israel*. New York: Random House, 2000.

Preston, Richard. *The Hot Zone: A Terrifying True Story*. New York: Anchor Books, 1994.

Price, Larry W. *Mountains and Man: A Study of Process and Environment*. Berkeley and Los Angeles: University of California Press, 1981.

Rald, Jorgen. *Rural Organization in Bukoba District, Tanzania*. Copenhagen, Denmark: C.A. Reitzel, 1975.

Rappaport, Roy A. *Ritual and Religion in the Making of Humanity*. Cambridge, United Kingdom: Cambridge University Press, 1999.

Reid, Ian. *Guide Book to Mount Kenya and Kilimanjaro*. Nairobi: The Mountain Club of Kenya, 1963.

Reining, Priscilla. "The Haya: The Agrarian System of a Sedentary People." PhD diss., University of Chicago, 1967.

Rhodes, Frank H.T. *Fossils: A Guide to Prehistoric Life (A Golden Nature Guide)*. New York: Golden Press, 1962.

Sabini, John. *Islam: A Primer*. Washington, DC: Middle East Editorial Associates, 1963.

Schoenbrun, David Lee. *A Green Place, A Good Place: Agrarian Change, Gender and Social Identity in the Great Lakes Region to the 15th century*. New York: Heinemann, 1988.

Schmidt, Peter R. *Historical Archaeology: A Structural Approach in an African Culture*. Bloomington: Indiana University Press, 1978.

——. *Iron Technology in East Africa*. Bloomington: Indiana University Press, 1997.

Simpkins, Annellen M., and C. Alexander Simpkins. *Zen around the World: A 2500-Year Journey from the Buddha to You*. Boston: Tuttle Publishing, 1997.

Smith, Houston. *The Illustrated World's Religions: A Guide to Our Wisdom Traditions*. New York: HarperCollins, 1994.

Stock, Robert. *Africa South of the Sahara: A Geographical Interpretation*. New York: Guilford Press, 1995.

Sundermeier, Theo. *The Individual and Community in African Traditional Religions*. Piscataway, NJ: Transaction Publishers, Rutgers University, 1998.

Taylor, Brian K. *The Western Lacustrine Bantu*. London: International African Institute, 1962.

Tenney, Merrill C. "The Zondervan." *Pictorial Bible Dictionary*. Grand Rapids, MI: Zondervan Publishing House, 1967.

Tzu, Lao. *Tao Te Ching*. Translated by D. C. Lau, New York: Penguin, 1963.

Williams, John G. *A Field Guide to the Butterflies of Africa*. Boston: Houghton Mifflin, 1969.

Withers, Martin B., and David Hosking. *Wildlife of East Africa*. Princeton, N.J.: Princeton University Press, 2002.

World History and Cultures in Christian Perspective. 2nd ed. Pensacola, FL: A Beka Press, 1997.

Zondervan. "New International Version." *The Holy Bible*. 1984.

About the Publisher

LANTERN BOOKS was founded in 1999 on the principle of living with a greater depth and commitment to the preservation of the natural world. In addition to publishing books on animal advocacy, vegetarianism, religion, and environmentalism, Lantern is dedicated to printing books in the U.S. on recycled paper and saving resources in day-to-day operations. Lantern is honored to be a recipient of the highest standard in environmentally responsible publishing from the Green Press Initiative.

www.lanternbooks.com

Awarded in 2011

green
press
INITIATIVE

Lantern Books has elected to print this title on Nature's Book, a 30% post-consumer recycled paper, processed chlorine-free. As a result, we have saved the following resources:

2 trees, 115 lbs of solid waste, 1040 gallons of water
2 million BTUs, and 227 lbs of greenhouse gases

As part of Lantern Books' commitment to the environment we have joined the Green Press Initiative, a non-profit organization supporting publishers in using fiber that is not sourced from ancient or endangered forests. We hope that you, the reader, will support Lantern and GPI in our endeavor to preserve the ancient forests and the natural systems on which all life depends. One way is to buy books that cost a little more but make a positive commitment to the environment no only in their words, but in the paper that they are printed on. For more information, visit www.greenpressinitiative.org.